The Politics of Landscape

JAMES TURNER

The Politics of Landscape

Rural Scenery and Society in English Poetry 1630–1660

HARVARD UNIVERSITY PRESS
Cambridge, Massachusetts
1979

Library of Congress Cataloging in Publication Data

Turner, James G., 1947–
  The politics of landscape.

  Includes index.
  1. English poetry—Early modern, 1500–1700—
History and criticism. 2. Landscape in literature.
3. Politics in literature. 4. Country life in
literature. 5. Literature and society—Great
Britain. I. Title.
PR545.L27T8   821'.4'0932   78–11027
  ISBN 0–674–68930–5

Printed in Great Britain

Contents

List of Illustrations

It is my comfort to escape the rude
And sluttish trouble of the multitude:
Flowers, rivers, woods, the pleasant air and wind,
With sacred thoughts do feed my serious mind.

  (Rowland Watkyns, 'The Poets Soliloquy')

The charming landscape which I saw this morning is
indubitably made up of some twenty or thirty farms.
Miller owns this field, Locke that, and Manning the
woodland beyond. But none of them owns the landscape.
There is a property in the horizon which no man has but
he whose eye can integrate all the parts, that is, the poet.

  (Emerson, 'Nature' I)

since the horizon's bought strange dogs are still.

  (Yeats, 'To Dorothy Wellesley')

Preface

The concerns of this book carry it beyond its immediate subject-matter. I raise questions of the status of the literary text, of the structure of thought it reveals, and of its relation to class, culture and ideology. These are now hot issues. Structuralism and the renaissance of Marxism have challenged the theoretical feebleness of traditional literary studies, and a gulf has opened up between new theorists and practitioners of the older kinds of literary history, "background" and the sociology of literature. I try, not to build a bridge, but at least to throw a line across. My conclusion attempts to draw a theory from my practice, and to look at recent critical models of the way literature operates in society. Is it myth? ideological apparatus? consumer durable? conspiracy of silence?

Critical writing on rural poetry is still relatively slight. I have not been able to find a satisfactory theoretical model of the relation between literature and the land. Most studies of landscape in literature deal with a particular feature or author; in the seventeenth-century field, the most perceptive are Kitty Scoular's *Natural Magic* (1965) and H. M. Richmond's *Renaissance Landscapes* (1968). Wider studies, like those of John Dixon Hunt and John Barrell, have concentrated on the eighteenth century. General works are often suggestive and exciting—Jay Appleton's *Experience of Landscape* (1975) or Gaston Bachelard's *Poetics of Space* (1957),[1] for example—but they tend to deal with the aesthetics of landscape and how the individual perceives it. This approach is too limited; landscape is a socialized image. It has a population and a social content, and it represents an ideal and harmonic structure whose basis is the land—a precise counterpart of the way seventeenth-century society was imagined by its rulers and poets.

Some critics recognize the social dimension of *topographia*, however. The political context of *Coopers Hill* has been thoroughly analysed. Maren-Sofie Røstvig's *The Happy Man* (2nd ed., 1971) gathers together the basic texts of retirement-poetry; unfortunately she assumes a real movement towards country life, and fails to penetrate sham rusticity. J. W. Foster attempts "a redefinition of topographical poetry" in *JEGP* (1970). He sees that topographical formulae are used to evoke "larger settings . . . . England, say, or the countryside in general" (p. 400); he defines a topographical poem as one in which space and time interact to provide a general morality, colouring the whole description. Charles Molesworth had already explored the conjunction of history, morality and landscape in his 'Property and Virtue' (*Genre*, 1968); he sees that the country-house poem integrates panegyric and topography, and converts history into a timeless model of virtue. He is also aware of the economic basis of property and virtue; unfortunately his grasp of economic history is weak—"the change to a monetary basis for property ownership" (p. 149) happened long before the seventeenth century. Raymond Williams goes much further with "the general problem of the relations between country writing and country history".[2] Williams is the Moses of this new field of study; fundamental principles can be extracted from the swirling clouds of *The Country and the City*. There is no longer any excuse for taking topoi at face value. He proclaims the courtliness of literary rurality and the spuriousness of finding a natural order in the country estate; he is correspondingly aware of metaphors of social order in "natural" description. He challenges the assumptions of charity and neighbourliness in country-life poems. He sees that landscapes are made by human labour and that idealization involves spiriting away the labourer. He shows that we can sometimes discover "a precise set of social relationships" (p. 55) behind the mystification of ideal landscape. He also raises a more difficult question: was the topos *ever* real? What was the relationship between what he calls Pastoral and Counter-pastoral? He argues that pastoral, acknowledged to be unreal, gradually gathers realistic details—rents, acreage, locality and so on; by the early eighteenth century it "can be offered as a description and thence an idealization of actual English country life and its social and economic relations" (p. 38). I will argue that *topographia* did this in all genres throughout the seventeenth century, and that its history cannot be written as a simple increase in actuality. It required sufficient realism to be convincing, and sufficient idealization to be dissociated from immediate reality; different political and economic conditions demand different ways of resolving this contradiction.

I would like to acknowledge my gratitude to all those individuals and libraries who made this work possible when it was a dissertation (especially Barbara Rosenbaum and Rachel Trickett); to John Carey, Brian Southam, John Dixon Hunt, Annabel Patterson and Martin Battestin for their comments and encouragement; and to Joan Welford for typing the manuscript.

Liverpool   *February 1978*

Introduction
The poetry of place

The subject of this book is *topographia*, the literary depiction of rural places and the life they support. I attempt to explain its form, its application to political thinking, and its unspoken assumptions and contradictions.

Rural poetry flourished in the crisis of 1630–1660. There is a great increase in the number and quality of retirement and garden poems, of rural celebrations like 'The Hock Cart', of poems on actual places or modelled on landscape painting. The theatre introduces landscape scenery and creates a topographical genre.[1] Amateur theatricals dramatize the setting of country houses. Long descriptions of imaginary landscape are introduced into fiction, either as similes or as settings for amorous retreat. Rural and topographical imagery is central to the poetry of this period. Yet it was a time of disaster in the countryside. Beyond the magic circles of Windsor, Belvoir and Penshurst was a land racked by bad harvests, unprecedented poverty and oppression, peasant rebellion and the devastations of civil war. The country was also a place of social and cultural bleakness,

> Perpetual *Winter*, endless *Solitude*,
> Or the society of men so rude
> That it is ten times worse.[2]

This picture of desolation is derived partly from historical sources but partly from those very poets who idealize country life elsewhere. Stuart culture was courtly and metropolitan, though its wealth was based on country estates. To resolve this contradiction, the rural element of the gentleman's life must be identified as exceptional, a *villeggiatura* or rustic episode in which the real business of life is left behind. Literature, with its separate reality and its watertight genres and topoi, plays an

important role in this ideology of dissociation. Country literature cannot be reduced to "depiction" of the actual state of the
countryside—that is its whole point. It works on historical
reality, and produces something different. It works, moreover, in a variety of ways—insisting on the irrelevance of the
world, or suppressing its painful contradictions, or interrogat-
ing, transforming or inverting it. This book tries to recon-
struct the meaning of rural poetry in its complex collision with
the economic processes of rural life and the theories evoked to
explain them in their own time.

The poem has a double status. It is an exercise in rhetoric,
elaborating purely literary and aesthetic effects, and it is a
version of the world, which is to say an interpretation, an
ideological statement. This may be seen in any piece of
rural verse, Katherine Philips's 'A Country-Life', for
example:

> How Sacred and how Innocent
>   A Country-life appears,
> How free from Tumult, Discontent,
>   From Flattery or Fears!
> This was the first and happiest Life,
>   When man enjoy'd himself;
> Till Pride exchanged Peace for Strife,
>   And Happiness for Pelf.
> 'Twas here the Poets were inspir'd,
>   Here taught the multitude;
> The brave they here with Honour fir'd
>   And civiliz'd the rude.
> That Golden Age did entertain
>   No Passion but of Love;
> The thoughts of Ruling and of Gain
>   Did ne'er their Fancies move.

This happy state is vanished from the world, but still lives on
in the country life:

> What Blessings doth this World afford
>   To tempt or bribe desire?
> Her Courtship is all Fire and Sword,
>   Who would then retire?

She praises the innocence she has achieved in retirement and satarizes the wretched entertainments of Hyde Park, Spring-Garden and the Exchange. She is "resolved from within, Confirmed from without"; only Friendship and Honesty are valuable in this life, and these can only be found in a country hermitage. Philips's poem is certainly amiable, and parts of it are honest—though not perhaps in the way she intended:

> Opinion is the rate of things,
>   From hence our Peace doth flow;
> I have a better fate than Kings,
>   Because I think it so.

This is true; the poem embodies an *opinion* of country life, though in the guise of an experience. If we take seriously its implicit claim to be a personal utterance, great cracks of irony open up:

> When all the Stormy World doth roar
>   How unconcern'd am I!
> I cannot fear to tumble lower
>   Who never could be high,
> Secure in these unenvi'd walls
>   I think not on the State . . . .

She is indeed "unconcern'd" with politics, and she does write "secure" within a country dwelling; but of what kind? Katharine Philips was a London merchant's daughter, "who never could be high" in a caste sense. She married James Philips, a parliamentary colonel who distinguished himself both during and after the civil war by ferocious suppressions of local royalist rebellions. The poet is therefore acutely qualified to attest the cruel world's "Fire and Sword", and the freedom of the countryside from tumult and strife. Did not the colonel himself guarantee this happy state, and bravely "civilize the rude"? The lack of Pelf and Thoughts of Gain in the local populace can also be attributed to James Philips. He personally sequestered at least eleven estates in South Wales. He became wealthy enough, through plunder and judicious marriage, to maintain a London home and a splendid country-house in Wales; this explains the poet's expertise in condemning the fashionable places of London, and throws some light on her recommendations:

> It is not brave to be possest
>   Of Earth, but to despise. . . .
> Them that do covet only rest
>   A Cottage will suffice.

This particular Cottage was roofed not with thatch but with lead; in fact colonel Philips stripped off the entire roof of St. David's cathedral and transferred it to his own house – the "Hermitage" where his wife felt able to praise the sacredness as well as the innocence of country life.

Katharine Philips was, of course, herself a victim of the colonel's sequestrations. We should not chide her too fiercely for having to gain financial security by marriage; no one would want to undergo the sexual and social abuse levelled at women who earned their living—especially if it was by the pen. Her poetry is designed to express her freedom of spirit, her ability to transcend the material base of her existence; the exact lineaments of that existence are nonetheless preserved in what she writes. Horace put the praise of country life into the mouth of a city money-lender in his Epode "Beatus ille qui procul negotiis", but this irony was too near the knuckle for most of his seventeenth-century followers. They could not tolerate explicit contradictions in the text, itself produced from contradiction: the graceful articulation of the *beatus ille* theme, the quintessence of rural poetry, was a mark of the writer's urbanity; Katherine Philips's life was the diametric opposite of what she purports to celebrate. The meaning of 'A Country-Life' cannot be adequately grasped without relating it to this matrix of contradiction and suppression.

Rural poetry always deals with society in general as well as the landscape and the peasantry, its immediate subjects. The literary countryside is a *bon à penser*, an instrument to think with; like any tool, it makes a task easier but it also determines the form of tasks to be done. This book pursues two questions, therefore. What kind of ideal countryside do poets depict, given their need to embody social doctrine this way? And what kind of thinking needs to be expressed in terms of landscape and rurality? What is "green Thought"?

This study began by looking at the social implications of landscape in Pope and his contemporary poets and horticulturalists. I traced this Augustan Georgic tradition back to *Coopers Hill* (1642), but this source turned out to be a watershed. Denham's poem appeared at a crucial point in the political crisis; it brings into focus the scattered topographical themes of earlier poetry – Jonson's moralized estates, Drayton's loose blend of regional history and geography, Waller's praise of royalist architecture. Denham adapts the clear water and rich vegetation of the *locus amoenus* or earthly paradise, and touches on the "happinesse of sweete retir'd content" – but these traditional topics are set in a new form; the poet tries to imitate the themes and patterns of landscape painting, a newly-discovered art in England then.[3] But *Coopers Hill, Upon Appleton House*, and, in inception, Milton's mnemonic, using real places instead of the artificial *loci* of memory-training. It is also prophetic; the prospect from a high place was well-established as an image of political foresight and inquiry. The word "prospective", in fact, could be used interchangeably for future options, distant views, telescopes, optical tricks and painted landscapes; it draws together all the new-found "arts of prospect". Such was the tool available to Denham at the outbreak of the civil war.

To study an individual poet was not enough, however. Nor did it seem worthwhile to render separate accounts of the acknowledged topographical masterpieces of this period— *Coopers Hill, Upon Appleton House,* and, in inception, Milton's Eden. I began to uncover, in major and minor verse alike, a repetitive network of descriptions and allusions. Did they have a common principle or structure?

Landscape art was a dominant unifying influence, not so much in its pictorial effect as in offering structural principles which could convert topography into a dazzling artefact. These aesthetic conceptions of the countryside were also sustained by a coherent ideology of Nature and Place, which had long been given the privileged status of a natural philosophy. "Land" and "place" are equivalent to "propriety" – meaning in seventeenth-century English both *property* and *knowing one's place*. The order of the universe, like the structure of society, was supposed to depend on a hierarchy of places from lowest to highest. Place is identity. Things out of place are not properly themselves, and move as living forces towards their natural home. Birds nest in trees, fish in water, and the salamander in fire; the needle turns to the North Pole, rivers flow to the sea, and the hearts of man, so the analogy runs, obey their God and King:

> every kyndely thyng that is
> Hath a kyndely stede ther he
> May best in hyt conserved be.
>   (Chaucer, *The Hous of Fame*)

All motion towards the proper place, in this adaptation of Aristotle's physics, is "natural", and all deflection is "violent". Violence is the sole reason for the deformity and decay of the natural world; "all violent Motions short do prove".[4] Comenius's personal emblem (title page) was a landscape in a cosmic circle, bearing the motto

> Omnia sponte fluant, absit violentia rerum
> Let all things flow naturally; away with the violence of things!

Violence is expunged from the perfect structure when "each part is fixt in's proper place And not *chaost* together".[5] This is poor physics but powerful social ideology. Beauty, Nature and political establishment are assumed to be sustained by the same forms of propriety; all opposition is hideous and violent. Opposition from the rural working class – the terror of landowners throughout this period – is therefore doubly violent, since manual workers were believed to be as ugly and brutal as their work. Landscape descriptions, idealizations and condemnations of country life, and political poems like *Coopers Hill* should not be treated separately; they all embody the concept of natural place and violence.

Landscape was often used for specifically political purposes. "Land" and "country" were synonymous with "nation", and "Landschap" meant "in English landship or expressing of the land".[6] The freshly-mown meadow at Appleton House was a "naked equal Flat which *Levellers* take pattern at". Royalists and Puritans were exhorted to learn from the landscape around Cooper's hill, and withdraw from the brink of civil war. Marvell and Denham sought different effects in different tones, but the process is the same in both their poems: landscape is read as a political lesson, as a "pattern" or exemplary structure. The analogy works reciprocally too; at the same time political institutions are "greened"—transformed into part of the natural order.

Topographia develops into an important system of images – a transformation of the land in all its aspects. It is used most fully between 1630 and 1660—partly because of a new fascination with landscapes and "prospective", and partly as a response to the political crisis, which began with a widespread fear that property in land would be swept away by rural insurrection. The art of *topographia* consists in reconciling the demands of realism and idealisation. When reality is permeated by violence, "nature" is asked to oppose, to criticise and if possible to replace it. The imaginary countryside is pursued as a "strong *Retreat*", a

> sure *entail'd Estate*
> Which nought has power to alienate,[7]

a land purged of trouble but recognizable as home.

> 'Twas here the Poets were inspir'd,
> Here taught the multitude.

Any work of imagination is distinct from the reality it embodies, and creates a world of its own. But rural poetry of the civil war period does not simply embellish or ignore the things of the world; it inverts them.

1

The Ideal Form of Landscape

New developments in seventeenth-century art and their effect on English writing

> *To view the Towring tops of Mountains, unaccessable Rocks,*
> *with ridgie extents, or suddain fractions, by some steepy*
> *abruptnesse: Here a valley so large that at the end of the plain*
> *it seems to meet Heaven, there a Grove, and here a Green*
> *pleasant Arbour . . . gently swelling Hillocks, high delightfull*
> *plaines, flowry meddows, pleasant streams, naturall fountains,*
> *gushing waters down the rocks, Stately Cities, famous Towers,*
> *large Bridges, spiring Steeples, intermixed with Orchards,*
> *Gardens, Walks and what not of these kinds, that delights the*
> *mind of Man?*
>
> (William Sanderson, *Graphice* (1658) p. 5)

These words call to mind Paul Brill's mountain landscape, reproduced on the endpapers of this book. They describe the same topography in the same spirit of visual adventure. Such prints appeared as an exciting novelty at the beginning of the seventeenth century, but by the time Sanderson published his treatise literate English people had learned to understand the visual arts and to foster a native school of painting. Landscape, a new word and a new genre, plays an important part in this renaissance. Not only does Sanderson praise individual landscape artists; his general introduction, from which these words are taken, uses landscape as a means of expressing the grand creative power of the eye itself. He promotes the new art form because it embodies a new experience—*seeing the world as a landscape.*

For most of this book I will use "landscape" as a literary term, to refer to a formal and structured description of topography. But first I must prove that this is legitimate by showing how literature adopted the concept, and what it was felt to mean.

Landscape began as a technical term of artists, though it was readily applied to real places; to describe a familiar view poets evoke the unfamiliar beauties of the new art:

> When Westwell Downes I gan to tread
> Where cleanely wynds the greene did sweepe,
> Methought a landskip there was spread . . .
> (William Strode, 'On Westwell Downes')

George Sandys on the road to Jerusalem sees "on each side round hils, with ruines on their tops, and vallies, such as are figured in the most beautifull land-skips."[1] Henry Peacham fills out his directions for the painting of landscapes with a touring artist's guide to the great "Landskips" of Europe and the Middle East.[2] A prospect like Windsor or Greenwich had a European reputation, attracting landscapists and increasing the prestige of their work. The interrelation of reality and artistic preconception is dense and fecund: Greenwich becomes a favourite recreation-place because of the view; visitors spread its reputation in their writings, which are strongly pictorial; these attract painters and printmakers, whose views carry literary inscriptions (Fig. 2); but why was it so exciting in the first place? Because it looked like a fine landscape painting.

Seventeenth-century literature is greatly enriched by the new experience of landscape. Pictorial views were occasionally attempted in earlier literature—the Carthaginian harbour in *Aeneid* I, for example, or the vine-clad slopes and hazy distances of Ausonius's *Mosella*. The fourteenth-century *Mum and the Sothsegger* contains a beautiful hill-prospect, crowded with keenly-observed details, but with very little indication of space. In the sixteenth century we find consciously pictorial treatments of *topographia*, which anticipate landscape in an undeveloped form. Sannazaro describes an extensive panel of "woods and trees" over the door of an Arcadian temple.[3] He gives far more prominence to the landscape than his model, Theocritus, suggests; but he makes no attempt to place it in perspective. By contrast, Montemayor and Sidney both describe views which evoke the space and tone of a landscape painting:

travelling one morning on her way, thorow the mids of a woode, and at the going out of certaine thick bushes . . . from the top of a high hill she beheld before her a most pleasant and greene Champaine that lay all along beneath the hill, and of such length, that she could scarce see to the end of it; for twelve miles right out it butted upon the bottoms of certaine hils, that might hardly be discerned . . .

a pretty height . . . gives the eye lordship over a good large circuit, which according to the nature of the country, being diversified betweene hills and dales, woods and playnes, one place more cleere, and the other more darksome, it seemes a pleasant picture of nature, with lovely lightsomnes and artificiall shadowes.[4]

Ruth Pitman notices a similar process in travellers' descriptions of America, which begin as accounts of the distinguishing features of a distant coastline, develop into formal portraits from a given point of land, and culminate in profound effects of colour and atmosphere.[5] There is an increasing readiness to discover pleasant pictures in Nature; in the seventeenth century this impulse takes an *organized* form. Contemporary landscape began to be constructed according to clearly-defined principles, guided by a body of theory whose influence can be traced in literature as much as in art.

The rudimentary landscapes of Renaissance literature depended on a single effect—particularity, depth of prospect, or dramatic contrast. The new landscape is composite. It is not a portrait of an individual place, but an ideal construction of particular motifs. Its purpose is to express the character of a region,[6] or a general idea of the good land. Peacham defines it as

in English landship, or expressing of the land by hills, woodes, Castles, seas, valleys, ruines, hanging rocks, Cities, Townes . . . within one Horizon.[7]

His practice matches his theory; in *Minerva Britanna* (1612) he creates a landscape emblem (Fig. 1), one of the first by an English artist, to illustrate his general idea of a place of retirement

> Such as we may neere princely *Richmond* see,
> Or where a long doth silver *Severne* slide,
> Or *Avon* courtes faire *Flora* in her pride (p. 185).

In *Salmacida Spolia* (1640) Davenant and Inigo Jones present a scene where

> in the Landskip were Corne fields and pleasant Trees, sustayn-ing Vines fraught with grapes, and in some of the furthest parts Villages; with all such things as might expresse a Country in peace, rich, and fruitfull (f.B4v).

We know from the surviving drawing that this scene was a mixture of classical motifs and familiar English scenery, fields, fences, cottages and church spires. Out of the mélange both artists try to create a plausible and unified effect—a *composition*, "expressing of the land . . . within one horizon."
    Landscape must also create an illusion of distance. Even before 1600 it was recognized that

> Landskip . . . expresseth places of larger prospecte, as whole contries where the eye seemeth not to be hindred by any objectes . . . but to passe as farre as the force therofe can pierce.[8]

Two kinds of perspective must be combined—geometric, which scales down objects, and aerial, which depicts haze. Peacham explains how to "shew a faire Horizon" by selecting dark green for the foreground, and then "driving it by degrees into a blew"; the result is "Landscapes, that seeme a great way off."[9] The landscape artist, according to Edward Norgate, should aim for "a certeyne aereall morbidezza, as Paolo Brill caules it, or dilicatt softenes"; by making the distance "appeare sweet and misty," and controlling the whole progression of light and shade, he can "remove the ground, and . . . extend the prospecte farr off."[10] Brill, as Norgate remembered in a later revision of his treatise, claimed that a landscape must "*Caminare*, that is move or walke away."[11] The illusion of distance is, quite literally, dynamic.
    But pure distance is not enough. John Barclay, trying to see why the view from Greenwich hill is so delightful, remarks that it "did neither suddenly debarre the prospect, nor suffer

the sight to be dispersed through the emptie aire."[12] For Henry
Wotton, analysing the perfect prospect, the eye

> can indure no narrow *Circumscription*; but must be fed both with
> extent and variety. Yet on the other side, I find vaste and
> indefinite views which drown all apprehension of the uttermost
> *Objects* condemned by good Authours, as if thereby some part
> of the pleasure (whereof we speak) did perish.[13]

The sight must be neither "limited" nor "lost", in Waller's
terms.[14] The best landscape is neither cluttered nor bleak; it
represents an Augustan ideal, the mean between two self-
destructive extremes.

Balance must not exclude contrast. Du Bartas's description
of a painted landscape, one of the earliest in literature, crawls
with antitheses:

> First, in a Mead he marks a frisking Lamb,
> Which seems, though dumb, to bleat unto the Dam;
> Then he observes a Wood, seeming to wave:
> Then th'hollow bosom of some hideous Cave:
> Here a high way, and there a Narrow Path:
> Here Pines, there Oaks torn by tempestuous wrath:
> Here from a craggy Rock's steep-hanging boss
> (Thrumm'd half with Ivie, half with crisped Moss)
> A silver Brook in broken streams doth gush,
> And head-long down the horned Cliff doth rush;
> Then, winding thence above and under ground,
> A goodly Garden it be-moateth round.[15]

Here contrast is pursued without organisation; the effect is
cluttered, like the clumsy mid-sixteenth-century landscapes it
describes. For William Browne, indeed, landscape *was* an in-
toxicating muddle; he uses it, in a long descriptive simile, to
denote turmoil.[16] The new landscape, by contrast, is a triumph
of management. Richard Corbett discovers a strikingly organized picture in the Trent valley:

> The ground wee trodd was Meddow, fertile Land,
> New trimm'd and levell'd by the Mowers hand;
> Above it grew a Roke, rude, steepe, and high,
> Which claimes a kind of reverence from the Eye:

Betwixt them both there glides a lively Streame,
Not loude, but swift . . .
This side the open Plaine admitts the Sunne
To halfe the River there did Silver runne:
The other halfe ran Clowdes, where the Curl'd wood
With his exalted head threaten'd the floude . . . .[17]

This concise and balanced scene is the model for Denham's version of Thamesside, and anticipates the half-hidden, half-open landscapes of *Pharonnida* and *Windsor-Forrest*. Henry More uses the same techniques with more spacious effect:

Fresh-varnish'd groves, tall hills, and gilded clouds
Arching an eyelid for the glowing Morn;
Fair clustred buildings which our sight so crowds
At distance, with high spires to heaven yborn;
Vast plains with lowly cottages forlorn,
Rounded about with the low wavering skie;
Cragg'd vapours, like to rugged rocks ytorn.[18]

The elements of the landscape must appear systematically arranged. Milton's "allegro" sees a measured landscape of

Russet Lawns, and Fallows Gray,
Where the nibling flocks do stray,
Mountains on whose barren brest
The labouring clouds do often rest:
Meadows trim with Daisies pide,
Shallow Brooks, and Rivers wide.

These details are framed in beautiful balancing pairs—but balance, tone and colour are all subordinate to the idea of great and small, summed up in the pairing of castle and cottage. Even in brief allusions to landscape the structure must be emphasized; here, for example, Thomas Randolph addresses a rich man:

Thou hast thy landskips, and the painters try
With all their skill to please thy wanton eye.
Here shadowy groves, and craggy mountains there;
Here Rivers headlong fall, there springs runne cleare . . .[19]

The elements of the picture are discriminated and recombined into a stylish unit. The essential distinctions are rough and smooth, shady and open, turbid and clear, vertical and flat; they are to be found with equal elegance in Denham's couplets on the Thames and in Marvell's *Appleton House*—

> In fragrant Gardens, shady Woods,
> Deep Meadows, and transparent Floods . . .
> Gulfes, Deserts, Precipices, Stone . . .

The new organization of visual experience is neatly summed up in Barten Holyday's *Survey of the World* (1661). He describes himself as a traveller who

> climbes a Hill,
> Lookes back, sitts down, and oft, if hand have skill,
> Landskippes the Vale with pencil; placing here
> Medow, there Arable, here Forest, there
> A Grove, a City, or a Silver-streame,
> As offring to yield beauty to his Scheme (f.A3).

The hard-won valley offers itself to his scheme; he *landscapes* it.

By selecting and placing features correctly the landscape artist created order. In painting this was achieved by the disciplined exclusion of the anomalous and the perverse—of double horizons, multiple systems of scale and shadow, excessive visibility, mixed seasons. Gombrich suggests that the genre is influenced by Vitruvius, who contrasted the realistic scenes that used to be painted on the walls of villas with the surreal trash of his own day;[20] this was to become "*Grotesco* or (as we say) *Antique-worke*."[21] The landscape defined itself alongside the grotesque, respectability emerging from chaos. The frames of tapestries and stage sets were made of "spruce Anticks,"[22] the "true prospect" is set in "gross rustick work."[23] Richard Ligon "was designing a piece of Landscape," but in prison

> being disabled to discern or judge of colours, I was compelled to expresse my designes in Black and White: So that now you will find exposed to your view, a piece of wild *Grotesco*, or loose extravagant *Drolorie*, rather than a Regular piece of Story or Landscape.[24]

Marvell contrasts "a rude heap together hurl'd" with the "more decent Order tame" of the Appleton estate. But this new order must not be regimented or severe; every outline and transition must show a casual elegance or "wild *Regularity*."[25] Literary topography affected "that orderly disorder which is common in nature."[26] Southwell describes a rocky valley which seems an artistic contrivance precisely because it reveals "such disordred order."[27] Style in landscape came to resemble a social grace; the "placing" must be entirely faultless and entirely unobtrusive.

Landscape must above all be a unity. Max Friedländer describes it as "a school where relativity is taught, since here the terms decide the issue less by their own shape and idiosyncrasy than by their relation to one another."[28] Until the 1590s the pictorial treatment of landscape was more or less *itemized*; from then onwards the predominant concern is with unity of structure, light and atmosphere, and the creation of "an organisational framework"—Donald Posner traces this process in his study of Annibale Carracci (1971). Disparate elements must seem intangibly bonded. Hollar's panorama of Greenwich (Fig. 2) invites the viewer to "behould, by Prospect, with what art" the castle on the hill, the palace below, the river and the distant city are made to appear "near and part" of one another. Margaret Cavendish's ideal garden includes a

> *Prospect*, which *Trees* and *Clouds* by mixing shewes
> Joyn'd by the eye; one perfect peece it grows.[29]

This was the principle which led Brill, Elsheimer, Domenichino and Claude to create a form of ideal landscape which dominated European taste for centuries; we see it also in the stage designs of Inigo Jones. The theatrical organization of light and dark, wings and backdrop, is essential to this style. It represents the triumphant fusion of three separate techniques—perspective, the proper contrasting of shades, and the organization of masses. Sidney finds "a pretty picture of Nature" in Arcadia because of its "lovely lightsomnes and artificiall shadowes"—but he does not mention distance. For Brill and Norgate chiaroscuro becomes a means of controlling the progression from foreground to background, so making

the picture "move or walke away." The principles of landscape composition do not operate singly, but contribute to
each other.

The new landscape influenced the style as well as the content
of literature. Poetry was described in terms of landscape.
Vaughan most impresses Katherine Philips when his "sacred
Muse diverts her Quill, the Landskip to design of *Sions* hill."[30]
Lucretius's *De Rerum Natura* reminds Evelyn of "the surprising artifice of some various *Scene*, curious *Landskip*, or delicious prospect."[31] Davenant explains what can be learned from
this analogy:

> . . . surely Poets (whose business should represent the Worlds
> true image often to our view) are not lesse prudent than
> Painters, who when they draw Landschaps entertaine not the
> Eye wholy with even Prospect, and a continu'd Flatte; but (for
> variety) terminate the sight with lofty Hills, whose obscure
> heads are sometimes in the Clowdes.[32]

Tone and style should imitate landscape, a harmonious composition of crags and plains, the lofty and the smooth; in this
way the poet can obtain "the Worlds true image" by means of
an ideal aesthetic structure. A topographical poem like *Coopers
Hill* is therefore doubly landscaped; it exemplifies the principles of aesthetic and stylistic variety which Davenant draws
from landscape art, and restores his metaphor to reality by
applying them to an actual landscape. This technique becomes
explicit in the central description of Egham wood, where

> the steep horrid roughness of the Wood
> Strives with the gentle calmness of the flood.
> Such huge extreams when Nature doth unite,
> Wonder from thence results, from thence delight.
> The stream is so transparent, pure, and clear,
> That had the self-enamour'd youth gaz'd here,
> So fatally deceiv'd he had not been,
> While he the bottom, not his face had seen.
> But his proud head the aery Mountain hides
> Among the Clouds; his shoulders, and his sides
> A shady mantle cloaths; his curled brows

Frown on the gentle stream, which calmly flows,
While winds and storms his lofty forehead beat:
The common fate of all that's high and great.
Low at his foot a spacious plain is plac't,
Between the mountain and the stream embrac't:
Which shade and shelter from the Hill derives,
While the kind river wealth and beauty gives;
And in the mixture of all these appears
Variety, which all the rest indears. (1655 version)

Like the landscape artist Denham uses *interrelatedness* to create an organizational framework.

The poet's duty, as Drayton proclaims in *Poly-Olbion*, is to expound the orderly variety of the face of the earth,

as the sundry soyles, his style so altring oft . . .
Now, as the Mountains hie; then as the Valley lowe:
Heere, fruitfull as the Mead, there as the Heath be bare.
(*Works* ed. J. W. Hebel IV pp. 468 and 30)

But *topographia* does not necessarily mean landscape. Though Drayton is keen to introduce the new concept and form, its influence is only fitful. In his description of Romney Marsh he draws attention to the word "Landskip" by defining it in the margin: "The naturall expressing of the surface of a Country in Painting." Nevertheless he depicts the marsh in old-fashioned terms, as a pageant-figure in decorated robes

Embost with well-spread Horse, large Sheepe and full-fed Neate.
Some wallowing in the grasse, there lie a while to batten;
Some sent away to kill; some thither brought to fatten;
With Villages amongst oft powthred heere and there;
And (that the same more like to Landskip should appeare)
With Lakes and lesser Foards, to mitigate the heate
(In Summer when the Fly doth prick the gadding Neate,
Forc't from the Brakes, where late they browz'd the velvet buds)
In which they lick their Hides, and chew their savoury Cuds
(p. 364).

This is a vivid and delightful passage; but the "landskip"—a genre-scene of cattle and still water—has to be extricated from the geography. Margaret Cavendish, whose verse is often chaotic, manages a clearer impression:

> *Nature* adornes this *Island* all throughout,
> With *Land-skips*, *Prospects*, and Rills that run about.
> There *Hills* o're top the *Dales*, which levell be,
> Covered with *Cattell* feeding *Eagerly*.
> Where *Grasse* growes up even to the *Belly* high,
> Where *Beasts*, that chew their *Cud*, in *Pleasure* lye,
> *Whisking* their *Tailes* about, the *Flies* to beat,
> Or else to coole them from the *soultry heat*.[33]

Drayton's strength and his difficulties may be gathered from his description of Charnwood forest, in the second part of *Poly-Olbion*:

> Who will describe to life a Forrest, let him take
> Thy Surface to himselfe, nor shall he need to make
> An other forme at all, where oft in thee is found
> Fine sharp but easie Hills, which reverently are crownd
> With aged Antique Rocks, to which the Goats and Sheepe
> (To him that stands remoat) doe softly seeme to creepe,
> To gnaw the little shrubs, on their steep sides that grow;
> Upon whose other part, on some descending Brow,
> Huge stones are hanging out, as though they downe would drop,
> Where under-growing Okes on their old shoulders prop
> The others hory heads, which still seeme to decline,
> And in a Dimble neere (even as a place divine
> For Contemplation fit), an Ivy-seeled Bower,
> As Nature had therein ordayn'd some Sylvan power (p. 254).

He has now managed to subordinate his geographical knowledge to the visual scheme, but he shows little sense of distance or the interrelation of parts. The same is true of the work it so strikingly resembles, the shaggy Alpine landscapes of Roelant Savery. Drayton's definitions of landscape insist on the *surface*, and his response to pictures is correspondingly shallow. Landscape, for Drayton and Browne, is a gimmick. Not until the 1640s and 1650s do we find poets who obviously respect the art. Lovelace includes "th'*Elizian* plain" in Lely's repertoire, in his 'Peinture: a Panegyrick to the best Picture of Friendship Mr

Peter Lilly'.[34] His friend Eldred Revett was equally at home in painterly circles. He is fascinated by the paradox of the painter's illusionism, but appreciates also his direct and sensual involvement with the subject; he writes 'To his ingenious Friend, Master *Maes*, drawing the flowres in their successive growth'

> When the first parting bud gives it self vent
> And opes for breath ev'n stifled in the scent,
> You catch the clean unsulli'd beauty (grown
> By your rare art the Zanye of its own).[35]

He was himself sensitive to visual effects—he writes, for example, 'on the sight of a Lady, walking in an Evening, in white Sarsnet'.[36] His poem 'The Land-schap between two Hills' is a tribute to the maturity of the form. The poem emulates landscape in its accuracy of colour and texture, changing with distance, and its uncluttered and stately composition. The tone is at the same time rich and light. The human analogues are those suggested by the landscape itself—the gestures of trees, and the passage from fever to serenity and then feebleness, according to the sweep of the valley. In the same way we talk of the youth and age of a river. I give the whole of this enchanting poem; to my knowledge it has never received critical attention.

> Plac'd on yon' fair though beetle brow
> That on the pleasures frowns below,
> Let us with sprightly phancie thence
> Teach the dumb Rhetorik Eloquence;
> And leave the Painters Art out-gone,
> Inliv'ning by transcription.
>   First then observe with levell'd sight
> A rising to this opposite;
> As if the wind in billow drave
> Here, and had rowld the earth in wave:
> The Aspen and the Bramble heaves
> And a white foam froth's in the leaves:
> That spot beneath, that lies so plain
> Schorch'd here and there, hath lost the grain:
> As Sol there dried the Beams he swet
> And stain'd the grass-green coverlet;

That Goat the bushes nigh doth browse
Seems the un-ravell'd plush to frowse;
And now let fall the eye it sees
A pretty storm of clowdy trees,
To us seem black and full of rain,
As they would scatter in the plain:
From hence the hill declineth spent,
With imperceptible descent,
'Till un-awares abroad it flow
Lost in the deluge spreads below.
    An Age-bow'd oak doth under-root
As it would prostrate at it's foot;
Whose thrown-out arms in length display
And a fair shady carpet lay;
On it a lad in russet coat
His soul melts through the vocal oate;
And near that black eyed Nymph doth draw
As if her eyes hung on the straw:
The scrip and leathern Bottle nigh,
(With guardian too *Melampo*) lie:
The flocks are round about them spread
In num'rous fleece have clad the Meade;
And now our eyes but weakly see
Quite tippled with varietie:
Here the grass rowls, and hills between
Stud it with little tufts of green:
There in the midst a tree doth stray
Escap'd, as it had lost the way,
And a winding river steals
That with it self drunk curling reels,
A cheaper flood than *Tagus* goes
And with dissolved silver flowes.
Some way the field thence swells at ease
And lifts our sight up by degrees
To where the steep side dissie lies
Supinely fast in precipice
Till with the bank oppos'd it lie,
In a proportion'd Harmonie,
As Nature here did sit and sing,
About the *cradle* of the spring.[37]

Revett's previous poem was on the successive growth of flowers and 'The Land-schap' leads us through the cycle of life to end with birth; the next poem is 'A Frost'.

As the century progresses artists and writers try to make the landscape *deeper*, spatially and emotionally. The principle of variety is obeyed dramatically, and in depth. Evelyn compares Lucretius to a

> curious *Landskip*, or delicious prospect where sometimes from the cragginess of inaccessible Rocks, uneven and horrid precipices (such as are found, respecting those admirable plains of *Lombardy*) there breaks and divides (as the Wandring Traveller approaches) a passage to his eyes down into some goodly and luxurious valley; where [all things] conspire to create a new *Paradise*, and recompense him the pains of so many difficult accesses.[38]

Landscape artists showed an increasing taste for emotive contrasts of light and dark, enveloping shade and distant sunshine, or shafts of light in the gloomy forest. Such contrasts can be found in earlier literature—Ausonius, for example, emerges from the dark forest to a glittering prospect in *Mosella*—but they are not fully developed until the 1650s. It is an effect particularly suited to a northern climate, where brightness and coolness are not incompatible, and shade may be ominous rather than a welcome relief; its adaptation in literature is the first serious challenge to the *locus amoenus*, with its fossil Middle Eastern climate, as an image of complete delight.

This chiaroscuro landscape can be seen at various stages in Milton. The brothers in the *Ludlow Mask*, lost "in double night of darkness and of shades", pray

> som gentle taper
> Though a rush Candle from the wicker hole
> Of som clay habitation visit us
> With thy long levell'd rule of streaming light,
> And thou shalt be our star of *Arcady*,
> Or *Tyrian* Cynosure (336+).

Milton's conception of the wood seems influenced by contemporary landscapes; scattered cottages in a dark forest are a favourite theme, evoking a mingled sensation of comfort and loneliness. When the scene becomes nocturnal, lit by a single lamp (Fig. 3), these emotions are greatly intensified. In 'Bermudas', for example, Marvell shows the oranges "Like golden Lamps in a green Night". Shadow is not normally green;[39] here we are to imagine oranges throwing a dim light onto the foliage, with the darkness beyond. In 'The Garden', however, the shade is green because the dense leaves are illuminated from behind by the sky. It envelops the poet, and its generosity is contrasted with the "short and narrow verged Shade" of the single tree. We progress from the shade of the grove to the bird-like soul, shimmering in "the Glories of th'Almighty Sun".[40] One image embodies the anxiety of a tiny island community, the other the reassurance of one for whom solitude is a game. Similarly, the brothers pray for a single light as their cynosure, and sink back on the mere sounds of the community for comfort; but the speaker of *L'Allegro* begins, as they ended, with cockcrow and the sounds of human activity—then, as light builds up, the "Lantskip" itself is revealed. The parallelism is exact, even to the "cynosure". One represents the shrinking of the hope of light, the other, progression out of the darkness.

The word *landscape* is rare in Milton. A descriptive passage in William Browne is annotated "a curious landskip";[41] it refers quite clearly to a painting. On the other four occasions the word denotes, not the countryside in general, but the procession from darkness to sunlit land. *L'Allegro* celebrates the landscape which emerges after the scattering of night, parallel to the defeat of a more sinister darkness. This dramatic element deepens in *Paradise Lost*, reflecting not only Milton's personal development but the increased profundity of landscape description in the 1650s. After their first disturbed night, Adam and Eve emerge "from under shadie arborous roof" (V. 137) into the sun's first rays,

> Discovering in wide Lantskip all the East
> Of Paradise and *Edens* happie Plains (V. 142–3).

A fiercer contrast is used in Book II, to show the relief of decision and the surge of confidence in Satan:

As when from mountain tops the dusky clouds
Ascending, while the North wind sleeps, o'respread
Heav'ns chearful face, the low'ring Element
Scowls ore the dark'nd lantskip Snow, or showre;
If chance the radiant Sun with farewell sweet
Extend his ev'ning beam, the fields revive,
The birds thir notes renew . . . (488+).

Satan's progress is marked by intense images such as these; it is impossible not to share their jubilance and relief. At his first sight of this world

                    as when a Scout
Through dark and desart wayes with peril gone
All night; at last by break of chearful dawne
Obtains the brow of some high-climbing Hill,
Which to his eye discovers unaware
The goodly prospect of some foreign land
First-seen, or some renown'd Metropolis
With glistering Spires and Pinnacles adornd,
Which now the Rising Sun guilds with his beams.
Such wonder seis'd, though after Heaven seen,
The Spirit malign (III. 543+).

The images progress according to the structure of the narrative; a darkened landscape which is then lit, the great city seen in glittering prospect, a wide and innocent landscape, and later, in Book IX line 445+, the great city as a foetid trap. This rise and fall is in turn framed within the descriptions of hell. The moment when Satan first approaches paradise is therefore the keystone of an arch; here the emotive simile becomes actual. Though the garden wall is higher than the tops of the trees, Satan sees it from *within* the forest, which "over head up grew Insuperable highth of loftiest shade" (IV. 138–9) and impedes him with its undergrowth. "Lantskip" has Milton's usual meaning—the sun on the golden trees, viewed distantly from deep in the forest, generating

Vernal delight and joy, able to drive
All sadness but despair (IV. 155–6)

Vaughan describes the same sensation:

> I felt through all my powr's
> Such a rich air of sweets, as Evening showrs
> Fand by a gentle gale convey and breath
> On some parch'd bank . . .
> So have I known some beauteous *Paisage* rise
> In suddain flowres and arbours to my Eies,
> And in the depth and dead of winter bring
> To my Cold thoughts a lively sense of spring.
>
> ('Mount of Olives II')

Like everything else in Milton's paradise, this landscape reviews and surpasses the typical effects of the art, the rainbow, the sun recovering after showers or touching the clouds at sunset – various forms of light piercing the gloom:

> a circling row
> Of goodliest Trees loaden with fairest Fruit,
> Blossoms and Fruits at once of golden hue
> Appeerd, with gay enameld colours mixt:
> On which the Sun more glad impress'd his beams
> Than in fair Evening Cloud, or humid Bow,
> When God hath showrd the earth: so lovely seemd
> That Lantskip (IV. 146+).

It is surely wrong to detect a hollow note, as if Milton has to assure us that he means his description seriously,[42] in this profound and consistent image.

The landscape artist and poet have the same purpose—to go beyond the pictorial without violating it. They both work up an idea of human geography, a view of country life or regional character. Each must use different means. There are no plurals in painting, and the artist generalizes by using ideal composite structures. The poet can throw his horizons wider, and suggest an endless array of scenes and places; the structure remains the same. In *Coopers Hill* the individual places are 180° apart, and the hill is sometimes a viewpoint, and sometimes an object; but the poem is still constructed as a landscape with contrasting masses to right and left, and a river leading from the middle-ground to the distant city. The heroine's island-retreat in William Chamberlayne's epic *Pharonnida* (1659) is described in a panorama of 360°. On one side her father's castle, conveniently near, with a flowery park in front and the city all round—

> that civil Wilderness,
> The pathless Woods and ravenous beasts within
> Whose bulk were but the Metaphors for sin.
> (I, i.e. first pagination, p. 144).

Chamberlayne's reaction to the city is like Denham's; his eye is fascinated but his social sense repelled. He induces us to share these feelings by placing the most glorious objects in the opposite direction:

> We turn to view the stately Hils, that fence
> The other side oth'happy Isle, from whence
> All that delight or profit could invent
> For rural pleasures was for prospect sent.
>   As Nature strove for something uncouth in
> So fair a dress, the struggling streams are seen
> With a loud murmure rowling 'mongst the high
> And rugged clefts; one place presents the eye
> With barren rudeness, whilst a neighbouring field
> Sits cloathd in all the bounteous spring could yield;
> Here lovely Landskips, where thou mightst behold,
> When first the Infant Morning did unfold
> The Dayes bright Curtains, in a spatious Green,
> Which Natures curious Art had spread between
> Two bushy Thickets, that on either hand
> Did like the Fringe of the fair Mantle stand,
> A timerous herd of grasing Deer, and by
> Them in a shady Grove, through which the eye
> Could hardly pierce, a wel-built Lodge, from whence
> The watchful Keepers careful diligence
> Secures their private walks; from hence to look
> On a deep Valley, where a silver Brook,
> Doth in a soft and busie murmure slide
> Betwixt two Hils, whose shadows strove to hide
> The liquid wealth they were made fruitful by
> From ful discoveries of the distant eye . . .
> Where the more lofty Rock admits not these

Domestick pleasures, Nature there did please
Her self with wilder pastimes; on those Clifts
Whose rugged heads the spatious Mountain lifts
To an unfruitful height, amongst a wild
Indomitable herd of Goats, the mild
And fearful Cony, with her busie feet,
Makes Warmth and Safety in one Angle meet.
   From this wild range, the eye contracted in
The Islands narrow bounds would think't had been
I th'world before, but now were come to view
An Angel-guarded Paradice . . . (I pp. 144–6)

This is a gallery of landscapes, but it is also a single piece, built up on the contrasts of rough and smooth, shady and open, deep and light. We recognize familiar themes—the unfolding dawn, the deer set within symmetrical groves, the lodge deep in the trees, the steep valley between two hills, vanishing into the distance, with goats climbing the barren rocks. The visual and the emotional are carefully related; the one anomalous detail, the rabbits, have a particular purpose in defining our sensations—comfort in the midst of enormous grandeur. The domestic security of the island turns space into a luxury.

The poet can develop landscape further than the artist because he can set it in a context. *Topographia* is no more than an episode within the heroic poem, and not an entity in itself. Its strength lies in its significant obliqueness to the main action. It interposes a different order of time; urgency is suspended, pleasurable idyllic, grief elegiac. The harbour in *Aeneid* I, for example, is suddenly human and peaceful, in a poem hitherto entirely Olympian and Titanic. It provides relief but hints at seduction and oblivion, suitably enough for Carthage. It is a picture of the desire to relinquish struggle. The pastimes on Pharonnida's island "did contract the day To pitied beauty; time steals away On downy feet", and the lovers are "rockt in the soft Armes of the calmest pleasures" (I p. 151). But the action of the poem soon crowds in—an appalling tangle of civil war and intrigue. The hero leaves for battle, and the heroine's father is tricked into imprisoning her:

> the pleasant Isle
> Whose Walks, fair Gardens, Prospects did beguile
> Time of so many happy hours, must now,
> A solitary Wildernesse whose brow
> Winter had bound in folds of Ice, be left
> To wail their absence, whilst each Tree bereft
> Of Leaves did like to Virgin Mourners stand,
> Cloathd in white Vails of glittering Icelets . . .
> the Meadowes green
> And fragrant Mantle withering lay between
> The grizzlie mountains naked armes. All growes
> Into a swift decay (I pp. 205–6).

The landscape criticizes and suspends the action, but is obliterated in its turn.

Paradise Lost is unique among heroic poems in that the description of paradise is not peripheral. In Milton's proposed tragedy (third draft) the "Chorus of Angels . . . sing the marriage song and describe Paradice" at the end of Act 2. In 'Adam unparadiz'd' the archangel Gabriel takes over the task, in the opening lines; a special emphasis is placed on his role, "the angel Gabriel as by his name signifying a prince of power tracing paradise with a more free office". Grotius's *Adamus Exul* begins with the arrival of Satan within prospect of Eden. His description is large and dramatic, but though it begins "Ecce" it does not subordinate information to visual realism—he tells us, for example, the minerals in the soil and the sounds of the leaves.[43] Andreini give Adam one "landscaped" description, of a river running through meadows and into an impassable flooded valley, bright with swans and orange-trees. The irony is twofold, dramatic and literary. This moment of relaxation comes just before Eve reveals she has eaten the fruit. The enticing river, and the deep valley into which he can look but not walk, are exact models of temptation and transgression. He is led by two doves, echoing the *Aeneid*; at the end of their trip both heroes find a tree which leads them to hell. Adam is the unwitting protagonist of a heroic poem, and, suitably, his description is an entrancing but localized episode, relating *obliquely* to the main action.[44] The play's stage designs resemble landscape only in this scene (Fig. 4); elsewhere description is confined to the formal terrace

(Fig. 5), to scattered references ("care valli, e foreste"), and to the conventional lists of delicious objects and absent plagues. The same applies to every earlier description of Eden in narrative verse, as far as I have read. In sacred iconography, by contrast, the garden of Eden had long become a landscape. Milton's originality is to treat paradise with the mastery that secular poetry had absorbed from landscape art. He now feels confident to take over from Gabriel.

Satan's progress, as we have seen, is marked by a series of landscape images which involve us in his success. They culminate when he approaches the border of paradise:

> So on he fares, and to the border comes
> Of *Eden*, where delicious Paradise,
> Now nearer, Crowns with her enclosure green
> As with a rural mound the champain head
> Of a steep wilderness, whose hairie sides
> With thicket overgrown, grottesque and wilde,
> Access deni'd; and over head up grew
> Insuperable highth of loftiest shade,
> Cedar, and Pine, and Firr, and branching Palm,
> A Silvan Scene, and as the ranks ascend
> Shade above shade, a woodie Theatre
> Of stateliest view (IV. 131+).

The distant mound grows into an "insuperable highth"—dishonestly, since he is to jump it with ease. Two dramas are to be distinguished; Satan is a character in the story of the fall, but he also dramatizes himself. "Silvan Scene" defines us as the audience; "woodie Theatre" is Satan's view from the footlights. Milton surely remembered his intention to begin a play at this point, and the passage reflects careful pondering of theatrical devices. "Scene" meant three things in succession: a curtain, framed within the proscenium and down-stage flats, concealing the inner stage and depicting a general and anticipatory landscape; the entire set, in deep perspective, stating the theme and mood of the piece to come; and the action itself. The second stage is introduced suddenly and followed by an interval of silent wonder, as the illusion and significance is allowed to sink in—"Men the silent *Scene* assist." The *silvis scaena* is not here the setting for an action, as in the *Ludlow Mask* and

Paradise Regain'd; it evokes its original context in Virgil's harbour (*Aeneid* I. 164), a static picture celebrating safe arrival, but anticipating a troublesome seduction. This is confirmed by its vertical arrangement, by its position among "hairie sides With thicket overgrown, grottesque and wilde", by the suddeness with which he leaps from one sight to the next, and by the "new wonder" of his languorous prospect in the proper scene of paradise. Satan is the presenter of his own drama, and uses all the fierce skills of his angelic nature; but he is overwhelmed by this momentous description, written and produced by the poet from an original idea by God. He takes up his position "for prospect" in line 200, and though he is "undelighted" in line 286, he is "still in gaze" at line 356, well into the dumb show. His perception—for once—coincides with ours, the audience. In this way Milton combines Grotius and his own early plans; Satan introduces the prospect, but it is the supreme work of Milton's own imagination, "tracing paradise with a more free office".

Heaven itself is landscaped in Milton's poem. The warring angels

> pluckt the seated Hills with all thir load,
> Rocks, Waters, Woods, and by the shaggie tops
> Up lifting bore them in thir hands (VI.644+).

This image is all the more stupendous because Milton is aware of how settled the countryside is; gravity and the slow action of geological forces "seat" the hills and "load" them with rocks, waters and woods. They become a miniature landscape, a standardized unit. However violent the action, he will not imagine them split; there is nothing as fearsome as Henry More's argument against the movement of the earth:

> If she should move about, then would she sling
> From off her self those fair extructed loads
> Of carved stone: The air aloud would sing
> With brushing trees: Beasts in their dark aboads
> Would brained be by their own caves; th'earth strowd
> With strange destruction.[45]

In keeping with the theme, Milton's approach is less practical, more formulaic:

> At [God's] command the uprooted Hills retir'd
> Obsequious, Heav'n his wonted face renewd,
> And with fresh Flourets Hill and Valley smil'd (VI. 781+).

Milton's havoc is reversable.
Earth is made in the image of heaven:

> For Earth hath this variety from Heav'n
> Of pleasure situate in Hill and Dale (VI. 640–1).

The variegation of hill-and-dale is conceived as an object in its own right, a single source of overriding pleasure. But this form must be properly clothed; the third day of creation is only complete when

> with high woods the hills were crownd,
> With tufts the vallies and each fountain side,
> With borders long the Rivers. That Earth now
> Seemd like to Heav'n, a seat where Gods might dwell,
> Or wander with delight, and love to haunt
> Her sacred shades (VII. 326+).

It is now recognizable to the archangel as a *seat*—a site, configuration or personal estate; Paradise is to be "a happy rural seat of various view".
      The earth is sweet also to fallen angels:

> With what delight could I have walkt thee round
> If I could joy in aught, sweet interchange
> Of Hill, and Vallie, Rivers, Woods and Plaines,
> Now Land, now Sea, and Shores with Forrest crownd,
> Rocks, Dens, and Caves . . . (IX. 144+).

Satan is addressing the earth, but he seems also to speak to the "sweet interchange" itself; just as we are made to read "Hill and Dale" as a unit, so here Satan perceives the landscape as one piece, built up of deliciously contrasting parts. He recognizes "a seat where Gods might dwell", and dissolves into self-pity:

> but I in none of these
> Find place or refuge; and the more I see
> Pleasures about me, so much more I feel
> Torment within me, as from the hateful siege
> Of contraries; all good to me becomes
> Bane (IX. 118+).

He articulates his misery in the same antithetical terms that he discovered in the landscape, though with pain instead of pleasure in their combination. Adam has no need for landscape; connoisseurship grows on the forbidden tree. Adam's reward is a greater prospect; Satan is consigned to

> Rocks, Caves, Lakes, Fens, Bogs, Dens, and shades of death,
> A Universe of death, which God by curse
> Created evil, for evil only good,
> Where all life dies, death lives . . . (II. 621+).

Hell is a wickedly accurate travesty of the ideal landscape; that monosyllabic list of places remains a jarring memory behind the shapely and mellifluous lines of earth

> Powrd forth profuse on Hill and Dale and Plain
> In Wood or Wilderness, Forrest or Den
> Through wood, through waste, o're hill, o're dale
> Among the Groves, the Fountains, and the Flowrs
> To Hill, or Valley, Fountain, or fresh shade
> In Forrest wild, in Thicket, Brake, or Den
> Hill, Dale, and shadie Woods, and sunnie Plains,
> And liquid Lapse of murmuring streams
> Ye Hills and Dales, ye Rivers, Woods and Plains
>   sweet interchange
> Of Hill, and Vallie, Rivers, Woods and Plains.[46]

Randolph's gentle trick has become Milton's *forte*—a landscape compressed into a harmonious phrase.

The successful description of Paradise must surpass all other landscapes. Milton makes full use of the rhetorical figure out-topping, which loco-descriptive poets had made into a beautiful and recondite game:

the Gardens of *th'Hesperides*,
Semiram's pensil'ones, *Alcinous'es*,
Lucullus's, nor *Seneca's* to boot,
Compar'd but unto this, were nothing too't . . .
For you *Thessalian Tempe's Seat*
Shall now be scorn'd as obsolete;
Aranjuez, as less, disdain'd;
The *Bel-Retiro* as constrain'd . . .[47]

He had to solidify the convention, but not sink under an accumulation of learned and sensuous details. The new ideal landscape aspired to be comprehensive *and* realistic, organized *and* relaxed. This was the framework on which Milton could construct his encyclopaedic rhapsody. Compared to a field, a grove, a spring, a river-island, and a mountain, it proves to be all five at once. Eden is comprehensive in the same way as Pharonnida's island; it is crammed with scenes of natural delight, but these are revealed in a great sweep of the eye, in leisurely and subtle contrasts, steep and gentle, solemn and glad, shady and revealed. The sound imitates this rhythm

As if the wind in billows drave
Here, and had rowld the earth in wave;[48]

sometimes it is tense and massive, sometimes mellifluous and diffuse. Paradise is still an enormous catalogue of delights, but set into a deeper space, visually managed. The brooks make serpentine patterns and hide themselves under the pendent shades, like the rivers in Montemayor and Chamberlayne. The fabulous plants are assigned to units of various size or shape according to the lie of the land; they are not ranked evenly, but "interposed" with an artist's hand. In this way Milton imitates the cause of abundance, and not just its outcome.

The principle of his landscape is this: the smaller the object the more fantastic it may be. Individual plants may have golden fruit or no thorns, the pebbles of the stream are jewels and the bower is mosaic; but the large self-seeding patterns of the plants, and the geological form of hills and valleys, are entirely credible. It is the precise opposite of a contemporary garden. The central and unifying force in this landscape is water. The ideal landscape picture is a model river system viewed from high land, precipitous nearby and sluggish in the plain, but continuous in rhythm throughout. The removal of fantasy was the rediscovery of geology. Even the simplest landscapes had headlong springs and rich rivers, different in mood. Pharonnida's prospect begins with violent streams in the rocks, and leads into the distance by way of a silver brook. Her island

> did stand
> Divided from the Continent by th'wide
> Armes of a spatious stream, whose wanton pride
> In Cataracts from th'Mountains broke;

the mount thus raised is a "type of Paradice", like "fair *Eden* 'mids the Springs of *Havilah*" (I pp. 143–4). Here, too, the pressure of the river against the mound creates a stream

> whose Spring did live,
> When from the Hils cool Womb broke forth, within
> A *Grotto*, whence before it did begin
> To take its weeping farewel, into all
> The various Forms restrictive Art could call
> Her Elemental Instruments unto
> Obedience by, it Courts th'admiring view
> Of pleas'd Spectators (I p. 147).

Superficially the two poets describe the same thing—a mount of paradise on a river, and a spring which takes every possible form as it flows to rejoin it. In Chamberlayne the water is made to seem fantastic, incidental, a mark of the division of land by human effort—precisely not what Milton intends. His art is the opposite of "restrictive": his river determines every form, visits every plant, and operates every emotional climax—the gushing and pouring of the flowery valleys, the murmurings, the thirst of the mountain soil, the darker passages through the mountain, and the mercurial stillness of the lake, where the waters unite. The syntax, too, is fluvial. One sentence contains the whole landscape, serpentine and inexorable: from "Southward" (IV. 223) it runs to the first colon, gathers itself at "Thus", multiplies to match the dispersing and varying of the stream, and closes at "unite their streams" after forty-one lines. The impetus of the description, the placing of the elements and their increasing size and depth, are all determined by the river.

Genesis insisted on the prominence of the rivers. Grotius's chorus has a long and beautiful address to the river Euphrates, and Adam's long and innocent description is supported by Andreini's Biblical notes. The conventional description of Eden embroidered hugely on three facts; the rivers, the centrality of the tree of life, and the presence of all good species. Milton creates a profound landscape by simple means; instead of considering his data separately, he combines them into a single proposition. Satan takes vantage on the central tree and sees a natural panorama carved by the river, clothed perfectly in all green things.

Critics have doubted whether Milton can be called a true landscape artist. Christopher Hussey finds no pictorial composition in *L'Allegro*; Roy Daniells finds Eden predominantly architectural; J. R. Knott appreciates the depth and variety which makes Milton nearer to *Coopers Hill* than to the *locus amoenus*, but finds Eden "never static, or simply pictorial" (what picture is?); Helen Gardner sees it as a landscape garden, "but its beauty and deliciousness is conveyed to us by appeal to the most immediate of our senses".[49] Pictorial landscape does not mean the removal of atmosphere, movement and sensual memories, however; it is a structure to evoke them.

Stanley Koehler, in *Milton Studies* VIII (1975), comes nearest to appreciating the fullness of Milton's landscape; he compares it to late eighteenth-century ideas. He does not realize that landscape theory and practice flourished in the first half of the seventeenth century. "The pictorial type of landscape", according to A. C. Judson, was "very rare indeed in the seventeenth century. . . . As yet landscape had scarcely been discovered."[50] Jean Hagstrum detects no influence of ideal landscape on English poetry before Thomson, and in this he is echoed by Mario Praz and Jeffrey Spencer.[51] I hope this has been sufficiently disproved.

Landscape was a new found land. It made unfamiliar demands on the viewer's emotions and sense of reality. John Barclay, enthralled by the view from Greenwich hill, asks himself

"What should it bee, that thus unawares had ravished mee?
Why should this prospect soe wonderfully please? What hid-
den force or reason had thus wrought upon my minde?"[52]
A painter has "powerful skill to cheate the Eye With cunning
Shaddows, and faire *Imagerye*":[53]

> Lanscape is nothing but Deceptive visions. The greatest con-
> ning is to beguile and cosson your own eyes . . . in such manner
> that many tymes in a table of not a spanne long a manns
> imaginacion may be quite carried out of the country over seas
> and citties by a surprise of his own making.[54]

Margaret Cavendish describes the visit of a "gentle harmlesse
Spirit, that us'd to haunt me in the dead of *Night*", bringing "a
vision of some fine Land-skip".[55] She is *haunted* by the vision.
Writers are not sure whether the new experience of landscape
is an angelic visitation or a Satanic delusion—but few imaginations could withstand its power and influence.

2

Green Thought

Social and intellectual applications of the concept of landscape

> *What hidden force or reason had thus*
> *wrought upon my minde?*
> (John Barclay, *Icon Animorum*)

Barclay's description of the Greenwich landscape is strategically placed, to draw the reader into his book. The passage is immediately attractive in its own right, as later allusions and plagiarisms show;[1] but the author's real purpose is to prepare us gradually for his main argument, a comprehensive study of social psychology and human geography. He sideslips easily from landscapes to people, from aesthetics to emotions, from the eye to the mind, from the individual to the social, and from human institutions to divine providence; one principle of structural balance and variety, he claims, governs all these cases. Landscape is an instrument of thought, a useful analogue for personal and social values. What are the properties of this mode of thought?

The distinguishing features of ideal landscape are attractiveness, realism, comprehensiveness and organized structure. It is particularly suited to panegyric—the ideal combination of virtues in the great man corresponds to the perfect visual experience:

> So thousand diverse *Species* fill the aire,
> Yet neither crowd nor mix confusedly there;
> Beasts, Houses, Trees and Men together lye
> Yet enter *undisturb'd* into the Eye.[2]

A landscape embodies its owner; the same structure is discovered in both:

> With such an easie and unforc'd Ascent,
> *Windsor* her gentle bosome doth present;

Where no stupendious Cliffe, no threatening heights
Accesse deny, no horrid steepe affrights,
But such a Rise as doth at once invite
A pleasure and a reverence from the sight.
Thy Masters Embleme, in whose face I saw
A friend-like sweetnesse and a King-like aw,
Where Majestie and love so mixt appeare,
Both gently kinde, both royally severe.
(*Coopers Hill*, 1642 version)

Ariamnes, in Chamberlayne's *Pharonnida*, combines all the moral virtues in his devotion to the golden mean; his estate reveals the same harmony of divers qualities:

In the composure of this happy place
Wherein he lived, as if fram'd to embrace
So brave a Soul as now did animate
It with his presence, strength and beauty sate
Combin'd in one (I p. 6).

The hill and grove at Bilborough express the composure of unlike qualities in Fairfax. Marvell's poem is as precise as co-ordinate geometry; "every mode of excellence is separated from its adjacent fault by a nice line of limitation", and each positive quality is contrasted with its negative form. Retirement is normally associated with littleness, and height with offensive grandeur. Hills are normally too bare, and groves too gloomy. But Fairfax's retirement combines the best of each:

Nor he the Hills without the Groves,
Nor Height but with Retirement loves.

The whole poem is an expansion of this formula. The hill combines stiffness and softness without falling into abruptness and hook-shouldered height. Its slope is soft and its height commanding but not rugged or heaven-daring. Terror, fear and wounding are here only in innocent versions, in groves not of pikes and mountains not of dying men. The trees feel both love and reverence, the desire to grow and modesty to restrain themselves; the same response is elicited from the reader. Bilborough remains, however, a living landscape.

Marvell is aware of the practical business of walking and shipping, of the variegated pattern of the land here and at Almescliffe, whose rocky outcrop against the horizon does look savage and deformed, and of the imposing power of fully-grown roots and trunks, which contrast so strangely with the animated whisper of their leaves. Personification and accurate descriptions are not at odds; the pleasing conflict of human qualities seems to bring Marvell's sense of landscape to fruition.

The art of landscape depends on "placing" the elements correctly. The social analogy was obvious to Anthony Gibson, writing in 1610 on John Guillim's *Display of Heraldrie*:

> As in a curious *Lant-schape*, oft we see
> *Nature* so follow'd as wee think it's shee,
> Trees, Rivers, Hils, Towers, Valleis, Country farmes
> Higher or lower plac'd; so heere are *Armes* (f.(a)3v).

The "Lantskip" of *L'Allegro*, as we saw, is organized on the contrast of great and small, lofty and low. It is in fact an assembly of topographical metaphors for social class; "russet" and "gray" were associated with peasant clothing, barren mountains with great men and meadows with the "labouring" poor.[3] These habitual metaphors have been turned back into actual topography, but they retain their hierarchic order. The human analogy "places" the landscape. In *To Penshurst* the division of the grounds into "lower land", "middle grounds" and the haunts of gods corresponds precisely to the social divisions within the hall. Richard Fanshawe echoes and develops Jonson's scheme; civilization, he believes, only began when society and the land were stratified. In the primaeval age men were communistic beasts and the landscape was correspondingly chaotic:

> Woods yet unto the Mountains did not passe,
> Nor Heards beneath in grassy Meadowes feed,
> Nor Corne inrich the middle Grounds; but Grasse,
> And weeds, and stifled corne, were shuffled in one Masse.[4]

This is no metaphor. Both poets uphold a doctrine of land management based on social subordination. Property and the orderly countryside are the same thing. In the composition of landscape practicality and aesthetics are allowed to melt together. As it develops in the seventeenth century from simple *placing* to complex *interrelating* it grows correspondingly richer as a means of displaying social doctrine. Denham's landscaping of the area round Cooper's hill, discussed in Chapter 1, depends on binding together disparate elements—hill, river, wood and meadow—by metaphors of mutual cherishing and by an aesthetic theory of contrasting values, rough, clear, threatening, calm:

> While the steep horrid roughness of the Wood
> Strives with the gentle calmness of the flood
> Such huge extreams when Nature doth unite
> Wonder from thence results, from thence delight.

The whole passage functions in the poem as a model for the restitution of political harmony by the integration of factions in the state and classes in society. Denham's landscape is a system of interrelated "values" in the aesthetic and painterly sense; he also intends them to be moral and social. This meaning is conveyed as much by the poem's texture, its verbal paintwork, as by its explicit content.

This enrichment and expansion of verbal description may be seen if we compare Jacobean to Caroline *topographia*. The traditional *locus amoenus*, for example, is transformed into an ideal landscape; the pleasure it yields develops at the same time from simple joy in grass, flowers and water to a complex structured emotion—pleasure of ownership, pleasure in the well-managed estate, pleasure of seeing everything in its proper place. Lovelace congratulates Lely on the realism of his landscapes:

> by thee
> As prepossess'd we enjoy th'*Elizian* plain,
> Which but before was flattered in our brain.[5]

The Jacobean imagination allowed for two kinds of topography. For Herbert the *locus amoenissimus* is paradise, which he conceives as a formal garden of fruit and flowers; he can use as synonyms "a treasure, a box of jewels, a ring . . . a garden in a

Paradise". The perfect place is a collection of dainties, "a box where sweets compacted lie", "*Natures Closet* of preserves".[6] The country house poem, on the other hand, stresses the serviceability of nature and its hierarchic arrangement; the controlling idea is "produce" rather than "pleasure". Landscape transcends this distinction. Amplitude combines with plenitude; the new *locus amoenus* includes spacious landscapes in its catalogue of pleasures:

> For all this *Place* is *fertile*, *rich* and *faire*;
> Both *Woods*, and *Hills*, and *Dales*, in *Prospect* are.[7]

Caroline taste began to reject freakish and "curious" pleasures, preferring to "enjoy at home what's reall".[8] The rich display of contrasting terrains evokes a sense of social well-being.

The gradual development of landscape may be illustrated from one work. George Daniel's historical poem *The Genius of this Great and Glorious Ile* (1637) begins in a typical *locus amoenus*, "By the Sweet Streame, with pleasant Mirtles crowned", representing England. The poet invites the Muses and the Gods to descend from heaven and "blesse, and be happie, in this fragrant vale":

> here Paradice on Earth is now,
> But 'twill be Heaven in All, when blest in you.

He appeals to them by evoking a future time when

> The wood-nymphs here shall waite you; here the Fawnes
> And prick-ear'd Satires shall your Groves frequent,
> Sporting themselves over your fertile lawnds:
> The naiades in Azure vestiment,
> With Hairs unbound, the willing Sand shall print.[9]

We anticipate the proper fulfilment of the land. The divine genius of Great Britain appears, and recounts the history of the previous two centuries: villains, closely resembling the present opposition, have been crucifying the country with civil war, but gradually she struggles from obscurity through violence to maturity and peace. Daniel expresses this progress through *topographia*. The opening scene is no more than a

symbolic frame to the action; the allegorical abode of Misery is
detailed but horrible; only under Caroline rule are we given a
real landscape, confident and rich:

> Now pleasant verdure cloaths my fertile Meads;
> And sun-burnt Ceres crowns the Plowman's toyle.[10]

Passing from symbolism to history is like passing from two
dimensions to three. The present is a Georgic landscape, where
the Gods of place and skill protect and bless the land— just
what we looked forward to from the start. Vicious creatures
are banished, and gentle ones restored:

> The well-clad Cunnie, and the harmles Sheepe,
> Here graze; and in full flocks the Hills do keepe.
> These on the Downs; birds cherup in the woods,
> The Tritons Joy and sport upon my floods . . .[11]

Everything rejoices in its proper place, "And Peace and Plenty
tell, a STUART reigns". The "genius of the land" is equally
political and aesthetic, a natural guide and unifying power in
both designs.

In a sense the new landscape *was* natural – scale and lighting
were consistent, and outlines were taken from the real forms
of trees, hills and rivers. Milton and Denham both give water
the central role in their landscapes. Human activities and
mythological creatures are presented as if in a natural habitat.
The sensation of naturalness, however, is easily confused
with nature itself. Landscape is an aesthetic contrivance,
even though its maker tries to palm it off as Nature's
work:

> Nature here hath been so free
> As if she said leave this to me.
> (*Upon Appleton House* st. 10)

The accidental affinity of topography and emotion is equally
"naturalised"; Cowley, for example, laments in a

> gloomy shade
> By Nature only for my sorrows made.[12]

The boundaries between subject and inanimate object become fuzzy:

> We're now become a fine coole shady walke . . .
> And if sad Soules would mallencholy tell
> Let them come, to visitt, where wee dwell,
> For wee're become a fine thick Grove of thought.[13]

> But I would see my self appear
> Within the Violets drooping head . . .
>
> (James Shirley, 'The Garden')

> Or turn me but, and you shall see
> I was but an inverted Tree.
>
> (*Upon Appleton House*, st. 71)

This mental vegetation is presented, with great sympathy, in Marvell's 'Garden'; the ecstatic dissolution of common-sense is seen as a response to the loveliness of the garden itself. "Green thought" appears to blur together the properties of nature and the properties of the mind. Such melting or softening is inherent in our response to landscape; it helps the social analogy to be accepted as natural.

This mushiness has to be offset by firmness – hence the insistence on structure and discipline. 'The Garden' ends with a different kind of green thought, the dial—a formal and constructive use of greenery. Milton tries to capture these two responses to landscape in the first conscious moments of Adam and Eve; Adam stands upright and gazes at the creatures of the world in strict hierarchic order, Eve is led by "a murmuring sound of waters" and crouches over her own reflection in a lake! Marvell and Milton both recognize the critical relationship between two tendencies—one structuring and objectifying, one blurring and falsifying. They can coexist happily in the state of nature.

Seventeenth-century users of landscape seem to be well aware of these opposing tendencies. "Landscape" came to be synonymous on the one hand with "a definitive model", on the other with "a pernicious delusion".

We have already seen how landscape was interpreted as the epitome of a region. It may also symbolize the world, a synop-

tic vision or an intellectual system; it is in fact equivalent to a
"Mirrour", "Prospective" or "Glasse"—all forms of encyclopaedia. I show elsewhere how the word *landscape* was held to
be synonymous with *prospective* and *perspective*.[14] Walter
Charleton's verse paraphrase of Helmont is a "transcriptive
Landskip of Magnetisme", a "translator's Landskip, or Abstract"; within every creature is "an adumbration or landskip
of the whole Univers".[15] London is "our England of England,
and our Landskip and Representation of the whole Island".
Cromwell is a "lantskipp of iniquity" (*OED* 4e). Fanshawe
published his translation of *Il Pastor Fido* "because it seems to
me (beholding it *at the best light*) a Lantskip of these Kingdoms
. . . as well in the former flourishing, as the present distrac-
tions thereof".[16] On this analogy the behaviour of the eye in a
fine landscape is practically equivalent to thought itself. Barclay's mind was as ravished as his eye by the prospect of
Greenwich. Denham's eye moves "swift as thought" from
Cooper's hill to the ominous haze of London in the distance.
Charles II, in Waller's poem on St James's Park, retires into a
grove to meditate on the new constitution; the park itself, with
its adjacent buildings, provides him with a model:

> His fancy objects from his view receives;
> The prospect thought and contemplation gives.

The "prospective"—a mountain-view or telescopic vision—is
almost invariably associated with the wide-ranging political
survey. William Browne, for example, compares his denunciation of court-parasites to a man scanning the landscape with
"a glasse prospective". The simile concludes with a pregnant
pun—telescope and political poem are both "an Instrument of
truth compos'd".[17] Landscape, with its wide scope and mastery of distance, suggests a vision of transcendant truth. The
kingdom of Christ appears to George Wither

> Described by a Patterne unto me,
> As if it painted, in dim Landskip, were;
> And my Unbounded soule runs rambling over
> So many objects that, if she should give
> Account of ev'ry thing she can discover,
> I should relate what few would yet believe.[18]

Such vision requires a special vantage-point. The heroine in Joseph Beaumont's *Psyche* (1648), is taken in an airborne chariot to the Holy Land as part of her theology lesson; she and her guide climb mount Calvary

> that that Prospect might
> Yield her with uncontrolled Libertie
> *Of Loves chief stations* an open sight (p. 221).

Landscape has become a didactic model, and prospect the equivalent of *synopsis*.

Proper use of landscape establishes the poet's authority. The panoramic view allows him to appear clear without plainness, inspired without fantasy, pious, visionary but strong on facts. He imitates, in fact, the prophet of ancient state religion—the *auspex*. This is the context for *Coopers Hill*;

> Nor wonder, if (advantag'd in my flight,
> By taking wing from thy auspicious height)
> Through untrac't waies and airie paths I flie,
> More boundlesse in my fancie than my eie. (1642 version)

The prospect lends grandeur to the verse, and induces Denham's claim to speak with a privileged voice. The argument imitates the visual field that evokes it—"one perfect peece it grows". Reason itself is

> that all-knowing powre that holdes within
> The goodly prospective of all this frame,
> (Where, whatsoever is, or what hath bin,
> Reflects a certaine image of the same).[19]

Time is landscaped as well as space. History becomes typology; past and present make one "certaine image"—a perpetual and beneficient *status quo* opposed to the perennial forces of evil, the future being accordingly dismal or glorious. One philosophical assumption embraces all these forms of prospect—"vision is only valid if it is elevated and disengaged". The position is familiar from Stoic writers, and from Lucretius:

Suave, mari magno turbantibus aequora ventis,
e terra magnum alterius spectare laborem (II. 1–2).
(How nice to be on the shore when the open sea is churned
by storm-winds, watching someone else in great difficulty.)

The philosophical man does not simply see *more*—he sees
through. From his vantage he sees deep contradictions in normal practice, but can reveal the single principle which explains
them. In a topographical setting, like *Coopers Hill* or Katherine
Philips's 'Resvery', the usual metaphors are restored to physical reality—"height", "situation" and "point of view".

Once the landscape has been established as a model of truth,
bad design can be equated with moral deviation. The prospect
must be neither cluttered nor bleak; both are associated with
extremism. Parliamentarians "streight Prospect scorne, and
Private View"; the tyrant "seems to cut down ev'ry Tree That
clouds th'ambitious prospect of his eye"; "Ambitious souls,
that climbing to the height, Enlarge their Prospect, with their
Appetite" end up in a precipice. Educational, religious and
political malpractice are all expressed as vast or constricted
prospects.[20] Pharonnida's eye delights in the expansion and
contraction of her island-landscape; the same effect in *Coopers
Hill* is associated with Puritan violence:

> casting round
> My wandring eye, an emulous Hill doth bound
> My more contracted sight, whose top of late
> A Chappell crown'd, till in the common fate
> The neighbouring Abbey fell, (may no such storme
> Fall in our times, where ruine must reforme). (1642 version)

It is his *brows* that contract, thinking of his enemies—but he
presents it as a reflex of the eye itself. Once again we see how
aesthetic and visual values slide into social ones. The "Lantskip
of these Kingdoms" must be viewed in *"the best light"*—
through the right perspective.

Vision and thought are not necessarily the same, as Henry
More observed:

> the whole world that Ope doth lie
> Unto our sight, not reason but our eye

> Discovers first, but upon that fair view
> Our reason takes occasion to trie
> Her proper skill.[21]

Reason and the eye may be at odds. Perspective may be false, the eye cheated, dazzled or blocked; Marvell even claims in 'Eyes and Tears' that the sight is "Self-deluding". Landscapes could be considered as a dazzling trick, as Suckling did in 'Farewell to Love':

> Well shadow'd Landskip, fare-ye-well.

In Marvell's *Further Advice to a Painter* "Landskip" means simply a trivial picture of cheats; in *Appleton House* (st. 58) it is an optical trick, "drawn in Looking-glass" and distorting the scale. The effect of distance is achieved by loss of clarity: Nashe describes Great Yarmouth "in dimme farre off launce-skippe", as early as 1599; the sins of respectable women "shew in landscip, far off and full of shadow"; the Jews "saw Christ presented in land-scept", rather than directly.[22] This dimness is often associated with deception:

> we'l present
> To him (as 'twere by Lanskip) your intent:
> We will imploy an Agent who shall speak
> By circumambitues, and slyly break
> The Ice of your desires.[23]

Drummond calls on the Scots in 1638 to abandon their

> few Months Liberty of Dancing to your own Shadows, in new Magistracies, Offices of State, imaginary and fantastical Councils, Landskips of Commonwealths, and an icy Grandeur, erected by your selves.[24]

In his religious verse he uses the same image of sombre evanescence:

> To me this World did once seem sweet and faire,
> While Senses light Minds Perspective kept blind;
> Now like imagin'd Landskip in the Aire
> And weeping Raine-bows her best Joyes I find.[25]

Landscape could be interpreted as a pernicious fantasy, dangerously beautiful.

The ambiguity of landscape imagery is shown in Denham's major works, *The Sophy* and *Coopers Hill*—published simultaneously in 1642. One was hailed by Herrick as a "prospective poem", and uses all the devices of landscape and prospect for political ends; the other is a private introspective tragedy, emphasizing the failures and limitations of worldly vision. Mirza, the hero of *The Sophy*, is a younger version of Gloucester in *King Lear*. He trusts excessively to material success and worldly reason, is captured and blinded by his own family, and is rescued from hideous destruction by an appeal to philosophic patience. Images of vision run throughout the play. At first they are obviously ironic, but these ironies are resolved when the blinded hero learns to differentiate between the false world and the true inner landscape. Happiness, he comes to believe,

> is something sure within us, not subjected
> To sence or sight, onely to be discern'd
> By reason my soules eye, and that still sees
> Clearely, and clearer for the want of these;
> For gazing through these windowes of the body,
> It met such severall, such distracting objects,
> But now confin'd within it selfe, it sees
> A strange, and unknowne world, and there discovers
> Torrents of Anger, Mountaines of Ambition;
> Gulfes of Desire, and Towers of Hope, huge Gyants,
> Monsters, and savage Beasts . . . (pp. 39–40).

He has "a world within himself", to govern more contentedly than the empire he has lost. "Man to himselfe," he concludes, "is a large prospect."

In these last examples the simple equation of humanity and topography breaks down; likeness is shown to be dubious, or negated altogether. Paradoxically, the landscape analogy is no less potent.

Barclay described the effect of landscape as a "hidden force or reason". The landscape artist must decide on his tactics—shall force and reason be harmonized or opposed? Landscape may be termed panegyric topography; it thrives on the

confluence of politics and imaginative description. The visible
scene and the political message may support each other, or
they may be mutually distracting. We must be made to accept
the naturalness of the landscape analogy – to melt into it; but
amorphous and unthinking assent is of no practical use in
political argument. Rigorously organized structures, on the
other hand, must not seem artificial. Both tendencies must be
held in equilibrium.

We can now begin to answer the original question – why did
landscape poetry thrive in an age of political conflict? It can be
simultaneously an idyll and a model, an escape and a solution.
If an aesthetic structure seems both convincing and comprehensive, as the new landscape aimed to be, then it will come
to be accepted as a form of reality – a version of the world.
Landscapes exert what Marvell calls a *viridis virtus*, a force

> Annihilating all that's made
> To a green Thought in a green Shade.

Things beyond this world become *unthinkable*.

3
Long Views
Prospect and historical perspective in two poems of place

*It seems to me (beholding it at the
best light) a Lantskip of these Kingdoms . . .*
(Fanshawe on *Il Pastor Fido*)

Denham's *Coopers Hill* appeared in 1642, and Marvell's *Upon Appleton House* was probably written by 1652. They are both true topographical poems,[1] elaborating on the description of an actual place, and bearing its name. They are very different in manner, but they both derive their structure from a transformation of ideal landscape. Both poems construct an image of country life, and draw upon "prospective" techniques to arrange multifarious material into a significant pattern. Denham confines himself to the emulation of landscape, though with unprecedented grandeur and dynamism; Marvell extends the range of techniques, and remodels topography in forms suggested by didactic emblems, theatrical scene-building, perspective distortions and architecture. Both use *topographia* for ideological purposes. Denham deals with national politics and Marvell with the internal politics of one family, but both poems are designed to serve a particular historical situation; "green Thought" becomes an instrument of extreme precision. I hope the reader will share my fascination with uncovering the details.

It is no longer necessary to establish that *Coopers Hill* is a political poem, or that it is constructed on the principles of *concordia discors*, antithesis and harmonious balance. Earl Wasserman demonstrated this in *The Subtler Language* (1959) and Brendan O Hehir has documented it fully in *Expans'd Hieroglyphicks* (1969), his edition of the various texts of *Coopers Hill*. My study is at once more particular and more general; I attempt to clarify the precise nature of Denham's politics, still in debate, but I also place the poem in a tradition of adapting landscape to social issues.

Denham began his writing career with a double first; "he came out," as Waller said, "like the Irish rebellion, three score thousand strong." *The Sophy* and *Coopers Hill* were published simultaneously in August 1642, only a few days before civil war was declared. The landscape poem is certainly political, but the tragedy, despite being set in a corrupt court, is unusually remote from the crisis. It does contain a reference to the troubles of England—the famous lines in Act IV on the seditious role of religion in extremist politics. But this is an interlude, spoken by the mouthpiece characters at the halfway point, written in couplets, and dealing with issues that occur nowhere else in the play; from that moment, we concentrate on the inward moral drama of the prince himself. It is a tragedy on the pure Aristotelian model, with faults, turning-points and sudden revelations; its principal purpose is to inspire pity and fear for the hero. The core of the play is Act IV, where philosophical courage struggles with ghoulish anger, rescuing Mirza just as his hands close on his unsuspecting child. "A reader in 1642" would not, I believe, "have leaped with one movement of the mind to a recollection" of Charles's disastrous attempt on the Five Members.[2] Denham's two works form a double essay on the theme of seeing; in both, the mind's eye looks down on the violence and contradiction of human life, and discovers a philosophy to maintain true vision and a harmonious existence. In the tragedy this insight is personal, inward, and reached by a series of hideous and ironic catastrophes; in the 'prospective poem' the message is political, explicit, and unrolled consistently from the beginning of the description.

Coopers Hill exists in several versions, some dating from the early 1640s, some from 1655–68; they are elaborately transcribed and compared in O Hehir's edition (Berkeley and Los Angeles, 1969: I refer to this work only when comparing drafts, and revert elsewhere to the original published texts, indicated by date only). All these versions begin with the same lines, a relaxed, familiar address to the hill where the poet has so often found himself:

So where the Muses and their Troopes resort
Parnassus stands; if I can be to thee
A Poet, thou Parnassus art to mee (1642).

As a way of proving how congenial this place is to the Muses,
Denham then shows how his thoughts embroider on the social
and political elements of what the hill allows his physical eye
to see; poetry and ideology are thus subtly linked from the
start. Once again, all versions do this. In the earliest draft the
'Parnassus' lines continue

Whose topp when I ascend, I seeme more high,
More boundlesse in my Fancy than myne Eye (p. 79).

He explains this by an extended simile: visionary scientists,
lifted into the stratosphere by magic or their imaginations, can
see foul weather forming before it shows on earth; Denham
likewise, gazing from his earth-bound hill at the fog which
surrounds London but having his "minde uppon the Tumult
and the Crowde", can see that fog as "a more dusky Cloud of
busines than of Smoke". Eye and Fancy—the faculties which
create optical and mental images respectively—are closely
linked; mental vision is higher and "more boundlesse" certainly, but only because it enjoys the full cooperation of the
eyesight, raised and enlarged by topography above the plain,
but not so high as to be remote from human affairs. Windsor
Castle is the next object to "swell into myne Eye", and again
the eye is an agent of interpretation:

such a Rise as doth at once invite
A pleasure and a Reverence from the Sight;
Thy Masters Embleme, in whose face I saw
A frendlike sweetnes and a Kinglike Awe (p. 80).

Ranging the horizon in a hungry search for new stimulus, the
eye alone is responsible for introducing the next topic—St.
Anne's hill, stripped of its abbey by the depredations of Henry
VIII (p. 83). This move is rather a dishonest one; since St.
Anne's hill is visually less prominent than Windsor and lies in
the opposite direction, the eye is obviously led by a political
argument and not vice versa. This politicization of vision

increases when, by grammatical sleight-of-hand, the eye is made
the subject of the emotion aroused by Puritan church-breaking:

> Partinge from thence twixt Anger, Shame and fearre
> (Those for what's past, and this for what's too neere)
> My Eye descending from the Hill surveyes
> Where Thames amongst the wanton valleys strayes (p. 84).

The reader comes perilously near to rejecting this trickery, and
only a certain grace and dynamism redeems it. Later in the
poem, in fact, Denham points out that only a "quicke poeticke
sight" (p. 87) can grasp his vision.

Later versions amplify this structure of vision without
changing it. Draft II breaks the flow of the opening lines to
insert a complement to Waller's poem on St. Paul's (p. 94), and
resumes the parallelism of eye and mind in a clumsy antithesis:

> Then London where my eye the place, the crowd
> My mind surveyes . . .

Denham also adds more lines on the self-contradictory frenzy
of City life—lines which are extended again in the first published version ("Draft III"). Here the tribute to Waller is more
skilfully blended in, and the implications of this prospective
vision more clearly stated:

> Nor wonder if (advantag'd in my flight
> By taking wing from thy auspicious height)
> Through untrac't waies and airie paths I flie,
> More boundlesse in my Fancie than my eie (p. 110).

The airy flights of his contemplations are possible only
because their objects are brought into physical view. Since this
elevation is both physical and mental, the ambiguity of the
next line is quite fruitful:

> Exalted to this height, I first looke downe
> On *Pauls* . . .

Nevertheless it is replaced in the fourth draft (1655) by a still
more fluent and comprehensible version:

> More boundless in my Fancy than my eie:
> My eye, which swift as thought contracts the space
> That lies between, and first salutes the place
> Crown'd with that sacred pile . . . (p. 139).

The Civil War had made Denham's prognostic function obsolete, and the meteorological simile is dropped. Tall clouds now have the connotation of diffuse grandeur, and their ominous aspect is downgraded to a creeping mist:

> . . . that sacred pile, so vast, so high,
> That whether 'tis a part of Earth or sky
> Uncertain seems, and may be thought a proud
> Aspiring mountain, or descending cloud . . .
>
> Under his proud survey the City lies
> And like a mist beneath a hill doth rise
> Whose state and wealth, the business and the crowd,
> Seem at this distance but a darker cloud (pp. 139–40).

This revision shows signs of partial rethinking of the relation claimed between eye and mind. The eye is merely *as* swift *as* thought, and it contracts the space between London and Windsor, several hours' journey, in the same way that a telescope does. It "salutes" the various places described in the poem, but this only denotes their visual prominence. The word "seems" is given greater emphasis. The transition from Windsor to St. Anne's hill is made more explicit and compact:

> Here should my wonder dwell, and here my praise,
> But my fixt thoughts my wandring eye betrays,
> Viewing a neighbouring hill (p. 145).

But this only brings out more clearly the paradox already noticed—it is Denham's *idée fixe* that betrays his visual realism, not vice versa. All other cases—Windsor, the Thames, the quick poetic sight—remain the same as in the poem's first conception.

In *Coopers Hill*, then, Denham is trying to establish his credentials as a seer. He is a logician, using his privileged synoptic vision to pierce the fog of error; he claims to lay bare a whole system of inherent contradictions invisible to those in their toils—

> False to their hopes, afraid to be secure,
> Those mischiefes onely which they make, endure,
> Blinded with light, and sicke of being well,
> In tumults seeke their peace, their heaven in hell (1642).

He compares himself to a natural philosopher, the happiest of all men according to the *Georgics*, and so confers a scientific colour on his analysis of London. Later, translating Mancinus's 'Of Prudence', he goes out of his way to refer to his own earlier poem. The original asks

> What is the use of researching into the various paths of the stars? You fool, why do you seek to know matters and causes? Why do you want to embrace innumerable sciences in your studies and to place correctly every location on earth?[3]

This becomes

> What need we gaze upon the spangled Sky?
> Or into Matters hidden Causes pry?
> To describe every *City*, *Stream* or *Hill*
> I'th World, our fancy with vain Arts to fill?[4]

But in *Coopers Hill* logic and science *do* serve the cause of prudence. As an *auspex*, Denham offers advice to kings, and laments the inadequate knowledge which leads to unnecessary bloodshed:

> Had thy great destiny but given thee skill
> To know, as well as power to act, her will . . .
> That bloud which thou and thy great Grandsire shed,
> And all that since those sister Nations bled,
> Had beene unspilt—had happy Edward knowne
> That all the bloud he spilt had beene his owne. (1642).

Denham seems to offer help to the victims of contradiction, and warning of what he sees in the clouds. He has the insight of the meteorologist, but the moral security of the countryman with whom Virgil pairs him. By conflating these distinct forms of philosophy, he persuades us that he deals in necessary truths.

We have seen how *Coopers Hill* resembles landscape; its prospective devices are as persuasive as its philosophical guise. The littleness of the City (in geometrical perspective) suggests its pettyness. The mist of aerial perspective corresponds to the malignant fog of Puritan business, and the romantic horror of the ruin-piece to political thuggery. How far can this visual analogue be taken? Landscape can depict contrasts, but not critical relationships, or the struggle of opposites. Typically, Denham profits from this limitation. In a landscape the eye is pleased more by the composition than by its members; this harmony from variety is transcendental, and can be intensified by the skilful use of ugly and disturbing patches. Equally, the threat of Puritan reformation has to appear as an aberration which, properly understood, can be nicely brushed into the landscape. The theory of harmony from discords discovered in the landscape of the Thames valley allows opposites to be seen as contrasts. More precisely, it allows the desperate opposition of Royalist to Puritan to expand into lofty and agreeable arrangements, and the opposition of Puritan to Royalist to shrink into a jagged outline or a little patch of mist, an episode in the entertainment. Trouble is seen in perspective.

Denham was aware that perspective imagery can be false or true, according to whether it is properly applied. On the one hand, the observer may shrink or expand the truth according to his affections; this is the theme of Saavedra's emblem of the telescope, warning against the "false Opticks" of the court,[5] the flattery and moral blindness which plays such a large part in *The Sophy*. He must equally avoid the appearance of idiosyncrasy, of "looking thorow the prospective of min owne imagination, that onely takes measure of other men's passions by that itselfe feeles".[6] On the other hand, correct perspective leads to a sound interpretation of history and society; heroes and villains may be given their proper stature and perhaps their vanishing point. To apply the telescope of history you must "sett. . . your eyes in method";[7] only a good prospective can extract a single image from confusion. Fanshawe's translation of *Il Pastor Fido* operates in this way; the play is trivial in itself, but "through the *perspective* of the *Chorus*" the real

political message is revealed—"a *Lantskip* of these Kingdoms
. . . as well in the former flourishing, as the present distrac-
tions thereof".[8] Fanshawe illustrates his method by describing
another kind of "perspective",

> a Picture (it is in the Cabinet of the *great Chancellor* [of France])
> so admirably design'd, that, presenting to the common be-
> holders a multitude of little faces (the famous Ancestors of that
> Noble man), at the same time, to him that looks through a
> *Perspective* (kept there for the purpose), there appears onely a
> single portrait in great of the Chancellor himself; the Painter
> thereby intimating that in him alone are contracted the Vertues
> of all his Progenitors; or perchance by a more subtile Philo-
> sophy demonstrating how the *Body Politick* is composed of
> many *naturall ones*. . . .[9]

Every perspective device has a "subtile Philosophy" of this
kind, an exclusive viewpoint which claims to reveal the true
form of appearances. Landscape is the subtlest form of prospective, for its trickery is unobtrusive and the resulting image
overwhelmingly clear. Denham can sometimes be seen dictat-
ing to the reader's eye:

> Under his proud survay the Citty lyes,
> And like a mist beneath a hill doth rise;
> Whose state and wealth, the busines and the crowd,
> Seems at this distance but a darker cloud:
> And is to him who rightly things esteems
> No other in effect than what it seems. (1655).

More often he assumes that his message is self-evident, a
property of the venerable landscape itself. In *The Sophy* vision
operates on a closed world, foreign, fantastic and subjective;
Coopers Hill is founded on the open vistas of the Thames
valley, on the solid masses of hills and the siting of ancient
buildings:

> So *Windsor*, humble in it selfe, seemes proud,
> To be the Base of that Majesticke load,
> Than which no hill a nobler burthen beares
> But Atlas onely, that supports the spheres.
> Nature this mount so fitly did advance,

We might conclude, that nothing is by chance;
So plac't as if she did on purpose raise
The Hill to rob the builder of his praise.
For none commends his judgement that doth chuse
That which a blind man onely could refuse. (1642)

Denham's task is to establish a single viewpoint equally free
from flattery and idiosyncrasy; his opinions will then appear as
natural and irrefutable as sight itself.

Denham imitates the Stoic philosopher as Samuel Daniel
described him, "that hath no side at all But of himself".[10] But
is he really "moderate . . . less partisan than philosophical and
reflective"? Is it true that "no tempers would be aroused" by
Coopers Hill?[11] It is certainly a poem of "anger, shame, and
feare", of stinging satire and sarcasm, directed on party lines.
The moderate *Commons Petition of Long Afflicted England*[12] calls
upon "the bright Sun-shine of our Parliament" to dispel "the
misty foggs of error", but Denham envelops the whole City in
a "darker cloud"; after the protection of the Five Members it
was enemy territory, and not even the guild leaders could be
counted on. Another moderate, Isaac Massy, tried to reconcile
the parties:

> Ther's some would go to ransacke *Hull* . . .
> Ther's others would go ransack *Lumbard-Street*,
> But fy upon them they shall never meet.[13]

Denham clearly belongs to the latter. Furthermore, he attacks
popular institutions. He echoes James I in disparaging Magna
Carta,[14] and reserves his fiercest satire for Henry VIII. If
Denham's Windsor grows into *Windsor-Forrest*, his Henry
grows into Achitophel. Antithetic couplets, which give
double praise to Charles, confound their victim with a double
charge—he does wrong while able to do right. In the moderate
and considered view, Henry was partly bad, but predominantly good.[15] For the vast majority he was a hero, a bulwark of
parliament, Old England, and the Garter. To attack him was
to ally with the lunatic fringe—with the papal nuncio Nicholas
Sanders or the ultra-royalist and provincial George Daniel.[16]
Denham's fury over the ruins of Chertsey abbey should be compared with Speed's description, or the ruin-pieces of Joseph Hall

or Marvell, recognizing the justice of the reforming hand.[17] Edward III, on the other hand, was popularly a great lecher, and considered by historians to be a mixture of virtues and vices.[18] He is, nevertheless, one of the heroes of *Coopers Hill*, which thereby joins the series of fulsome historical poems commissioned by Charles himself in the 1630s. Thomas May's *Edward III* (1635), written "by his Majesties command", anticipates most of Denham's themes—Windsor as the seat of Mars and Venus, the splendour of the Garter, St George as "Saint and Souldier", the captured kings of France and Scotland, and above all the needlessness of the Scots campaign, revealed in a vision of Charles's glorious reign.[19] Denham's opinions are those of a fully-committed Royalist; it is hard to accept him as non-partisan.

Coopers Hill, like the landscape it describes, appears to be balanced and moderate. This was typical of the royalist point of view. John Taylor the Water-Poet's *Humble Desired Union Betweene Prerogative and Priviledge* (1642), for example, shows how the doctrine of balanced opposites became part of the vocabulary of coarse royalism. John Spelman, recruited by the King as early as January 1642, published *Certain Considerations Upon the Duties Both of Prince and People* a year later; despite this insistence on checks and balances,[20] Spelman's real message is that no subject may oppose or criticize a king, however absolute. Throughout 1642, Charles insists that he upholds the "true old legall way", the true Protestant religion,[21] and the balance of powers: on January the 20th he gives equal priority to parliamentary privilege and royal income; on March the 15th he proposes that each side should be "tender" to the other's privileges; on May the 14th he concludes by quoting Pym's own words—if prerogative overcomes liberty, the result is tyranny, and if the reverse, anarchy and confusion. Parliamentarians were used to this "moderation", and learned to read beneath it.[22]

Coopers Hill is in fact closely attuned to the successive crises of 1642, and to Charles's own messages of response. The opening of the poem is dominated by the contrast of London and Windsor. It must surely be engendered in the aftermath of the Five Members affair, after Charles had been driven out of Whitehall and Hampton Court by furious London crowds.

The episode rankled for the rest of Charles's life, and raged on after his death.[23] It is the nub of the propaganda battle of 1642; Parliament frequently calls him back to London, and Charles rebuffs them, arguing the danger to his family.[24] There is thus a particular point to the description of Windsor

> where *Mars* with *Venus* dwels,
> Beauty with strength;

one manuscript even adds the note "the Kinge and Queene there", confirming its topicality.[25] These issues remained alive after Charles moved north from Windsor, and the poem must be imagined accumulating during the following months. The praise of the Garter is appropriate for a Windsor setting, but it would be more sharply focused by the King's attempt to move the Lords to York, on the pretext of a Garter feast. Denham's sarcastic exposure of contradictions is matched in Charles's writing from May onwards, especially in the *Answer to a Printed Remonstrance of May 26*. There, too, Charles emphasizes his obedience to what Denham called

> that Law, which teaches Kings to sway
> Their Scepters,

reprinting the relevant part of his coronation service. In the winter months his tone is conciliatory, but increasingly from the end of April he uses a different style; he adopts a tone of profound patience, but at the very end hints that he may be provoked to overwhelming violence.[26] *Coopers Hill* ends in precisely the same way.

In these latter months, Charles seems to be running hand-in-hand with his propagandists. Denham's poem echoes the King's threatening patience, and the King's *Declaration*, published a few days later on the 12th of August, uses the effect more strongly than ever. July saw several proposals of conciliation by independent commoners; Isaac Massy foresaw pacification and unity, and the *Propositions of Accommodation* begs the King to return to Whitehall and govern by law only—a reference to the inflammatory commissions of array. Some royalists adopted the same persuasive tone, in a last-minute attempt to demoralize the enemy. John Price's *Few and Short Considerations on the Present Distempers* calls on parliament to surrender gracefully over Hull:

> squeez'd and exorted things in the commerce of life are not welcome to us: what willingly we accept of, must come willingly . . . When they shall see their undoubted and undaunted Soveraign in the head of an adverse Army, shooting forth Rayes of Majesty, and thundering out a *Durum est contra stimulos calcitrare*, what man can promise that they will not be appall'd, dazled, blinded? . . . His Majesty, like a Royall Dove, in a former return of his from the North parts of his Dominions brought us back an Olive-Branch, a token of peace with our Neighbours, and their reconcilement to us; an assurance that the Torrent which had swollen high was fallen and dryed up; if readily and humbly he be complyed with in his now-proposalls, his next return hither will bring better tidings, That the waters of his own displeasure are abated, a deluge more formidable then that other, to loyall and obedient hearts (such as we all professe to have) . . .
>
> The tie which I have as an honest man, and the right which I have as a free man, of speaking what I think conducible to the weale publike, hath invited me in the crowd of others who blot paper . . . to commend to all men, specially to the wisdom of our great Councell, these few particulars . . . Such is the weak, but hearty and most humble assistance, which in stead of Plate, Money and Horses, is presented, if not from the head of an able man, from the heart (at least) of an honest man, one whom no apprehension of possible private losses . . . no by-respect of advancing his peculiar interest, nor adulation of Monarchique power hath mov'd in this way to speak himself, . . . but a lively and deep sense of the common danger, a soul labouring with Anxiety from the just and too certain estimate of impendent ruine.

Denham's poem matches this pamphlet closely, in its warning tone, its attack on extorted gifts, its awesome presentation of the King's military power, its flood-imagery, and its character of virtuous objectivity.

Denham, like a good patriot, has placed his equipment entirely at the disposal of the authorities. We should not assume him to be spurious. If any fault is to be found, it is with Charles's belief in the efficacy of style,

> in his artificial-heav'n,
> Which flatring *Poets*, and his *Painters* made.[27]

A poet's first loyalty is to his art, and Denham's political loyalism gave him two excellent qualities. The first is breadth —the quality he praises in Fanshawe, and the opposite of

> Cheap vulgar arts, whose narrowness affords
> No flight for thoughts, but poorly sticks at words.[28]

The second is congruity—the ability to fuse description, interpretation and style into a single compatible image. These qualities offset his faults. The machinery of his "political optics" is sometimes all too visible, and his arguments are often tissues of loose analogy and innuendo. His themes are not original: Camden, Drayton and Speed combined vivid description of Windsor with antiquarian history; John Hepwith used a topographical title for political pamphlet verse, in *The Calidonian Forrest* of 1641; P. J.'s *Scottish Journie*[29] begins with an imposing castle and its noble prisoner, uses a ruin to lament the destructiveness of Puritans and a town to satirize their greed, describes a hunt, and ends with direct political comment. But *Coopers Hill* transforms them. For those already of his persuasion, Denham provides a valuable service. He offers them the landscape as a way of coping with the collapse of their political world—not a random and clumsy allegory, nor just a glimpse of idyllic country scenes, but a whole aesthetic system, succinct and adaptable, an elaborate display of the art of prospect.[30]

The prospective poem need not be rooted in a single spot. One function of a prospect, as Joseph Beaumont recognized, is to "yield an open sight" of the "chief stations" of a subject. *Upon Appleton House*, the longest and most complicated topographical poem in English, is a series of such "stations".

To what genre does Marvell's poem belong? To call it a "country-house poem" begs the question. Previous examples of this kind are panegyrics, like Herrick's *Pemberton*, or epistles, like Carew's *From Wrest*, or extended epigrams, like *To Penshurst*; Marvell's title implies an epigram, but the poem's length denies it. It is a typical locodescriptive poem of the post-war years, describing a solid and familiar landscape in a light and fantastic manner. Cotton's *Journey to the Peak*, Fane's *Summerly*, Thomas Winnard's *News from Newcastle*, Emerson's facetious descriptions of Orkney—these are consciously entertaining poems, quite different from the grave impending tones of *Coopers Hill* or *White-Hall*. But *Appleton House* is more coherent than these. The sight imposes an order on it. *Coopers Hill* resembles Hollar's *Graenwich* (Fig. 2) in its broad panorama of contrasting masses, its view of distant London and its flattering concentration on the royal palace; Marvell's poem is in the manner of his *Albury* (Fig. 6), a suite of small realistic landscapes which celebrate the retirement of a great lord. Both show unspectacular places hallowed by personal associations and affections, walks, woods, villagers intent on their own business, reflections in water. But Hollar's plates are only connected by locality and tone; Marvell is able to make a single theme run through all his locations:

> While with slow Eyes we these survey,
> And on each pleasant footstep stay,
> We opportunly may relate
> The Progress of this Houses Fate (st. 11).

The sight of each place evokes the past and future of its owners, and the poet arranges them in proper perspective; in this respect, *Upon Appleton House* is a prospective poem.

Marvell's long poems are both organized in the same way. The opening shows the dominant image of the poem, in detail, with particular attention to the principles of decorum which sustain it. He then states the subject of the poem, as succinctly as possible. The episodes which follow are all multiplications or inversions of the initial principle, just as architecture is created by the correct application of one module; this unites them. To conclude, the principal character is introduced in a suitable dramatic frame, and the poet expounds his theme directly. *Last Instructions*, as Michael Gearin-Tosh has shown,[31] depends on the successive distortions of State Painting; but this is not the only structural device. Marvell also provides a synopsis for our guidance, explaining in four lines

(121–4) the deceit which the entire poem seeks to parody and expose. The "argument" is stated with equal clarity in the earlier poem. Appleton house is an acceptable model, just as the vaulted brain is a false one. Why?

> Him *Bishops-Hill*, or *Denton* may,
> Or *Bilbrough*, better hold than they:
> But Nature here hath been so free
> As if she said leave this to me.
> Art would more neatly have defac'd
> What she had laid so sweetly wast;
> In fragrant Gardens, shady Woods,
> Deep meadows, and transparent Floods.
> While with slow Eyes we *these* survey etc.

These are grounds for believing Appleton superlative, and these, correspondingly, are the basis of the poem. Its subject, in a single line, is "the Progress of this Houses Fate"—but only inasmuch as the estate reveals it. The family's future is severely restricted, but within those limits it is glorious and all-pervasive, a subject to be talked about, not hidden away. Marvell reduces topography and panegyric to the same rules. Progress cast in a visible form is more beautiful and more clearly understood; it may only be related "opportunly", as the parts of the estate give occasion, but it is manifested equally throughout the place, in all the scenes provided. Few critics read these explanatory lines correctly. "This House" is taken to refer only to the nunnery-building, although we are clearly told that he will survey every place, and make relation as he goes; or else he is supposed to "turn aside" and "digress" from the topography. Even when panegyric topography is recognized, Marvell is denied a coherent structure; he must be content with hermetic allegory or creative disintegration. This is to ignore what Marvell himself tells us; *Upon Appleton House* is a progressive structure determined by the eye.

All the prospects I have discussed require leisure to expiate—"slow Eyes" and "pleasant footsteps". But relaxation must be offset by concentration; the ideal prospect is an equilibrium, in which the eye is neither bored by dispersal nor cluttered and confined. In *Coopers Hill* political controversy contracts the eye and gives it zest. In *Pharonnida* the wide landscape is set off against the contracted delight of the island garden. But in the low-lying Appleton estate, "slow Eyes" cannot refer to the scanning of a distant panorama. In fact, Marvell's eyes are quick and accurate. The usual epithets are crossed over; the poet's footsteps are slow, and his eye *plaisant* and keen. In this way, he provides the necessary mixture of detail and breadth, stringency and relaxation. The properties of eye and foot[32] are interchangeable; the quickness of his eye increases in direct proportion to his physical sloth. In the wood he picks out the tiny leaves and fruit of wild strawberries, the throstle's eye, the fallen fledgeling, the expert-looking "thumbs" of the wood-pecker, and the attentive bird. These details are of course common knowledge, part of natural history; but the sharpness of the visual impression retrieves them from that store. By the river he observes the moister colour of the grass, the mud in the stream, gradually clearing, and the gnarled, undermined osiers. A relaxed human being cannot "hang" in branches (st. 81), but the flood would have left weed draped over them. Observation provides an image for limp immobility, just as, in the wood, immobility provided images for observation—such details may only be seen by keeping still.

The kingfisher simile is the last of these attentive and silent moments:

> So when the Shadows laid asleep
> From underneath these Banks do creep,
> And on the River as it flows
> With *Eben Shuts* begin to close,
> The modest *Halcyon* comes in sight,
> Flying betwixt the Day and Night;
> And such an horror calm and dumb
> *Admiring Nature* does benum.
>
> The viscous Air, wheres'ere She fly,
> Follows and sucks her Azure dy;
> The gellying Stream compacts below,
> If it might fix her shadow so;
> The stupid Fishes hang, as plain

As *Flies* in *Chrystal* overtane,
And Men the silent *Scene* assist,
Charm'd with the *Saphir-winged Mist* (st. 84–5)

This is sometimes misunderstood, so I will examine it in some detail. We read that "Maria has her own bird to accompany her" . . . "the halcyon fuses with Mary Fairfax, as the two enter the scene together and jointly arrest the landscape".[33] This approach seems to forget that we are dealing with a simile, and so ignores important questions. What does Marvell describe? In what respect is Maria's entry like the kingfisher's? The image is obviously of structural importance; as in *Last Instructions*, Marvell induces a "calm horror" to usher in his conclusion. It concludes a series of trance-like observations, and at the same time announces a new style and attitude, spruce and prepared. What kind of a conclusion, then, does it make?

Firstly, the image is accurately and beautifully observed. Marvell selects the moment when even the low banks begin to throw a shadow. All along the western edge[34] of the stream these shadows "begin to close", like the first pair of hinged shutters on a house-window or picture—not, I think, like the shutters of stage scenery, which close simultaneously. The sun being low, its reflection appears close to the further bank, and the shadows are "Eben" by contrast; nearby the water is free from reflections, and illuminated by oblique rays. Only in these conditions may fish be seen "plain", and then only if the observer does not startle them. The water is calm, at evening, and unusually slow, for the fish are able to stay still without exerting themselves against the current. Though it is not explained, Marvell seems to think of the turn of the tide, still perceptible at Appleton; "gellying" describes it well. The whole description, in fact, is less fantastic than is often supposed. The kingfisher's colour is made by fine prismatic scales on its feathers, and actually seems to stand away from it; from a different angle its body is drab. Hence flying fast it is a streak of dye, hanging in the air, but its reflection in the water is a grey "shadow", impossible so to "fix".

In what respect does Maria's entry resemble this evening scene, so keenly noted? Obviously, there is conventional flattery; the freshness and sleekness of the evening are made to suggest an adoring creation, and the glassy sea of *Revelation*. But admiration remains within strict limits. "The word *Miraculum* importeth a thing moving stupor and admiration",[35] but the fish are "stupid" because they see no-one, not because they see Maria. (In the same way, Marvell pretends that the bird in st. 72 is an ideal pupil, attentive to his presence; in fact it is attentive to his apparent absence). Nothing happens against nature; though the sun is "aware" of Maria, this only makes him turn red at the usual time. Marvell makes careful use of a hyperbole which normally shows marigolds turning, leaves falling, suns setting in the morning, and nature generally pleading for the lady's attention. Maria's eyes do not scorch the grass and strike lovers dead; they are judicious and surprising, and Samuel Cooper's portrait shows this to be literally true.[36] She can therefore appreciate that the simile is just as important for its negative and unflattering respects. The kingfisher is so gorgeous that everyone stops to gaze— passers-by, salmon-fishers, guests, "Men" in general. Maria, on the other hand, is screened from public view. Creatures do not "charm themselves at" her, as Marvell suggested in another homage to girlhood, 'The Picture of Little T. C. in a Prospect of Flowers'; she is too old to be Little T. C., and too young to be the spectacularly dangerous mistress of adult love-poetry. The charm of her presence is compared to something much less grand—to the joy of gazing at a little dumb thing, iridescent and easily startled. In this way the flattery is chastened and suffused with less hectic emotions—peace, demureness and innocence. The predominant effect of the simile is glassy—cool, lucid and easily shattered. These qualities are transferred to Maria. Marvell's description suggests the anatomy of the eye itself, with its compact aqueous and vitreous humours, and blue colouring. The physical purity of the eye is a model for all the episodes of the poem:

> This 'tis to have been from the first
> In a *Domestick heaven* nurst,
> Under the *Discipline* severe
> Of *Fairfax*, and the starry *Vere*;
> Where not one object can come nigh
> But pure, and spotless as the Eye (st. 91)

Appleton house is a moral laboratory; Marvell's task is to prepare specimens, "ere they approach the Eye".

Slow eyes and pleasant footsteps produce a vivid mixture of clarity and lethargy. Marvell represents the state of suspended wonder in which we discover things. It is a teacher's poem, part dream and part sermon, on the text "be still and know". The emphasis is on rapt obervation. These "wonders" may be seen not by the virtue of the things themselves, but of the situation, the time, and the observers behaviour – the "Posture, Hour, or Place".[37] In *Last Instructions* the same theme appears in satiric reversal. The calm horror is painted, the virgin enters, but conditions "ill agree"; the lesson is learnt by default. In *Upon Appleton House* the conclusion is reached more happily. The visible and the moral concur. Shadows, for example, perform several functions; they make vivid pictures, announce and close the final section, and reinforce its message. These images are not menacing; the shadow-shutters are "laid asleep" and the coracles are like tortoise-houses. Nevertheless, they force us to be aware of closing-time, of the final reckoning. Each appearance of shadow is associated with sudden recollection, and the panegyric between them is strenuous, formal and moralistic. There is work to be done. The language tutor, of all people, cannot remain dumb in front of his pupil. Fairfax, Maria and their workers must gather, build and enumerate. Marvell's survey encourages them to build on moments of vision, to despise the lethargy but keep the clarity and delight.

The topographical poem is a didactic model, using the natural analogy to "teach Youth by Spectacle Innocent", as Marvell himself puts it in *Last Instructions* (line 389). Each section teaches what to avoid and what to espouse:

> may no such storme
> Fall on our times, where ruine must reforme
> (*Coopers Hill*, 1642)

> Oh happinesse of sweete retir'd content!
> To be at once secure, and innocent . . . (*ibid*)

> Fair quiet, have I found thee here,
> And Innocence thy Sister dear!
> (Marvell, 'The Garden')

Social doctrine is anchored in topography. "Security" is not a diffuse or sentimental desire; Denham's grounds, his propriety, his station are all discovered in the land around Cooper's hill. "Innocence" is no less concrete. For the Mower it is "wild and fragrant", a concept endowed with the physical quality of leaves and flowers. The Thames running by Cooper's hill deposits a "genuine, and lesse guilty wealth" than the Tagus. After the flood at Appleton

> the Waves are fal'n and dry'd,
> And now the Meadows fresher dy'd;
> Whose Grass, with moister colour dasht,
> Seems as green Silks but newly washt.
> No *Serpent* new or *Crocodile*
> Remains behind our little *Nile*;
> Unless it self you will mistake,
> Among these Meads the only Snake (st. 79).

Marvell makes the water represent the life he praises, a privileged and local innocence:

> And for his shade which therein shines,
> *Narcissus*-like the *Sun* too pines (st. 80).

Denham's river is equally appropriate for his theme, fore-knowledge:

> The streame is so transparent, pure, and cleare,
> That had the selfe-enamour'd youth gaz'd here,
> So fatally deceiv'd he had not beene,
> While he the bottome, not his face, had seene (1642).

The staghunt in *Coopers Hill* is "a more Innocent, and happy chase" than political struggle. Hunting is

> a Princely sport
> And much resembles warre . . .
> It shewes us pretty dangers, and acquaints us
> With scituations.[38]

Denham is calling the opposition to their senses, and asking them to contemplate their own heroic defeat—but in an image which disavows war, significant for not being what it closely resembles. Similarly, the first Lord Fairfax[39]

> when retired here to Peace,
> His warlike Studies could not cease;
> But laid these Gardens out in sport
> In the just Figure of a Fort (st. 36).

Marvell always uses military imagery to show the gulf between a certain mentality and the destructive machinery used to represent it. In a government minister, this discrepancy is scandalous, but in Thomas Fairfax or Uncle Toby it is a sign of moral excellence; all depends on their situation.

Shandeian innocence depends on the sheer absence of evil thoughts; it is sweeter but less intelligent than the Fairfax tradition, which requires expertise to unmask villainy:

> I know what Fruit their Gardens yield,
> When they it think by Night conceal'd (st. 28).

Marvell's models retain all the matter-of-fact details of the hideous routines they replace:

> The Mower now commands the Field;
> In whose new Traverse seemeth wrought
> A camp of Battail newly fought:
> Where, as the Meads with Hay, the Plain
> Lyes quilted ore with Bodies slain:
> The Women that with forks it fling,
> Do represent the Pillaging (st. 53).

This picture is as clearly marked as the scenes in *Orbis Pictus*; one page of this children's encyclopaedia (Fig. 7) does indeed show the camp, the bodies and the pillaging, identified by numbers. Throughout the poem educational virtues are put into practice—study, precision, application, discrimination. The praise of Maria at the end is arranged as a mnemonic, the elements of the landscape numbered and repeated in various orders. He attacks the "useless Study" of vain girls, who care only about their looks (st. 92). In the wood he shows the importance of sorting the essential from the accidental—

> And unto you *cool Zephyr's* Thanks,
> Who, as my Hair, my Thoughts too shed,
> And winnow from the Chaff my Head (st. 75)—

and of retrieving one's information—

> No Leaf does tremble in the Wind
> Which I returning cannot find (st. 72).

The birds of the wood are model pupils, especially the nightingale, practising her songs "and studying all the Summernight".[40] The military garden is thus a tribute to the first Lord's "warlike Studies" and an extension of their principle.

As I suggest elsewhere,[41] Marvell shows exemplary expertise in military technology, but uses it to undermine the military mentality. In the extended metaphors of the garden the vehicle—military life—evokes such powerful memories of civil war that it threatens to overthrow the tenor. The meadow, though equally permeated with military imagery, restores our sense of proportion. It celebrates a world where "the *Gardiner* has the *Souldiers* place", and a new Georgic régime has expropriated the old machinery of war; in the earlier garden episode this state of affairs could only be dreamed of (st. 43). The paradoxical combination of the military and the horticultural was already the subject of an emblem (Fig. 8) in the widely-propagated *Idea de un Principe Politico Christiano* of Saavedra. It deals with the education of the prince, particularly in languages and army drill; the garden illustrates the need for exercises, models and games to sweeten this harsh task—"learning has bitter roots, even if its fruits are sweet". At the age of 14, the prince should be placed in the hands of four tutors, representing learning, sobriety, equity and the discipline of war. The lesser world of Appleton contains all these—but there is no prince. Marvell seems to draw on the doctrine of this emblem – strikingly similar to the real five-bastioned garden he describes – while dexterously shifting its meaning for the benefit of a family with no son to continue its martial tradition. The gardener and the soldier are not complementary but opposed; the soldier's obsequies are sung (st. 55), and the gardener has his place.

Fairfax's position was strange, puzzling even his panegyrists.[42] There is something paradoxical about their praise. The man who makes the walls swell with his greatness is physically shy and diffident in voice, once described by Charles I as too "mean" and "inconsiderable" to hand in a petition.[43] His greatest military victory was over his own ambition and glory.[44] From the worldly point of view, his farming is equally crazy,

> For he did, with utmost Skill,
> *Ambition* weed, but *Conscience* till (st. 45).

"England's Fortress"[45] had not only resigned his command but "layd down his Place",[46] and so foregone the chance to restore the garden of England by civil means. To his detractors, he had failed by his own standards. The strategist was tricked out of office.[47] The great leader of men was a *"He Her Excellence"* who butchered Lucas in revenge for the scar which spoiled his looks.[48] The ancestral honour had been dragged down:

> If in the Rabble some be more refin'd
> By fair Extractions of their birth or mind,
> Ev'n these corrupted are by such allays,
> That no Impression of their Vertue stays . . .
> Else had that Sense of Honour still Surviv'd
> Which Fairfax from his Ancestors deriv'd;
> He ne'r had shew'd Himself, for hate or fear,
> So much degen'rous from renowned Vere
> (The Title and Alliance of whose Son
> His Acts of Valour had in Holland won).[49]

His own brother-in-law showered him with abuse, and ridiculed the looks and pretentions of his "whelp" Maria.[50] His grandfather accused him of seeking to "destroy the house" of Fairfax by his plans to elevate Mary to the status of full heir[51]—a terrible accusation in a family so conscious of lineage and masculine virtues. Marvell's task was delicate. The morality, the structure, the "progress" of the poem must be tailored to this unusual situation—the wounded Knight and his sole daughter.

The usual progression is from meadows and woods to cities and camps, from bucolics to heroics; Marvell must imitate Fairfax's inversion of this.

> Virgil forsook the pleasant Shade
> Of his broad Beach, and Contry Spade,
> To sing of Arms: Our Bard doth chuse
> A better methode for his Muse;
> First sings of warr, and then of Peace.
> He quits the camp, to Live at Ease.
> Retreats with honour: which is far
> The best and hardest part of war,

as Brian Fairfax wrote of Edward the translator.[52] Marvell encourages the reader to reject the obvious, and spot the true value hidden in things of small repute. The objects of the estate become moral exempla contrasting the common estimation of things with proper knowledge, subtler and more elevated. Throughout the poem the same mental drama takes place; the obvious gives way to the recherché, low ignorance to the awareness of higher things. The house reveals its clownishness by striving to be huge, not realizing what its master wants at this particular time. The rail's death is "unknowing" and "untimely", and gives the reader pause; but it soon becomes clear that superstitious grief is also clownish. By the river, Marvell suddenly remembers Maria, and pulls himself together. Nature "it self doth recollect", and strives to look presentable. The sun is "of her aware", and behaves more modestly. The wood provides a screen without Maria's ordering it; it is considerate and aware of her needs, not clownish. It seems to say, as nature did in the beginning, "leave this to me". Creatures seem to act in a subservient way, as if they seek approval of a higher witness. The flower-gatherers

> bring up Flow'rs so to be seen,
> To prove they've at the Bottom been (st. 48).

The woodpecker

> walks still upright from the Root,
> Meas'ring the Timber with his foot;
> And all the way, to keep it clean,
> Doth from the Bark the Wood-moths glean.
> He, with his beak, examines well
> Which fit to stand and which to fell (st. 68).

He does nothing of the sort, as Marvell well knows; but in the course of the conceit we are tactfully reminded of diligence towards higher goals, and Maria is confirmed in her own priorities:

> For *She*, to higher Beauties rais'd
> Disdains to be for lesser prais'd.
> *She* counts her Beauty to converse
> In all the Languages as *hers*;
> Nor yet in those *her self* imployes
> But for the *Wisdome*, not the *Noyse*;
> Nor yet that Wisdome would affect,
> But as 'tis *Heavens Dialect* (st. 89).

Proper knowledge is a secret staircase, shifting away from vulgar opinion at each upward step.[53] Only thus can the Fairfax family make their destiny their choice, and accept Maria as a full and sufficient bearer of the ancestral virtues, the leader of her own new model army, and the master of Appleton and its dynasty.

This house's fate is to progress through obliquity, to go forward by slipping sideways. Conventional progressive deeds are made to seem inconclusive; the "successive Valour" of the Fairfax ancestors marches towards toy forts and half-dry trenches. Old Lord Fairfax "could not cease" his warlike studies, and "restless *Cromwel* could not cease In the inglorious Arts of Peace"—but with opposite results. In his depiction of Cromwell, Marvell stresses powerful movement in a straight line, marching or falling hard:

> March indefatigably on . . .
> So when the Falcon high

> Falls heavy from the Sky . . .
> Much rather thou I know expectst to tell
> How heavy *Cromwell* gnasht the earth and fell . . .
> Thou *Cromwell* falling, not a stupid tree,
> Or Rock so savage, but it mourn'd for thee:
> And all about was heard a Panique groan,
> As if that Natures self were overthrown . . .
> It groanes, and bruises all below that stood
> So many yeares the shelter of the wood . . .[54]

Fairfax's great tree does something different. The holtfelster does not fell it. It falls like a city tired of seige:

> With these Articles the Commissioners returned to Sir *Thomas Fairfax*, certifying further how joyfull that poore Town of *Leicester* was at hearing of the said agreement, and that they should be rid of the Cavaliers.[55]

In the same way Appleton house "to *Fairfax* fell" by legal assent, not by the siege (st. 35). Gentle paradox is happier than aggressive straight-forwardness. *Appleton House* has its strong decisive movements, but never from A to B; the heroic tone is reserved for the morning and evening stroll, the mowers "Traverse", the circular motion of the stars, and the ornamental lane in the wood, leading nowhere.

Progress can only be through Maria, and she, by the sexist doctrine of the time, must limit her triumphs to private morality and fruition. Maria is not Elizabeth Drury; she inherits the ancestral virtues because she is alive and able to procreate. On the other hand, she is not Queen Christina or Oliver Cromwell. She does not confront the world,

> But knowing where this *Ambush* lay,
> She scap'd the safe, but roughest Way (st. 90).

The estate must become "Paradice's only Map",[56] read by the help of coordinates and contours; the path is often diagonal and obscure. This *paysage moralisé*, like its pictorial equivalent, is arranged in obliquely contrasting masses;[57] the argument proceeds by comparison and assessment. We progress from the past to the present; from celibacy to fruition; from the nuns to the Fairfaxes; from the sweet flowers and bitter evocations of the garden to the fruitful and confident labour of the meadows, which sweetens them; within the wood, from the nightingale to the mournful doves, and then to the active woodpecker, housing and feeding his young; then from the deliquescent poet of solitude to the spruce and recollected admirer of Maria; finally to the moment when

> Fate her worthily translates,
> And finds a *Fairfax* for our *Thwaites*.

The poem is clearly progressive. Why, then, does it seem devious to many readers, its episodes seductively long, and its wit metaphysical and tortuous? Marvell certainly intercepts himself, in the garden, for example, and by the river:

> None for the *Virgin Nymph*; for She
> Seems with the Flow'rs a Flow'r to be . . . (st. 38).

> But now away my Hooks, my Quills,
> And Angles, idle Utensils . . . (st. 72).

But these apparent swerves only concentrate our attention on the potential importance of Maria. His absorption in the nunnery and the wood serve the same purpose; he explores byways the more precisely to define the true virtue of the Fairfax heir. If the nun's speech were not so hypnotically beautiful, and nearly convincing, William Fairfax's deliberation would be a charade:

> What should he do? He would respect
> Religion, but not Right neglect (st. 29).

Careful discrimination is thus back-dated as a Fairfacian virtue. In these ancestors, justice and religion combine with fruition, and the celibates turn out to be witches and gypsies—"Twas no Religious House till now" (st. 35). This was in the corrupted past. Now the same process must be re-enacted in the present, and the same choice presented to Maria; mercifully it can be a "Spectacle Innocent". In this instructive game, Marvell offers himself as author and actor.

The wood is a "secret Schoole". The poet marks the leaves, winnows mental chaff, converts the natural scene into "one History" and "strange *Prophecies*". The troublesome institutions of the outside world are reduced to greenery by these "studies"; old Lord Fairfax had done the same. The birds teach by example – the diligent pupil, the good workman, the prompt tenant, the provident family, and the couple who moan without just cause. Marvell would be presumptuous to offer these directly, so he excuses himself by clowning. Alone in the wood, the house-poet pretends to be a lord:

> But I have for my Musick found
> A Sadder, yet more pleasing Sound . . . (st. 66).

> Then as I carless on the Bed
> Of gelid *Straw-berryes* do tread,
> And through the Hazles thick espy
> The hatching *Thrastle's* shining eye,
> The *Heron* from the Ashes top,
> The eldest of its young lets drop,
> As if it Stork-like did pretend
> That *Tribute* to *its Lord* to send . . . (st. 67)

> Under this *antick Cope* I move
> Like some great *Prelate of the Grove* (st. 74).

His pleasure in sad music, his carelessness and his emotional posing remind me of Orsino, or even a Byronic hero:

> Then, languishing with ease, I toss
> On Pallets swoln of Velvet Moss;
> While the Wind, cooling through the Boughs,
> Flatters with Air my panting Brows (st. 75).

His character is vegetative and his philosophy dilettantish, making grossly exaggerated claims for random or trivial concurrences. Not even Ralph Austen believed that all the bible and all the philosophers were hidden in the trees. Marvell regarded Mexique paintings as trash,[58] and castigates Clarendon's "Palace Mosaick"; he also hated prelates. This woody bishop lounges on swollen pallets; his entertainments are nocturnal, private and fantastic—"Mask" and "masquerade" have deceitful connotations in Marvell. His costume is "antick"—perversely ordered and botched up, contrasting with the orderly scenes of the meadow. He is so feeble that ivy overwhelms him and sedge is "heavy" on his brow. His retirement is suspect, for he congratulates himself on the moral safety he enjoys behind his barricade, and takes pleasure in galling the horsemen of the active world; it fails by the standards set in 'Bill-borow'—modesty and ease of access. Like Joseph Beaumont's Psyche at the nadir of her development, he

> does day by day
> Riot and Surfet in delicious smart;[59]

Like Musidorus in Sidney's *Arcadia*, his contemplation unites him with the plants—"me thought my feete began to grow into the ground . . . I might easilie have bene perswaded to have resigned over my very essence";[60] but this is a disaster, caused by extreme depression. Above all he is celibate, a Noah who takes care to find an ark "where all Creatures might have shares, Although in Armies, not in Paires", a parody of Adam in the character of 'The Garden'. He leads the life of a Catholic princely hermit; religious landscape art shows the same lavish acts of penance in deep woodland solitude—chains, briars and nails (Figs. 9–11).

Like the nunnery, the woodland episode shows bewitching artistry, power and fascination; but it should arouse suspicion as well as admiration. In both cases delusion and self-indulgence leads to a stunning rebuke from "Fairfax". There has been a progression from evil to innocence—the nun's pleasure was a deceitful promise, and to accept it would have led to real trouble—but even within the purified world of Appleton "we may stick in the Briars".[61]

Throughout the poem, Marvell lends his voice to attitudes which the Fairfaxes must criticize and reject—to the nun, to the lament over the dead bird, to the ecstasy of the wood. He follows the moral scheme proposed by Edward Calver,[62] who çontrasts Passion and Discretion in each age of man; his own acts represent the figure of passion. Generally, he gathers together traditional themes of debate—for and against fruition, the active and contemplative life, passion and discretion—and co-ordinates them. The result is a parallelogram of forces, in which oblique progress can be seen as the result of several excellences, normally distinct. In this way the poem becomes a precise and instructive model world.

The lessons and images of *Upon Appleton House* are angled towards one theme, Maria's sole responsibility for the upkeep of the dynasty; this is the perpective it offers. Marvell compares *Last Instructions* to a telescope, applied to the sun's spots (l. 949+); *Upon Appleton House* may be compared to other kinds of perpective, optical trick-pictures.[63] In stanza 1, the bulging brain and arched eyebrows recall anamorphoses, slanted portraits which seem normal when viewed from the side. The initial confusion of the meadow and the wood resembles a chaotic blur which becomes a picture when a specially-shaped mirror is inserted. The meadow is presented as a series of conventional tableaux, but these in turn are compared to crazier effects—microscopic plates, trick landscapes which turn into faces, Davenant's imaginary murals,[64] and perhaps Lely's unsuccessful plan to decorate Whitehall with the victories of the parliamentary forces, by "choice Artists in representing Personages, Battles and Landscapes";[65] the canvas is stretched, but remains empty. The wood is like a camera obscura, where daylight is barred so tightly that "light Mosaicks" of the outside world are projected. More generally, the obliquity of the poem's imagery works like the separate prisms of the Paris perspective, as described by Fanshawe; properly grouped, they reveal a single person where a cluster once appeared. Hobbes applied the same device to the author of *Gondibert*:

> I beleeve (Sir) you have seene a curious kind of perspective, where he that lookes through a short hollow pipe upon a picture conteyning diverse figures sees none of those that are there paynted, but some one person made up of their partes, conveighed to the eye by the artificial cutting of glasse. I find in my imagination an effect not unlike it from your Poeme. The vertues you distribute there amongst so many noble Persons represent (in the reading) the image but of one man's vertue to my fancy, which is your owne.[66]

This concentration of many persons into one may be pure imagination:

> Each thinks his Person represents the whole,
> And with that thought does multiply his Soul.[67]

In Maria's case, however, fantasy becomes reality:

> Fairfax in's children doth Himselfe survive
> Nor can He dye, whiles kindly they derive
> That influence of Grace which earst was His,
> Now theirs by a blest metempsychosis.[68]

She possesses the virtues of her ancestors in every sense; she bears the flame alone. But whereas her masculine ancestors blazed throughout Europe, her *fax* will have to be a marriage-torch.[69] She must accept the "holy bounds" of matrimonial duty,[70] and so fulfil the ancestral promise

> That there may be one of their seed to goe
> Henceforth for ever 'fore thy people soe.[71]

This is the Fairfax perspective. The visual machinery of the poem provides hints and analogues of its single theme.

In the seventeenth-century imagination all these perspective arts had a single purpose—the construction of a visual world on geometric principles, applied to the structure and continuity of human life. For Marvell, the chief of these is not landscape painting, but architecture. *Upon Appleton House* is permeated with architectural references. Fairfax's house is built of local materials, is perfectly proportioned, suits its owners as the nest suits the bird, and expresses their social relationships; these were the main requirements of classical architectural theory, as found in Vitruvius. Marvell deals at first with the building only—an incongruous old-fashioned little house which looked nothing like the classical ideal.[72] Vitruvius's principles are fulfilled on a moral level, *despite* the house's physical appearance; Marvell presents this paradox in suitably outrageous imagery. But the house is only a small part of the poem; its real significance is unfolded as we walk through the grounds. The estate as Marvell interprets it is "one perfect peece"; every part of it contributes to the prospects of the

Fairfax dynasty. Local materials are built up into an integral
structure, expressing the virtues of its occupants; it is a model
of *oeconomia*. The whole poem, in short, is a perfect Vitruvian
building.

Marvell's 'Bill-borow' is a descant on hills and groves; this
poem, like his 'Clarindon's House-Warming', concentrates on
the idea of the *house*. In normal language the meanings of
"house" are diverse; the word may refer to a building or its
grounds, to the present household or its ancestors and descen-
dants, or to a moral or religious institution. Marvell, however,
invites us to imagine a world in which all these meanings are
one. "House" is the common denominator of his imagery, in
all its permutations.

As the poem progresses, for example, outdoor scenes are
presented more and more as domestic interiors. The foliage of
the wood provides a bed, a library, a wardrobe, even a cat and a
dog—the shrinking thorns of stanza 65 and the ivy of stanza
74. After the flood subsides the river licks its back like a
cat—we expected a snake—and the meadows look like fresh
laundry. The river has *"Eben Shuts"*. To conclude, the entire
estate offers itself to Maria as an interior –

> The Meadow Carpets where to tread;
> The Garden Flow'rs to Crown *Her* Head;
> And for a Glass the limpid Brook,
> Where *She* may all *her* Beautyes look;
> But, since *She* would not have them seen,
> The Wood about *her* draws a Skreen (st. 88).

The grounds seem to turn into a human institution—another
meaning of "house". The birds form model households. Vegetation behaves like servants and soldiers on parade. Marvell
loses his human qualities and merges into water and trees, but
Maria gives them her own purity and straightness. The garden
expresses the mind of both lords Fairfax, and the wood is made
of family trees,

> Of whom though many fell in War,
> Yet more to Heaven shooting are:
> And, as they Natures Cradle deckt,
> Will in green Age her Hearse expect (st. 62).

It is impossible to distinguish trees from ancestors here; Marvell prepares us for the climax of the poem, when this metaphor is used to the full:

> Hence *She* with Graces more divine
> Supplies beyond her *Sex* the *Line*;
> And, like a *sprig of Misleto*,
> On the *Fairfacian Oak* doth grow;
> Whence, for some universal good,
> The *Priest* shall cut the sacred *Bud*;
> While her *glad Parents* most rejoice,
> And make their *Destiny* their *Choice* (st. 93).

When the didactic message emerges in its clearest form, the parallel of house and grounds is most clearly declared:

> Mean time ye Fields, Springs, Bushes, Flow'rs,
> Where yet She leads her studious Hours,
> (Till Fate her worthily translates,
> And finds a *Fairfax* for our *Thwaites*)
> Employ the means you have by Her,
> And in your own kind your selves preferr;
> That, as all *Virgins* She preceds,
> So you all *Woods*, *Streams*, *Gardens*, *Meads* (st. 94).

The poem is literally *consummate*; it culminates with the summing-up of its principal themes.

Each episode of the poem is conceived as a natural building. The meadow is a theatre, part Vitruvian, part recollecting the fashionable private theatres of London.[73] The wood is a "Temple green", the choir of a church, and then a private house—with a heron for the stork on its chimney. The design of this temple suggests extravagance and disproportion; outside the columns are pycnostyle or "So closely wedg'd As if the Night within were hedged", but inside

> It opens passable and thin,
> And in as loose an order grows,
> As the *Corinthean Porticoes* (st. 63–4).

By Vitruvian standards this is doubly offensive; the crowded pycnostyle and widely-spaced araeostyle should be avoided, and even if used, should never be combined on one building.[74]

The looser order of this episode recalls the laxity of the nuns; their architecture, however, is more seriously amiss. "Vice infects the very wall"; the whole nunnery is bound together by perversity:

> Were there but, when this House was made,
> One Stone that a just Hand had laid,
> It must have fall'n upon her Head
> Who first Thee from thy Faith misled (st. 26).

Upon Appleton House, like heaven, seems to have many mansions; each one provides a moral lesson.

In his first stanza Marvell hints that the whole poem should be interpreted as architecture:

> Within this sober Frame expect
> Work of no Forrain *Architect*.

Vitruvius provides a model for the whole work—the *frons scenica* of the Roman theatre. Of its five doors, the outermost are fitted with *periaktoi*, revolving flats for sudden changes of scene. The inner side doors represent the abode of strangers. The central opening corresponds to the principal characters below and to the intervening deity above. Marvell approaches the centre from each side: first from the house, whose shape miraculously changes, to the alien nunnery, to the family in the garden; then from the meadow, with its revolving scenes, to the wood, the poet's house, and to the final display of Maria's celestial influence. The poem is loose in parts, but the final panegyric binds it tightly together; here again Marvell seems to be guided by Vitruvius. The whole estate is subjected to his rules for the tight construction of family monuments:

Ita enim non acervatim, sed ordine structum opus poterit esse sine vitio sempiternum,
For thus the work will be able to last for ever undamaged, being built not in a heap, but according to order.[75]

> 'Tis not, what once it was, the *World*;
> But a rude heap together hurl'd . . .
> Your lesser *World* contains the same.
> But in more decent Order tame.[76]

Fig. 1 Henry Peacham, *Minerva Britanna* (1612) p. 185 (photo: Liverpool University)

Fig. 2 Vaclav Hollar, *Graenwich*, third state (British Museum)

Fig. 3 Jan Sadelaer after Martin de Vos, *Oraculum Anachoreticum* (Venice, 1600) pl. 16 (Bodleian Library)

Fig. 4 Giovanni Batista Andreini, *L'Adamo* (Milan, 1617 ed.) p. 65 (Bodleian Library)
Fig. 5 *Ibid* f.c4v (Bodleian Library)

In these stanzas the poem is compacted and squared-off.

Marvell gives a lesson in *oeconomia*, in the politics of a good household; its central principle is concord.

> Musique is Concord, and doth hold allusion
> With everything that doth oppose Confusion,
> In comely *Architecture* it may be
> Known by the Name of *Uniformity*,
> Where Pyramids to Pyramids relate,
> And the whole Fabrick doth configurate:
> In perfectly proportion'd Creatures we
> Accept it by the title *Symmetry*,
> When many Men for some design convent,
> And all concentre, it is call'd *consent*:
> Where mutual hearts in sympathy do move,
> Some few embrace it by the name of Love:
> But when the Soul and Body do agree
> To serve their God, it is *Divinity*.[77]

Harmony is made from discord in the landscape of *Coopers Hill* and in the topographical architecture of *Upon Appleton House*. Perversity and obliqueness, the crosses of fortune or human folly, must be turned to profit; the essence of good building is the control of stresses. Cromwell, in Marvell's *First Anniversary*, knew that stubborn self-seeking men are like obliquely-cut stones; badly placed, they will crash down, but in properly-constructed governments they form an arch, stronger than ever, balancing lateral stresses by their opposition:

> The crossest Spirits here do take their part,
> Fast'ning the Contignation which they thwart.

Marvell's poem is constructed on this principle; obliquity turns out to be progress. The architecture of the poem, its topography and its moral lesson are exactly congruous. By integrating building, dynasty and lands, Marvell recommends the idea of their unity; "the Progress of this Houses Fate" is one perfect piece, and the estate enshrines it. The Fairfaxes must strive to be at one with their circumstances, to live *in* their daughter and their small estate, and not merely *with* them.

"*Domestick Heaven*" is not a condescending term. *Coopers Hill* was devoted to the prospects of the state; *Upon Appleton House* is a domestic poem, dealing with the house in all its aspects, private and homely in manner. But it is a prospective poem too—a visual survey of places which reveal the argument of past and future. The Fairfaxes must reconcile themselves to what Marvell celebrates—a world where the only prospects are domestic ones.

4

The Happy State

The politics of land and landscape

> *when a man's state is well,*
> *'Tis better, if he there can dwell*
>   (Jonson, *To Sir Robert Wroth*)

I showed in Chapter 1 that the art of landscape was a powerful influence on literary descriptions of the countryside, emulated not only in surface details but in its deeper structure. Chapter 2 demonstrated the potential of such landscapes as instruments of thought. Chapter 3 examined them as patterns of thought in which topographical realism and social doctrine are finely matched. This chapter attempts a general survey of the common ground between *topographia* and political theory. The peaceful country estate is a model commonwealth; yearning for political settlement is expressed as a blessed land or earthly paradise. Both pursue the state of happiness.

Topography has for a long time represented the state; the garden-scene in *Richard II* is a well-known example. But in our period we see a new and profounder correspondence between landscape and politics, in which metaphor merges into reality. Ownership of land becomes the sole condition for membership of the commonwealth, the "happy Garden-state" of England. France according to Henry VII was a great kingdom, "but *England* in his mind was a fine Seat for a *Countrey Gentleman*, as any could be found in *Europe*".[1]

Throughout the political debates of the revolution property in land is considered fundamental. Winstanley deduces his whole system from this principle.[2] Ireton allows the right to walk the lanes and breath the air to "any man that is borne heere", but unless he has "a locall and permanent interest in the Kingedome" he must be strictly excluded from "that power that shall dispose of the lands heere, and of all things heere".[3] This doctrine is most clearly expressed in Harrington's *Oceana* (1656):

Domestick Empire is founded upon *Dominion*. Dominion is Propriety reall or personall, that is to say, in Lands, or in money and
goods. Lands, or the parts and parcels of a Territory, are held by
the Proprietor or Proprietors, Lord or Lords of it, in some
proportion; and such (except it be in a City that hath little or no
Land, and whose revenue is in Trade) as is the proportion or
ballance of dominion or property in Land, such is the nature of
the *Empire* (p. 4).

The contribution of city wealth is negligible; "propriety . . .
should have some certain root or foot-hold, which, except in
Land, it cannot have, being otherwise as it were upon the wing
(p. 5)". The true character of Britain is agrarian. James I
ordered the gentry to return to their country estates:

> The Cuntry is your orbe and proper sphere:
> Thence your revenues rise, bestow them there.[4]

Bacon praised these Georgic policies which uphold country
estates

> with such proportion of Land unto them, as may breed a Subject
> to live in convenient plenty, and no servile condition, and to
> keep the Plough in the hand of the owners, and not meer
> hirelings: and thus indeed (saith he) you shall attain unto *Virgil's*
> Character which he gives of ancient *Italy* (*Oceana* f.B1v).

Harrington quotes Bacon with approval, and proposes further
agrarian laws to fix power permanently in the hands of the
smaller landlords, natural rulers of the country (pp. 10, 13–14).
Although banking and foreign trade were increasingly important, the vast proportion of the nation's wealth was in land,
and the profits of trade were invested in country estates.
"Common-wealths upon which the City life hath had the
stronger influence, as *Athens*, have seldome or never been
quiet, but at the best are found to have injured their own
businesse by overdoing it", but a nation of country squires and
yeomen "produceth the most innocent and steddy Genius of a
Common-wealth, such as is that of *Oceana* (f.B1v)". Harrington's ideas are anticipated with remarkable accuracy in *Coopers
Hill*; the violent and self-destructive city is an aberration, and

the true genius of the country is represented by the Thames
and its valley, "innocent and steddy", commanding the Ocean
but dedicated to the prosperity of its local fields and woods. So
the estate is assumed to be the basis of the state.

At the same time the converse is true; the country estate is a
miniature state. Richard Baxter, describing the unrelieved
exploitation of the husbandman, declares "I believe that their
great Landlords have more command of them than the King
hath".[5] Marx was drawing on traditional thought when he
saw that "for those belonging to it, the estate is more like their
fatherland. It is a constricted sort of nationality".[6] The gar-
deners in *Richard II* "keepe Law and Forme, and due Proportion, Shewing as in a Modell our firm Estate (II. iv)".
Overton claimed that "all men are equally born to like propriety, liberty and freedome . . . every man by nature being a
King, Priest and Prophet in his own naturall circuite".[7] Free
men, in Milton's phrase, should "dispose and *oeconomize* in the
Land which God hath giv'n them"[8] like Sir Lewis Pemberton
in Herrick's *Panegyrick:*

> No, thou know'st order, Ethics, and ha's read
> All Oeconomicks.

The well-managed country household was an *"Oiconomick-
Government"*,[9] an example for the whole nation,

> Where plenty, neatness, and a right
> Well-govern'd house yield full delight;
> Wherein you and your Lady give
> Example how the good should live . . .[10]

Both estate and country were ideally self-sufficient. Drayton
draws an explicit parallel between estate management and
regional economics:

> To *Mendip* then the Muse upon the South inclines,
> Which is the onely store, and Coffer of her Mines:
> Elsewhere the Fields and Meades their Sundry traffiques suit:
> The Forrests yeeld her wood, the Orchards give her fruit.
> As in some rich mans house his severall charges lie,
> There stands his Wardrobe, here remaines his Treasurie;

His large provision there, of Fish, of Fowl, of Neat;
His Cellars for his Wines, his Larders for his meate;
There Banquet houses, Walkes for pleasure; here againe
Cribs, Graners, Stables, Barnes, the other to maintaine:
So this rich country hath it selfe what may suffice;
Or that which through exchange a smaller want supplies.[11]

Bristol, according to Cowley, is "herselfe alone a *Province*
large and wide".[12] Drayton praised the self-sufficiency of
ancient Britain and Waller continues the theme in his
Panegyrick to my Lord Protector:

Our little World, the Image of the Great,
Like that amidst the boundless Ocean set,
Of her own Growth has all that Nature Craves,
And all that's Rare as Tribute from the Waves . . .
Things of the noblest kinde our own soyle breeds,
Stout are our men, and Warlike are our Steeds;
Rome, though her Eagle through the world had flown,
Could never make this Island all her own.

Waller wants home produce and colonial import to be happy
partners, one supplying natural tastes, the other rarities;
Drayton could only hark back to a pre-imperialist state, when
hardly a foreigner "defil'd her virgin breast". Colonial avarice
leads only to ruin:

Through her excessive wealth (at length) till wanton growne,
Some Kings (with others Lands that would enlarge their owne)
By innovating Armes an open passage made
For him that gap't for all (the *Roman*) to invade.[13]

The self-sufficient country estate is a model of the pristine
national community; food is local and abundant, cash is never
seen and far-fetched desires are as unheard-of as luxury
imports. Saxham in Carew's poem is

full of native sweets, that blesse
Thy roofe with inward happinesse . . .
Such rarities that come from farre,
From poore mens houses banisht are.

The flowers at Wrest

> diffuse
> Such native Aromatiques, as we use
> No forraigne Gums, nor essence fetcht from farre.

But this happy state is susceptible to invasion and decay.

Since the state of the nation is intimately linked to affairs on the estate, any disturbance in one is felt in the other. The threat of the levellers, according to Marchamont Nedham, is that "this Plea for *Equality of Right* in Government, at length introduceth a Claim for *Equality of Estates*".[14] Heneage Finch, on the other hand,

> practised the annihilating of Ancient and Notorious Perambulations of particular Forests, the better to prepare himself to annihilate the Ancient and Notorious Perambulations of the whole Kingdom, the Meets and Bounders between the Liberties of the Subject and Sovereign Power.[14]

In literature also topical issues are presented in terms of the landscape they affect. Mildmay Fane's *Candy Restored*, for example, is an allegory of the political crisis of 1640 (ed. C. Leech, Louvain, 1938). His characters look back to the "Halcion daies (p. 105)" of James I, when

> the people, each contented with his owne,
> past their tymes friendly; shepards on the hills
> whilst their flocks fed made musick to them freely:
> And those broake up the ground, with cheerfull hopes
> promisd themselves a future crops reward;
> Nor was there feare in anything (p. 104).

The sun shone with a kind aspect and rain-clouds

> scattered silver drops and pearle
> mingled together, which sowen on the mead,
> I know not by what art or chimestry
> Nature did use, cam up in Golden flowres
> amidst the grasse, which daggled to the knees (*ibid.*).

The disastrous régime of Charles I has filled the land with such "obnoxiousnesse"

> that grove, nor forrest,
> although ther briers now and thornes abound
> wher Olive once was chiefe, can harbour give
> suffitient to protect from the fierce stormes
> such furie menaceth . . . (p. 105)

> Temples, Downes and every feild
> with novelties are soe defilde –
> Nay the meade and grove below
> cannot scape this overthrow . . . (p. 116).

Suddenly the scene is transformed; the military figures on stage are replaced by "fresh greenes and faire garden Landskips" (p. 101):

> the cold wett moneths are past and May
> with her Flora who adornd
> the yeare with bewtie are returned.
> Fluttering winters flaky raine
> 's fled and melted, grass againe
> on the mead doth growe and dye
> it, into a fresh green livery (p. 133).

Parliament has been recalled.

Fane's independent provincial conservatism made him hate arbitrary taxation; he could not have foreseen the violent outcome of the crisis he then thought solved—

> but now, ah now,
> Intruding *Mars* molests the active *plough*! . . .
> Oh miserable *tillage*![16]

> We Ord'nance Plant and Powder sow.[17]

In the Isle of Man, where war has not penetrated,

> The Husbandman buryes his seed without fear
> O'th'Sequestrators sickle, nor does e're
> Doubt who shall share the Flock, or milk the Kine
> He fosters, or shall eat the fruit of's Vine.[18]

But in England

> the Drum shall speak
> In every Village warre, the Rurall swaine
> Shall leave his tillage, Shepheards leave the plaine.
> . . . the Glebe Land
> Shall unmanured and untilled stand.
> The plough shall be neglected, and the corn,
> By th'horse hoofe trampled, fade before full born
> 'Tis fit for sickle. Graziers sell away
> Their beasts, lest kept they prove the souldiers pay.[19]

Margaret James describes the crippling effect of free quarter on the economy of the countryside; passages like these are not mere rhetoric.[20]

Political disaster is commonly presented as a Fall, ruining the landscape as the first Fall was supposed to have done. Primitivism has a prescriptive function; imaginary topography shows us not only a vision of the land but a theory of its proper use. For Winstanley the tyranny of private landlords began with the fall.[21] For Hobbes the pristine land was a disgusting wilderness. For Harrington it was a natural agrarian oligarchy, whose foundations were only shaken when land came to be bought and sold; "*Alienations*" and violence are the result (*Oceana* pp. 4–5). Commercial greed and newfangled imports destroyed the happy state of Britain, according to Drayton. Gold, fire and alcohol are variously blamed for the fall. In the golden age

> No want appeares; th'officious Vine doth stand
>   With bending clusters to our hand . . .
> The Apple ripe drops from its stalke to thee,
>   From taste of death made free
> The luscious fruit from the full Fig-tree shall
>   Into thy bosome fall.
> Meanewhile, the Vine no pruning knife doth know,
>   The wounded earth no plow,
> The Corne growes green alone, and th'unhurt land
>   Doth white with harvest stand.[22]

Supreme fertility and happiness are therefore attributed to whatever age the poet admires with nostalgia.

In royalist propaganda the outrages of the Star Chamber and the fury of evicted peasants are rapidly forgotten. According to Margaret Cavendish, under Charles I there were

> Few Crimes committed, Punishments scarce known;
> The nobles liv'd in state, and high degree,
> All happy, even to the Peasantry;
> Where easy Laws, no Tax to make them poor,
> All live with Plenty, full is every Store . . .
> Their Lands are fertil, and their Barnes are full,
> Orchards thick planted, from whence Fruit may pull;
> Store of Cattle feeding in Meadows green,
> Where chrystal Brooks run every Field between;
> Where Cowslips growing, which makes Butter yellow,
> And fatted Beasts, two inches thick with Tallow;
> And many Parks for fallow Deer to run,
> Shadow'd with Woods, to keep them from the Sun;
> And in such Kingdomes, Beasts, Fowl, Fish, have store,
> Those that industrious are, can nev'r be poor.[23]

Peter Hausted appeals to the same memories:

> O those were Golden dayes! all things were quiet . . .
> How richly were yee blest in House and Field
> With all the store that a fat Land could yield . . .[24]

Whitehall palace, in Henry Glapthorne's poem, describes the glorious time, under Elizabeth and the Stuarts, when she resembled

>   that happy ground
> Pregnant with Aromatick Balme and Spice,
> The first created, long lost Paradise.
>   (*White-Hall* (1643) f.A3)

During this time there was "no civill broile or forraigne feare", no monopolies or powerful favourites, no arguments about religion, no foreign and gaudy costume, no false hair or makeup, and

> No tumults then attempted were by th'rude
> And many-headed beast, the Multitude:
> (To whom the present times seeme ever worst,
> Praising the past they never knew) . . . (ff.B1-v).

Reduced to such absurdities, nostalgic primitivism is self-defeating.

The political fall, unlike the original, leaves spots untouched:

> Heaven, sure, has kept this spot of earth uncurst,
> To shew how all things were created first . . .
>> (Waller, *The Batell of the Summer Islands*)

> If *Eden* be on Earth at all,
> 'Tis that, which we the *Country* call.
>> (Vaughan, 'Retirement')

It may be redeemed by good husbandry, as Walter Blith implies in his *England's Improvement, or Reducement of Land to pristine Fertility* (1649 running-title), or by the arrival of a ruler well-disposed to one's own interests:

> Mirth shall attend on Health, and Peace shall Plenty kisse:
> The trees with fruite, with flowres our gardens fill'd,
> Sweete honey from the leaves distill'd.[25]

Panegyric topography is thus a means of reconstructing the golden age under the benign eye of a present patron.

The ideal landscape is a little world. The orderly placing of its parts resembles divine creation; Chaos was

> a rude load
> Where scuffling seedes of things misplact aboad.
> Where springs, ponds, lakes immense, and hewtes curl'd
> Were with things hot, dry, humid, frigid hurld . . .
> When out of this dull masse
> By heavenly Alchymie extracted was
> A world well ordered, and methodicall.[26]

Society and the ordered landscape are born together; in Chaos

> *Each Thing* was wroth, and snarled with his Brother;
> When *Heav'n* and *Earth*, tumbled in one blinde Heap,
> Struggled and strove to stifle one Another,

but after "seasonable Love" has done its work,

> All rest contented with the Stations thou
> Appointedst Them.[27]

Fanshawe describes the primeval origins of the landscape in *The Progresse of Learning*, which has survived in an early and a revised version. He begins:

> Before the Earth was held in severall
> Twas one great feild where all the creatures fedd.
> As in a Common (therefore termd the All)
> Men mixt with beasts together in one shedd
> Upon the ground did take a homely bedd:
> Things were not sorted yett, for then there was
> No Groves where shady trees were billetted,
> Nor grass distinguisht from the corne, butt grass
> And corne and shady trees were shuffled in one Masse.[28]

Nature is "greiv'd to undergoe A second Chaos", and begs Jove for a son to "improve her mangled state" by husbandry. In this version Wit (or human intelligence) scorns anything so menial, and the field is left open to Craft, who introduces corruption. In his revised version, Fanshawe resolves the contradiction he has stumbled into, and links social doctrine and landscape even more closely:

> As now they are, things were not sorted then,
> Nor by division of the parts did breed
> The publique harmony. For how should men
> Manure the ground, their minds being choakt with weed?
> Or adde the last hand, which themselves did need?
> Woods yet unto the Mountaines did not passe,
> Nor Heards beneath in grassy Meadowes feed,
> Nor Corne inrich the middle Grounds; but Grasse,
> And woods, and stifled Corne, were shuffled in one Masse.

Nature complains "what availes my store Heapt in a common field?" Abundance is made to seem horrible when it is shared; only by class division can man attain his true nature,

> For till by worth some difference can be showne
> Twixt man and man, twixt man and beast there will be none.

Division is not simply a moral question, for the "good" are placed in dominion over the bad. Only when a Harringtonian system is established can Wit safely introduce agriculture, and retire

> Leaving the Countryes in propriety
> To such as were by him for Rule inspir'd.[29]

Describing primeval times, Fanshawe projects a dream of undiminished squirearchy.

Political terms intrude into the landscape even when it is supposed to represent a perfect quiet life, far removed from vicious affairs of state; invidious greatness is always in view. Argalus and Parthenia, in Quarles's poem,

> Would climbe th'ambitious *Tower*,
> From whose aspiring top they might discover
> A little Common-wealth of land, which none
> But *Argalus* durst challenge as his owne . . .[30]

an innocent state, certainly, but with the lineaments of the great one. Fanshawe persuades court ladies to take up a country life by discovering every feature of the court in nature:

> The Lillie (Queene) the (Royall) Rose,
> The Gillyflowre (Prince of the bloud)
> The (Courtyer) Tulip (gay in clothes)
> The (Regall) Budd,
> The Vilet (purple Senatour) . . .
> ('Ode upon Occasion of His Majesties Proclamation')

When Lovelace's Aramantha walks in her garden

> The flowers in their best aray
> As to their Queen their Tribute pay
> 　　　　　　(*Aramantha, a Pastorall*)

Each flower has a function in this court, like the garrison of flowers at Appleton house. Like Marvell himself, Aramantha passes from the garden to the meadow, and then to the wood, discovering in each place the household rituals suitable for that time of day. In Marvell, as we saw, each episode is a different type of house, and the metaphors are closely controlled to pay tribute to the destiny of the Fairfaxes, supreme in littleness. Lovelace's poem, despite a considerable resemblance on the surface, has no such control. Aramantha is congratulated on the innocence of her life, in contrast to courtly sterility; but she displays in metaphor all the pomp she is supposed to have eschewed. The cows are "Yeomanry", and they give her a civic reception; the grove is a "Pallace", the "Court oth'Royall Oake, where stood The whole Nobility", and so on. *Aramantha* is a two-dimensional *Appleton House*, written, as it were, by the Marvell of the wood before he is brought back to his senses by Maria. One poem is serious about love but frivolous about affairs of state, the other serious about social duties but frivolous with love; but both see their destiny in "a little commonwealth of land".

The creatures were frequently shown to have a form of society. Bees and ants were taken seriously as "Politicall creatures",[31] and birds form church choirs, funeral parties and parliaments. Every rank and occupation is depicted in the commonwealth of birds. The falcon is a

> Fair Princesse of the spacious Air,
> That hast vouchsaf'd acquaintance here,
> With us are quarter'd below stairs.
>   (Lovelace, 'The Falcon')

On Mildmay Fane's country estate the song-birds correspond exactly to the participants in a lawsuit, and crows and jackdaws to the clamouring left-wing—

> For you must know't observ'd of late,
> That Reformation in the State,
> Begets no less by imitation,
> Amidst this chirping feather'd Nation.[32]

Flowers organize themselves in Herrick's 'The parliament of Roses'; the rose is elected queen, but only to be Julia's maid of honour. Traditional science graded all plants and animals according to their nobility, so it was perhaps inevitable that they should become by-words for social hierarchy:

> In th'umble valley better be a shrubb
> With secure peace, than, on th'aspiring top
> Of a proud hill, a Cedar, still expos'd
> To certaine danger.[33]

Henry More's green chapel in *Psychozoia*, an allegory of the state church, is made up of a "higher hedge of thickn'd trees" and "a lower rank . . . of lesser shrubs".[34] Cowley hails the "old *Patrician* Trees, so great and good" and the "*Plebian* under wood" ('Of Solitude'). In Joseph Beaumont's Eden

> no crook-back'd Tree
> Disgrac'd the place, no foolish scrambling Shrub,
> No wilde and careless Bush, no clownish Stub.
>> (*Psyche* (1648) p. 85)

The trees at Somerley stand in their social ranks:

> The usefull Ash, and sturdy Oak are set
> At distance, and obey; the Brambles met
> Embracing twine int'Arbours . . .
> The Nobler Plants, as Firre, Deal, and the Pine
> Weeping out Rozen, bleeding Turpentine,
> Like the Life-guard, upon the Hall attend
> At nearer distance.[35]

Herrick describes the oak as if it were a monarch—

> The proud *Dictator* of the State-like wood:
> I meane (the Soveraigne of all Plants) the Oke;
>> ('All things decay and die')

Howell, on the other hand, deals with the commonwealth as if it were a forest, *Dodona's Grove*. Mountains are obvious and universal symbols of social and literary status. The bitter polemic of the civil war was often couched in allegories taken from Nature:

> there's a Toleration now; the *Hill*
> Levell'd to a Plain.[36]

Left-wing hatred threatened the fall of great cedars and oaks.[37]

> The *Commons* of the *aire* conspire to throw
> Their *Soveraign* down, and will not fly so low
> As formerly; but are resolv'd to be
> Oppugnant to the *Eagles Majesty*.[38]

Such terms are used equally by "moderates" and "extrem-ists"; Morforio and Pasquin, two conservative merchants in Mildmay Fane's *The Change*, discuss the monarchy:

> You'ld have the Winde a Monarch then and those
> his Royall Subjects bent att his Command?
> Yes; But an emptye or Titulary—
> His violent Raigne hath done the Forest mischeife.[39]

Coopers Hill is clearly speaking the natural language of its time.

On the country estate this symbolism may become more real. The king does "mischeife" to the nation's "Forest"; but Fane's chief grievance against him was his arbitrary applica-tion of the forest laws. The fortunes of a great house really are bound up in their timber, and trees may be planted to mark the birth of a child, like Sidney's tree at Penshurst, and indi-vidualized with carved initials and names; they are a living memorial to ancestors

> Of whom though many fell in War,
> Yet more to Heaven shooting are;
> And as they Natures Cradle deckt,
> Will in green Age her hearse expect.
> <div align="right">(<i>Upon Appleton House</i> st.62)</div>

James Howell, for example, writes on a child born at Ken-wood

> May this new-born *Diana* like *Cane-wood*
> Grow up and taper, Germinat and Bud,[40]

and Fanshawe's 'Ode' entices the gentry into the country with the thought that they can "plant Trees" and "see them shoote up with your Children". On this more intimate scale, trees can stand for the *moral* qualities that sustain society,

For they ('tis credible) have sense,
As We, of Love and Reverence,
And underneath the Courser Rind
The *Genius* of the house do bind . . .
Yet now no further strive to shoot,
Contented if they fix their Root.
Nor to the winds uncertain gust,
Their prudent Heads too far intrust.
(Marvell 'Upon the Hill and Grove at *Bill-borow*')

William Basse's *Metamorphosis of the Wallnut-Tree of Borestall* is a private poem of this kind. The haughty forest trees have nothing to do with the funeral of the "old and fruitfull Wallnut", and it is left to the humble nut-trees to bury him properly. These useful creatures represent "true and noble freinds", striving for the good of others, while the forest trees are parasitic—

The gallants of the groves, Th'Elme long and lazie,
The wavering Aspe, the Popler as unstable,
The hungry Maple, brittle Ash and crazie,
The gosling Sallow, and the Boxe unable,
Vague Willow, and the like inumerable,
A sort that yeild no fruite but proud neglect:
Who would no kindesse shew, can non expect.[41]

The landscape is presented as if it were capable of personal dealings with people and response to political events. Fields and groves may be "loyall Secretaries" and "Witnesses"; brambles catch hold of a nymph "and seem t'arrest thee at my Sute"; at Woodstock, Henry II's love-nest for Rosamund,

The place it selfe did seeme his sute to move,
And intimate a silent plea for love.

Shropshire "impropriates" a noble patron, instead of the reverse; whole regions languish when Charles I is absent; rivers run wild with joy when a new ship is launched, or when the poet's mistress bathes in them; they climb hills out of love for great financiers, flee in terror at civil war, run smoothly for the Duke of Devonshire, and even, passing by a stately palace, "kiss her base".[42]

The landscape of the country estate is thoroughly mythologised. The power of Orpheus,

> That voice which taught dispersed Trees to move
> Into an orderlie and well pitch'd Grove,[43]

is equated with the power of estate management. Grounds are designed to show the obedience of Nature, walks and avenues representing servants in attendance,

> While, like a *Guard* on either side,
> The Trees before their *Lord* divide.
> (*Upon Appleton House* st.78)

Orphic mythology allows trees to move of their "owne inclination",[44] responding to the presence of the lord and his beautiful heirs:

> Where ere you walk'd trees were as reverend made
> As when of old Gods dwelt in every shade . . .
> (Cowley, 'The Spring')

Even natural growth is a quality of this presence:

> 'Tis *She* that to these Gardens gave
> That wondrous Beauty which they have;
> *She* streightness on the Woods bestows;
> To *Her* the Meadow sweetness owes . . .
> (*Upon Appleton House* st.87)

Maria's influence over the landscape is not sheer fantasy, but an abbreviated version of the economic process. Previous generations of Fairfaxes have bestowed a special quality on the estate, by excluding commoners and ordering their labour to plant gardens and tend fields; by primogeniture Mary inherits all their power. The same divinities preside over the national government and the little commonwealth of the estate. Waller explains that

> Had *Dorothea* liv'd when Mortals made
> Choice of their Deities, this sacred shade
> Has held an altar to the power that gave

The peace and glory which these Allyes have;
Embrodered so with flowers where she stood,
That it became a garden of a wood.

('At Pens-hurst II')

"Her presence" is endowed with a supernatural power which inspires even the wildest trees to form lanes and arbours "Like some well marshall'd and obsequious band":

> *Amphion* so made stones and timber leape
> Into faire figures from a confus'd heape.
> And in the symmetry of her parts is found
> A power like that of harmony in sound.

Waller uses the same lines to celebrate Charles I's restoration of St. Paul's:

> He like *Amphion* makes those quarries leape
> Into faire figures from a confus'd heape:
> For in his art of regiment is found
> A power like that of harmony in sound.

('Upon his Majesties repairing of Pauls')

Both cases are absolutist; reality is presented as the emanation of a single powerful person.

The hyperbolic landscape is both domestic and political; topography provides an attractive and flexible means of idealizing society and absolving oneself from its problems. It embodies the desire to invest the state with the qualities of nature, innocent, self-renewing and inviolable. The natural, in seventeenth-century terms, means what has not been forced from its paths by violence. Consequently, if an entire system regains its natural state it will stay perfect for ever.[45] The political establishment of England, according to Royalists and Parliamentarians alike, was "naturally" made up of those who had a "locall and permanent interest in the kingdome"—*local* being invested in the natural wealth of a country estate, and *permanent* being exempt from alienation, disputed title, or popular invasion. In reality, the countryside was continually involved in struggles of this kind. Political theory and the ideal landscape both require a state of Nature, purporting to be a myth of origin, but in fact a rallying prescription for their cause.

This imaginary kingdom of nature is manifestly more coherent than the real political world. The various parts of the landscape are closely interrelated:

> The Christall Brookes which gently runne betweene
> The shadowing Trees, and as they through them passe
> Water the Earth, and keepe the Meadowes greene
> Giving a colour to the verdant grasse.
> (Cowley, *Constantia and Philetus* 229–32)

The valleys support life, but only because the hills give them shelter; trees protect the fields which feed their roots. Rivers descend from mountain springs and nourish the banks which guide them to the sea; but in turn the sea feeds the springs by exhalations and secret conduits.

The course of a river is easily moralized; we all "lose our selves in the insatiate Maine", but some, like the lady in Habington's elegy, can do so graciously—

> since shee perfum'd all
> The banks she past, so that each neighbour Field
> Did sweete flowers cherisht by her watring yeeld,
> Which now adorne her Hearse.[46]

The circulation of waters lends itself to financial metaphor:

> For all those various streames which do entombe
> Themselves within the Oceans liquid wombe
> The Sea payes Impost, and an interest brings
> Back to the Earth, when it refines to Springs
> The brackish billowes, and those waters straines
> To Brooks, and weaves them into all her veines.[47]

Thomas Washbourne explains political change in terms of natural circulation—of the blood, of the seasons, and of waters:

> Rivers which borrow from the main
> Their streames, do pay them back again . . .
> The like in bodies doth befall
> Civil as well as natural.[48]

Fulke Greville, like Denham in *Coopers Hill*, proposes "mutual ties" between monarch and subject, based on self-limitation; the subject should not ask too much, nor the monarch take too much. If this fails, society is destroyed by extremes of tyranny or democracy, but

> if Pow'r within these sceptre lines
> Could keep, and give as it would be repaid,
> These mutual fed, and mutual feeding mines
> Would still enrich, could hardly be decayd.[49]

"C.I." turns to the landscape in his *Commons Petition* of 1642, to express the ideal constitution that will avert the coming crisis:

> Princes, like the Sunne, should from the floods exhale
> The wealth they raise: then in a showre let fall
> In every place, as they see cause, a share,
> And not consume them in the worthless aire;
> Their full Exchequers should like Conduits be
> Open to all, but to the poore most free.
> And subjects should, like fields, be full of springs,
> That naturally still fall toward their Kings.
> The Common-wealth should alwayes be in motion,
> Seas flow to brooks, and brooks should fall to th'ocean;
> Such Royall and such loyall community,
> Keep Kings and subjects still in unity (f. A4).

This system breaks down when parliament, ungrateful for royal bounty, "return'd in Poyson, what He shed in Dew"[50]—a hideous parody of natural circulation. The inter-related landscape provides an organic model for society, emphasizing the mutual relationship between its members.

This relationship was not always harmonious:

> And as our surly supercilious Lords,
> Bigge in their frownes, and haughty in their words,

> Looke down on those whose humble fruitfull paine
> Their proud and barren greatnesse must susteine:
> So lookes the Hill upon the streame.
>
> <div align="right">(<i>Coopers Hill</i>, 1642 version)</div>

This is not intended as a denunciation, but as a conventional picture of pride and humility. Out of such discords, Denham claims, the harmony of the state is made, just as the contrast of hill and river makes an agreeable landscape picture. The river Usk is imprisoned by its banks but waters them despite their savage cruelty—teaching Thomas Vaughan to be Christian to his enemies.[51] In Henry More's rural retreat the sound of a stream reminds him of the behaviour of great men in a crowd:

> Hard at my feet ran down a crystall spring
> Which did the cumbrous pebbles hoarsly chide
> For standing in the way. Though murmuring
> The broken stream his course did rightly guide
> And strongly pressing forward with disdain
> The grassie floor divided into twain.[52]

But even this conventional "wild harmonie" disturbs the social metaphor. The landscape must be completely harmonized; this is the source of its didactic power. It must be clearly identifiable with righteousness and just society:

> Here learn ye Mountains more unjust,
> Which to abrupter greatness thrust . . .
> Learn here those humble steps to tread,
> Which to securer Glory lead.
>
> <div align="right">(Marvell, '<i>Bill-borow</i>')</div>

> I care not, I, to fish in seas,
> Fresh rivers best my mind do please,
> Whose sweet calm course I contemplate,
> And seek in life to imitate;
> In civil bounds I fain would keep
> And for my past offences weep.
>
> (William Basse, 'The Anglers Song')

In the first version of *Coopers Hill* Denham allowed his hill scenery to suggest the injustice and violence of the rich towards the poor; but in the political landscape all violence must be associated with the opposition, with moral evil, political hubris, and mere oppugnancy. In his revision of 1655 the proud mountain becomes grand, tragic and sympathetic, and the river "gentle" and "kind". They are no longer exploiter and victim, but happy partners in a scheme to nourish and protect the meadows between.

A calm river, for William Basse's Angler, represented civil obedience. A flooded river, or a raging sea, is a universal symbol for the machinations of one's political enemies, and the civil war which inevitably follows extremism:

> a tame *stream* does wild and dangerous grow
> By unjust force; he now with wanton play
> Kisses the smiling Banks, and glides away,
> But his known Channel stopt, begins to roare,
> And swell with rage, and buffet the dull shore.
> His mutinous waters hurry to the *War*,
> And *Troops* of *Waves* come rolling from afar.
> Then scorns he such weak stops to his free source,
> And overruns the neighboring fields with violent course.[53]

Usurpation and the good land are the themes of Edward Thimelby's pindaric ode *Upon Occasion of the Overflowes of Po and Tyber:*

> Hark, how the tyrant water foaming roares,
> > Disdaining hills for shores;
> > Each element his seate confounds,
> > > Where rivers brooke no bounds:
> > > Thos streams, who, lesse, could yeeld
> > Rich pasture to each gladsome field,
> Lyfe to each jolly swaine, now greater growne,
> And swolne more high, both feeld and shepard drowne.
> Alas! how rare a thing is moderate
> > To an unweldy state!

He then surveys the social and political disasters of immoderate state. The millionaire, "born to his friends and countrys good",

> Swells, rages, overflowes, depopulates,
> Confounds his owne, ruins his neighbors states.

Parliament once elected becomes a tyrant,

> braves Cesar to his face,
> And then usurpes his place,
> And puft so prowdly high
> Above the brinkes of mortality
> Even dares the Gods to reparation,
> And carves new currents to religion.

The army "like a torrent overflown . . . 'Gainst its own citty turnes th'ungratefull flood". It is as if the closing lines of *Coopers Hill* had been put into effect. Like Denham, Thimelby discovers in the landscape and its disturbance a detailed analogy to current affairs. Like Denham, too, he claims to be loftily objective, but is in fact partisan; under Charles I the landscape was a model of mutual cherishing care, and people enjoyed the promised land:

> A people seated in a fayre aboad,
> Where milke and nectar flowd,
> Where peace and justice fild the Cupps of blisse,
> In a perpetual kisse,
> Drunk with that ill-bestowed successe
> Of their owne happinesse,
> And pamperd bove ther hight,
> Kick downe the bankes of just and right . . .[54]

Every nuance of political rancour was expressed in terms of landscape.

Topographia is a recourse to those who are not prepared for rigorous argument. It is well suited to the emotive politics of the *ancien régime*, for it allows the old order to seem permanent, orderly and universally agreeable. The creatures "naturally" form households, commonwealths and hierarchies, and are tied together by mutual nourishment and protection. They are a "sweet society",[55] who cannot but do right since they are part of Nature's Kingdom; the converse is "no society"[56]— flood, starvation and mutual destruction. This polarity belongs more to party mythology than political philosophy. In mythological thought conformity becomes truth, and truth becomes sweetness. *Topographia* turns subjective values into apparent facts.

"Genuine society . . . right society . . . inviolable concord"—these are the preoccupations of the period. The landscape is described in terms of public ritual, the ceremonies of mutual faith and the social gathering that marks them. The confluence of rivers becomes a society wedding, complete to its last detail.[57] The sun and the earth make up an ideal home in Margaret Cavendish's *Island*, flowers being their children and Apollo the dutiful father

> Who takes great care to *dresse* and *prune* them oft,
> And with *clear Dew* he washes their *Leaves* soft.
> When he hath done, he wipes those *drops* away,
> With *Webbs* of heat, which he weaves every day . . .[58]

Morning and evening are marked by a ceremonial turnout of the guard at Appleton house. Birds which "bow as twere Cursey-homage shewing" augment the pageantry of welcome to a country estate. In snowy weather the arrival of Jove is heralded by "whole showers of Sugar plums", like a secular monarch's. The coming of spring is an event in the social calendar, when the earth "like some rich wanton heire" prepares for "vanities".[59] Spring is given the ostentatious bustle of the City preparing for a king's birthday or lord mayor's show:

> Fresh cloaths of State she spreads upon
> The Downes, in hope you'l walke thereon,
> And many faire *flowers* she doth create
> Your fair cheeks to imitate,
> Then borrowes perfumes for her Birth
> From the Spicery of your *Breath* . . .
>
> Thaw'd are the Snowes, and now the lusty Spring
> Gives to each Mead a neat enameling.
> The Palms put forth their Gemmes, and every Tree
> Now swaggers in her Leavy gallantry. . .

> The lofty Mountains standing on a row,
> Which but of late were periwigd with snow
> D'off their old coats, and now are daily seene
> To stand on tiptoes, all in swaggering greene. . .[60]

Nature is bound together by social bonds and commercial dealings, and unified by the excitement of a gathering. In the same way Cowley contrasts the sterile river of gold, devoid of fish and unable to "feede the neighbouring wood", with the sociable river of "pleasant poverty":

> Here waves call waves, and glide along in ranke,
>   And prattle to the smiling banke. . .
> *Dasyes* the first borne of the teeming Spring,
>   On each side their embrodery bring;
>   Here *Lillies* wash, and grow more white,
> And *Daffadills* to see themselves delight.
> Here a fresh arbor gives her amorous shade
>   Which *Nature* the best *Gard'ner* made.
>
>   ('That a pleasant poverty is to
>   bee preferred before discon-
>   tented riches')

The desire to present a "sweet societie" is cleary more important than convincing observation.

The elements of the landscape are close bosom friends among themselves, and courteous and altruistic to others. This conceit is already well developed in Gervase Markham's *English Arcadia* (first part, 1607):

> the trees did not overgrow one another, but seemed in even proportions to delight in each others evennesse: the flowers did not strive which should be supreme in smelling, but communicating their odours, were content to make one intyre sweet savour; the beddes whereon the flowers grew disdained not the grassie Allies, but lending to them their lustre, made the walkes more pleasant: the faire ryver *Penaus* would at no time overflow his bankes to drowne their beauties, but with gentle swellings wash them like a dewie morning: the springs did not challenge the river, because his water was not as theirs, so wholesome, but paying their tribute into his bosome, made him able to beare shippes of burthen. . . (f.K3)

The landscape "is, in a word, a world of sweets, that live in a Faire Communitie togeather".[61] In later poetry this community of attitude is replaced by one of action. "The whispering Foliage conspires" to sooth Eldred Revett's mistress; Mathew Stevenson's 'Jovial Journey' is delightful because "the Sun, Wind, Birds, Raine, Earth and Flowers conspire" to create a perfect environment for travelling.[62] The hill at Bilborough, in Marvell's poem,

> Not for it self the height does gain,
> But only strives to raise the Plain.

The Thames in *Coopers Hill* is ideally considerate to the fields along his banks,

> O're which he kindly spreads his spacious wing,
> And Hatches plenty for th'ensuing Spring,
> Nor with a furious and unruly wave
> Like profuse Kings resumes the wealth he gave:
> No unexpected Inundations spoyle
> The Mowers hopes, nor mock the Plough-mans toyle.
>   (1642 version)

The castle of the virtuous Ariamnes in Chamberlayne's *Pharonnida* (1659)

>   stood
> Upon a hill, whose Basis, freng'd with wood,
> Shadowed the fragrant Meadows, thorough which
> A spatious River, striving to enrich
> The flow'ry Valleys with what ever might
> At home be profit or abroad delight,
> With parted streams that pleasant Islands made
> Its gentle current to the Sea conveyd (I.6).

As I showed in Chapter 2, "the composure of this happy place", where "strength and beauty Sate combin'd in one", corresponds exactly to the owner's qualities of mind. His household is a model of the same cooperative virtues—size without vastness, plenty without surfeit, modesty, usefulness and· domestic harmony.

This conspiracy of nature is not necessarily amiable. Margaret Cavendish's '*Island*' is destroyed because all the elements "conspired to work *her Ruine*".[63] The bereaved lover cries out to the woods where he once spent happy days:

> Can trees be green, and to the Ay'r
> Thus prostitute their Flowing Hayr?
>
> (Lovelace, *Aramantha*)

The community of animals increases Milton's mourning for Damon. Tarquin, in John Quarles's poem, is punished by being sent to "a place of no society" in the country, where the gregarious sociability of the creatures tortures him still further:

> Ah! how these silent fishes seem to sport
> And revel in their cool aquarian Court. . .
> Whilst I am parboyl'd in a Sea of blood!

At the climax of the poem metaphor becomes reality; the nightingales gang up on him, drive him mad with their singing, and finally "flockt about him, and pickt out his eyes".[64]

In seventeenth-century language, Bilborough hill "communicates" its greatness by striving to raise the plain; in a different sense, the trees communicate their memories of Fairfax's career:

> Onely sometimes a flutt'ring Breez
> Discourses with the breathing Trees;
> Which in their modest Whispers name
> Those Acts that swell'd the Cheek of Fame.

Nature is supposed to share the poet's dominant concern:

> Lie downe, and listen what the sacred spring
> In her harmonious murmures strives to sing
> To th'neighbouring banke . . . sings she not of her?
>   Let no darke grove
> Be taught to whisper stories of thy love.[65]

The fame of Captain Dover's Cotswold games is echoed by local rivers, then told to the Avon, who tells it to the Severn, and thence to the Isis, Thames, Ocean and the world.[66] In

Paradise Lost the winds steal from the trees and whisper among themselves at Satan's arrival (IV.158), and whisper to the woods at the marriage of Adam and Eve (VIII.516); each case signals a major event, where ceremony is called for. In *Lycidas* Milton tries to involve the fellowship of Nature in a non-existent funeral ceremony "to interpose a little ease":

> call the Vales, and bid them hither cast
> Their Bells and Flourets of a thousand hues.

Cowley invokes the same fellowship in order to expunge it as a token of his grief:

> Henceforth no learned *Youths* beneath you sing,
> Till all the tuneful *Birds* to your boughs they bring;
> No tuneful *Birds* play with their wonted chear,
>   And call the learned *Youths* to hear.
>   ('On the Death of Mr. William Hervey')

Death breaks the sociable reciprocal patterns in the life of nature:

> How silent are the groves? No aire doth move
> To make the boughs each other kisse in love,
> Nor doe the leaves (as they had jealous feares)
> Whisper into each others joying eares.[67]

But even grief can be communicated. Crashaw 'on the death of Dr Porter' tells the river Cam to "murmur forth thy woes to every flower", teach the birds to sing dirges and the stones to "untie their shackled tongues", and generally "discharge thy struggling groanes" to the entire landscape it passes through. In the pathetic fallacy, creatures not only sympathize but share the bereavement:

> The neighbouring river mourn'd to heare her Fate,
> The blustering winds did chide the hollow trees,
> While they consulting to participate
> Her griefe doe all their verdant garments leese.
> The birds tell heaven, and heaven to show its pitty
> Bids *Philomela* sing a mournfull Ditty.[68]

Nature provides a network of communications to sustain the poet.

Ariamnes was the "Soul" of his well-composed estate; the lady of Beedome's poem is "like the Queen of earth"—wild beasts bow to her, birds gather and sing, and

> The now-growne-gentle Satyres did invite
> The wood-Nymphes to compose a measur'd dance.[69]

The sweet society of nature is invariably "composed" by a higher power; it is an idealized monarchy, whose members unite in paying tribute. The virgin land of America, according to Thomas Morton, is blessed with an ideally subservient nature, its springs and rivers

> Jetting most jocundly where they doe meete
> And hand in hand runne downe to Neptunes Court
> To pay the yearly tribute which they owe
> To him as sovereigne Lord of all the spring.

The conceit is appropriate, for the author is inviting the reader to join him on a colonial expedition. Possession and Lordship is the inescapable counterpart of the ideal cooperative landscape:

> Not such
> Another place, for benefit and rest,
> In all the universe can be possest;
> The more we prove it by discovery
> The more delight each object to the eye
> Procures, as if the elements had here
> Bin reconcil'd.[70]

Morton is sometimes presented as a villainous opportunist, but his imagery has a respectable philosophical background. In *The first Anniversary* Donne laments that the whole world

> Is crumbled out againe to his Atomies.
> 'Tis all in peeces, all cohaerance gone.

Only supernatural power can bond communities and systems together, and that has gone with Elisabeth Drury. In fine landscapes, however, a fragment of universal coherence might be preserved. Thomas Philipott borrows from Donne's lines to describe the garden of a dead lady:

> This piece of winnow'd earth, which she did strew
> With Roses, and pale Lillies, where they grew
> In kind and reconciled mixtures, is
> Now crumbled to a heap of Atomis.[71]

Appleton house remains exempt from the general decay:

> 'Tis not, what once it was, the *World*:
> But a rude heap together hurl'd. . .
> Your lesser *World* contains the same.
> But in more decent Order tame (st. 96).

Reconciliation is the central concept here. The elements are reconciled in the cosmos and in the perfectible landscape of earth, in Appleton house and Cooper's hill. They teach an important political lesson—for the Fairfaxes reconciliation to "this Houses Fate", and in public life the reconciliation of warring classes and religious conflict.

The Augustan poet believes that "we were commanded to be all as one".[72] Topographical poetry promotes this commandment by a cult of harmonizing power, that

> Through all the parts divided made them One:
> Gave to each Part t'it self Proportion,
> And to the whole; and in that Union
> Made Life and Order, Strength and beauty joyn.[73]

It is discovered in the glorious presence of court ladies and the glorious policies of the Stuart kings, proclaiming Georgic retirement and rustic sports:

> *Lords, Knights, Swaines, Shepheards, Churles* agree,
> To crowne his sports, *Discords* make *Harmony*.[74]

Above all it appears in the land itself, the national landscape. England herself is imagined saying

> what a combining bliss
> It was to live united, and to praise
> That God of Peace, that blest my peaceful days
> With large increase. . .
> Must I be now *divided*, that was never
> Divided yet? Must I be lost for ever? . . .
> Must I be now dispers'd? Must my own hand
> Destroy the bounty of my Fruitful Land?[75]

The readership is presented with a choice. On the one hand is "sweet societie", the natural well-watered landscape, "the Land redeem'd from all disorders" that Vaughan celebrates in 'To the River *Isca*' and Denham in *Coopers Hill:*

> Such Royall and such loyall community,
> Keeps Kings and Subjects still in unity.[76]

On the other hand is a flood, "a rude heap together hurld", a chaos, a dissident city—everything that Peacham, in the poem that accompanies his first landscape emblem (Fig. 1), condemns as "a body severed in a thousand parts".

We have seen how closely landscape and statecraft match; politics is reduced to questions of land, and rural matters are presented in political terms. Both kinds of "Estate" should display self-sufficiency, hierarchy, mutual co-operation and communication, subordinated to one powerful lord. Both evoke a prelapsarian past, and suggest that it is regained "here only", as a mark of special grace. But above all both are partisan, and conceal their partisanship under a universal doctrine of Nature. The writer arrogates to his own persuasion everything natural, harmonious, and unified; the other side is violent, chaotic and therefore against nature. The landscape is equally polarized. Every harmonious detail of *Coopers Hill*, for example, is matched by something rough, "Stupendous" and extreme, in order to discredit the opposition—the gentle hill of Windsor versus the ruin at Chertsey, the mellifluous Thames versus the final evocation of flood. Political enemies are placed in gloomy and hideous landscapes to hatch their plots, and in the civil war period these are meticulously contrasted with the good landscapes of orthodox Royalism;[77] the anonymous

Stipendariae Lacrymae, published in the Hague in 1654, is based entirely on two such contrasting visions—a dream of Charles I in Elysium, and a "deep melancholick" nightmare of the vale of woe that Britain has become (p.32+).

The art of landscape insists on continual harmony; it claims to display a model of the blessed land. Nature, landlord and monarch are celebrated in the same terms:

> All that are harsh, all that are rude,
> Are by your harmony subdu'd;
> Yet so into obedience wrought
> As if not forc'd to it, but taught. [78]

It was widely recognized that force is engrained in the state—its edifice built, like the temple in Jerusalem, with one hand on the sword. [79] But violence is disgraceful; the landscape must appear "as if not forc'd", and all disturbance must be transferred to an alien state. The savage wilderness and the pleasant place are mutually defining opposites; the one is invoked to exorcise the other. Political *topographia* often pursues the byways of ritual, mythology and propaganda, but it never strays completely from the philosophical road. Comenius expressed his scheme for universal peace and wisdom by means of an emblematic landscape (title page). His motto—

Let all things flow naturally; away with the violence of things!

—expresses equally well the aspirations of English poets engaged in the struggles of civil war and agrarian revolution. They merge the ancient *locus amoenus* and the ancient image of the state as a garden into a unified political landscape, a wishful Happy State, secure against decay.

5

Country Values

Villainy and innocence in the economic life of the countryside

Mankinde doth on God Pluto call;
To serve him still is all their pleasure;
Love here doth little, Money all,
For of this World it is the measure.[1]

This chapter deals with the economic processes that mould the landscape and determine the forms of rural society, as they appear in the poetry of country life. Landscape, as I suggested in Chapter 1, grows out of the fertile intercourse of reality and artistic preconception. The same is true of the literary structures derived from it, when *topographia* is organized into hierarchic, interrelated and antithetical forms so as to recommend a similar order in intellectual or political life. Rural poetry is *topical* in two senses: it is a response to historical events in the countryside, and it consists of *topoi*, traditional exercises of rhetoric. Charity and oppression, the benevolence of the good landlord and the violent pride of the rackrenter and the encloser, were stock subjects of satire and panegyric. In seventeenth-century English poetry these topics are given a new structure and beauty, both orderly and vivid, realistic in detail and rich and balanced in language. These are the qualities we find in *To Penshurst, Coopers Hill* and 'The Hock Cart.'

Can we disentangle rhetorical devices from "reality"? Not without gross naïveté. Historical reality is mainly available as a tissue of contemporary and modern documents, themselves rhetorical. And the conventions of literature are not empty forms but "mental sets", perceptual devices which frame and label an area of experience. Sometimes a seventeenth-century poet explicitly dissociates his words from reality—but it is equally common to find no sense of disjunction. We should expect no simple marriage of literature and history. We can, nevertheless, observe their complex relationship, and note happy correspondences, strains, fissures and contradictions between different parts of an author's work, or between literary descriptions and those made at the same time in another mode—historical, polemic or economic. We can identify these modes by referring to literary tradition and by discovering evidence of intention in the writer's own words. We can, in short, apply texts to texts. The fissures thus revealed are sometimes gaping, and my response is sometimes emotional or moralistic; I cannot disavow that "awareness of our indissoluble links with, and difference from, the past" which Vincent Newey identifies in Raymond Williams's work (*E in C* XXVII (1977) p. 370). But literature cannot be arraigned. It is evidence of nothing but itself. My intention is not to denounce aesthetic and rhetorical attitudes but to clarify them.

Violence is expunged from the ideal countryside by attributing it to enemies; rural poetry is always partly satirical. Moral, social and economic values are not distinguished, for they all generate the same outrage. Such values can be seen in 'The Mower against Gardens', for example—though Marvell also allows us to be amused at the speaker's earnest singlemindedness. Most rural poets, like the mower, attack luxury, mercantile greed, enclosure and doubleness of mind. They too lament the fallen world, but find local innocence exempt. Carew at Wrest will have

> No forraigne Gums, nor essence fetcht from farre,
> No Volatile spirits, nor compounds that are
> Adulterate;

the mower denounces strange perfumes, forbidden mixtures and adulterate fruit. Both dismiss statues and claim to have the gods themselves at their service. The fauns and fairies operate on the landscape like Waller's Saccharissa or Pope's nymph, "more by their presence than their skill". The poem is Augustan, too, in its allusion to Virgil, its satire against cosmetic vanity, its love of decorum and its hatred of extremes, of luscious stagnation and the feverish pursuit of trivia. Marvell is not belittling the mower by giving him absurd or heterodox ideas. Nor does he make him rustic or incompetent. The argument and structure of the poem are well matched. Luxury, stagnation, doubleness, pretence, forbidden dealings, tyranny and vexation—all these are forms of violence against nature, and violence forms the crux of the argument and pivot of the poem: "Tis all enforc'd. . ." After this line (31) the poem becomes as clear and lyrical as it was hitherto turbid and threatening; the mower puts his professed ideals into practice and his writing is plain and pure.

Upon Appleton House is punctuated by satirical episodes; Marvell burlesques the nuns, parodies the woodland poet and denounces fashionable women and foreign architects. The poem ends on the characters of women, having begun with Timon's windy villa. The purpose in each case is to recommend the correct form of progress for the Fairfax family by highlighting the ways of error. The opening is therefore particularly important, as it sets standards for the conduct of the poem; it tells us what to "expect". Like his mower, Marvell is championing the plain and the pure; both poems begin by contrast with the foreign, the villainous and the excessive—"luxurious Man . . . superfluously spread". 'The Garden', too, begins with the acrid fury of public life, and the hill at Bilborough is contrasted with the gigantic violence of "Mountains more unjust". *To Penshurst* begins with sterile pride and *From Wrest* with a hideous desert, imitating on a domestic scale the epic structures of the *Divina Commedia* and *Paradise Lost*. Like the *repoussoir* in painting, this guarantees vividness; but it should also be a logical unit, briefly defining the problem to be answered at length in the body of the poem. The first stanza is a "module" for the whole of *Appleton House*. The poem submits itself to architectural criteria—constructive skill, decorum, proportion—but with a particular emphasis on the "native" qualities of country simplicity. It must be a "great Design", but not "in pain", not chaotic or disturbing. The "Forrain *Architect*'s" crimes are threefold: he violates the regular placing of the landscape by turning quarries to caves and forests to pastures; his work fosters the pride it should moderate; and he indulges in unsupported fantasy, building on the vault of his conceited brain. All these qualities have been ascribed to *Upon Appleton House* itself by modern critics. But Marvell intends his first lines as a set of guiding principles.

Painful memories and associations, like those of war, should be remodelled. Conceited fantasy, like the swelling house or dumbfounded nature, should be tested against common experience. Luxurious and tortured pride, like the poet's in the wood, should be chastened by sobriety and ease. Marvell invites us to cope with discordant elements in a spirit of constructive optimism.

Marvell avoids the usual topics of the country house poem—variations on the theme of good housekeeping—but his satirical opening is firmly in that tradition. The honest, plain and provident home is contrasted with "ambitious Pyles, th'ostents of Pride"[2]—compilations, in both senses, of gilded roofs and gleaming marble pillars. The theme is Horatian, and is obligatory for the poet who praises moderation and humility:

> I live in *low Thatcht House, Roomes* small, my *Cell*
> Not big enough for Prides great Heart to dwell:
> My *Roomes* are not with *Stately Cedars* built,
> No *Marble Chimney-peece*, nor *Wainscot* gilt,
> No *Statues*. . .[3]

In such a humble dwelling, even the earl of Westmorland leads a life of plain integrity:

>   as the night draws on
> Its sable Curtain, in I'm gon
> To my poor Cell; which 'cause 'tis mine
> I judge it doth all else out-shine,
> Hung with content and weather-proof,
> Though neither Pavement nor roof
> Borrow from Marble-quarr below,
> Or from those Hills where Cedars grow.[4]

The house of poverty is as delightful as its counterpart is monstrous—

> The *littlenesse* doth make it warm, being close
> No *Wind*, nor *Weather cold*, can there have force.
> Although tis plaine, yet cleanly tis within,
> Like to a *Soule* that's pure and cleare from *Sin*.[5]

In these places a moral quality becomes a sensation. The mower's doctrine of "wild and Fragrant" nature appeals to the irresistible love of refreshment; the house of humility evokes a wintry equivalent, snugness. The proud man lives in the bleakest of houses "where Winds as he themselves may lose", but the poor farmer is imagined

> to live round and close, and wisely true
> To thine owne selfe; and knowne to few.
> (Herrick, 'A Country life')

This is the "fitness" of Appleton house, the serious idea behind Marvell's playful images.

Rich building is a sign of the villain:

> In roofes which Gold and Parian stone adorne,
> Proud as the Landlord's minde, he did abound.
> (Cowley, *Constantia and Philetus* 535–6)

John Taylor attacks the false worship which thrives in the rich man's house in terms which anticipate Pope; the chaplain is servile and the décor overpowering (*Differing Worships*). The good and pious man chooses more "dwarfish Confines"

> Where neatness nothing can condemn,
> Nor Pride invent what to contemn.
> (*Upon Appleton House* st.8)

Reading carelessly we assume that these lines describe the absence of pride; the general drift of moral satire encourages us to do so. In fact they say that pride is satisfied by Appleton house and cannot find fault. Marvell suggests, unobtrusively, that pride and humility can happily coexist.

Consistency of attitude is rare. We often find humble and proud places in the same author's work, praised equally though they are supposed to be mortal enemies. Ausonius, the father of the locodescriptive poem, attacks the folly of building in marble and mosaics when nature does just as well in the pebbles of the Moselle; but he glorifies the rich villas and marble-factories along its banks (*Mosella* 48–54 and 283+). Samuel Daniel despises proud and invidious palaces but

assumes that virtue needs "an eminent and spacious dwelling" to be properly herself.[6] Fanshawe, who recommends
Georgic retirement so eloquently in his 'Ode', devotes a whole
poem to the Escurial, a byword for luxury. Habington scorns
riches and praises the country life both in his love-poems to the
Powys heiress and in his devotional work; God visits "the cold
humble hermitage" but not "the lofty gilded roofe Stain'd
with some Pagan fiction" nor "the gay Landlord . . . whose
buildings are like Monsters but for show". But his highest
terms of praise are "th'Epitome of wealth" and "the cunning
Pompe of the Escuriall".[7] In the deepest pastoral retreat we
come across fantastic buildings of jewels and marble—in Margaret Cavendish's *Description of Love and Courage*, for example,
or Chamberlayne's *Pharonnida*.[8] In fact rural poverty and
wishful opulence seem to go together. Cotton's rustic court-
ship of Phyllis leads to a summerhouse of marble, porphyry,
silver, ebony, gilt, cedar and tapestry—the familiar list of
proud materials disclaimed ('The Entertainment to Phillis').
Aston Cokaine's simple house is "a Palace fit for Jupiter" ('A
Journey into the Peak') and prince Philoxipes retires to a palace
entirely "built from the marble quarry" ('Philoxipes and
Policrite'). The most ostentatious wealth is presented as modest comfort. Statius's revolting villas are "comfortable and not
luxurious". Chatsworth is "neat and commodious" as well as
splendid and immense; Hobbes tells his Muse not to list the
marble features but to go straight to the lord and his family,
morally above such things (*De Mirabilibus Pecci*). Argalus and
Parthenia retire to the familiar modest house, "not capacious,
as neat"; but Quarles continues

> Yet was it large enough to entertaine
> A potent Prince, with all his Princely traine.
> *(Argalus and Parthenia)*

The two statements are in flat contradiction. The suspicion
grows that the plain and modest dwelling is no more than a
figure of speech. George Wither dismisses

> *Houses*, builded large and high,
> Seel'd all with *Gold*, and pav'd with *Porphyrie*. . .

He is content to live in a shed and to take his recreation in hedgerows and footpaths; his liking makes them groves and palaces. But he is aware of the conventionality of what he is saying; he protests that his feelings are "not alone in show, but truly such",[9] referred to on p. 187 below. He seems to recognize that the confident display of humility is itself a form of ostentation.

The traditional image of the proud house is accompanied by an equally traditional tirade against enclosure and oppression. The cruel landlord pillages churches, hoards grain, fleeces the poor, devours whole villages and waters his field with their sweat; he drinks the blood of widows and dines on "the spoils . . . of beggar'd orphans, pickl'd in their tears".[10] The poet's patron, however, is always exempt:

> Thou pluck'st no houses down, to rear thy own. . .
> Thou not inclosest to fence out the poor,
> But an inclosure art to keep their store.
> Sheep eat no men, thy men thy sheep do eat;
> In tears of others wil'st not stew thy meat;
>
> Yet thou thy just inheritance did'st by
> No sacrilege, nor pillage multiply.
>
> You have the basis of no structure fixt
> On widdowes ruins, or the mortar mixt
> With Orphans tears; you wish the melting skies
> May wet your fields, and not your tenants eyes.
>
> Have you one grudging Tenant? will they not all
> Fight for you? Do they teach their Children,
> And make 'em too, pray for you morn and evening? . . .
> What Hariots have you tane from forlorne Widows? . . .
> What Acre of your thousands have you racked?[11]

Conventional as it is, this image of naked economic power bears some relation to reality. "The violence of great *Oppressors*"[12] had been an emotive issue since Elizabethan times; it was fiercely denounced by conservative and radical moralists and inspired the political movement of the poor. J. S. Morrill has "found evidence of enclosure rioting in twenty-six English counties in the years 1640–44" alone.[13] But our poets do not enter these struggles. Their argument is diffuse rather than particular; it is not clear what differentiates the good man from the oppressor apart from the obvious intention to make one hated and the other loved. The image of the evil landlord is the same in all authors, a pantomime ogre. No one could identify with such a Pharaoh; the picture is so fantastic that it comforts what it purports to attack. We are given the sensation of villainy without the analysis to support it.

Satire and panegyric are closely linked; they work together to dissociate the writer and his circle from an economic system recognized to be unjust. Old-Rents in *The Jovial Crew* is "th'onely rich man lives unenvied"; every other landowner is assumed to be a monster. Brome does not explain how Old-Rents came to be so wealthy while Hearty, who delivers the speech, is "a decayed Gentleman".[14] Habington accepts the wealth of the earl of Argyll because no one was harmed by it,

> And though your roofes were richly guilt,
> Their basis was on no wards ruine built.
> Nor were your vassals made a prey,
> And forc't to curse the Coronation day.
> And though no bravery was knowne
> To out-shine yours, you onely spent your owne.[15]

But the Argyll estates, so huge that their owner was a virtual monarch, were acquired by unremitting slaughter and brutality. Habington addresses a man who was imprisoned for "oppressioun alledged to be committed by his folkes", "almost extirpated" the Macgregors and "suppressed" the Clandonalds, receiving their entire territory by act of parliament (*DNB*). He is not a cynical or moronic poet; in the presence of awesomely successful violence rationality is replaced by the deferential gestures of panegyric. Denham is nearer to the truth in his analysis of the troubles of mediaeval England, when

> Kings by grasping more than they can hold,
> First made their Subjects by oppressions bold;

if they can hold it, they may grasp it.[16] But Denham speaks from the elevation of Cooper's hill.

It was widely recognized that economic injustice was not the work of a few demons, but a product of the existence of a landed gentry:

> we cannot enjoy the benefit of our labors ourselves, but for the maintenance of idle persons, slow bellies who raigne and ride over the common people in every Parrish, as Gods and Kings. Weep and howl, ye Rich men. . . . God will visit you for all your oppressions; you live on other men's labours . . . extorting extreme rents and taxes. Who are the oppressors, but the Nobility and the Gentry; and who are the oppressed, is not the Yeoman, the Farmer, the Tradesman, and the Labourer? . . . The rich and mighty [have drawn] most of the land of this distressed and enslaved nation into [their] clawes . . . yea, and inclosed our commons in most countries. Enclosure of land . . . hedges in some to be heirs of life and hedges out others; poore people are constrained to work in the very fire, for the maintenance of them that do live Deliciously, if not very viciously, as too many of the Gentry have done.[17]

This analysis is not confined to the agrarian left; conservatives and radicals agree in their description of society. "The poore man payes *for all*", according to a ballad of that name—the sentiment was clearly thought appropriate for the genre. The poor "labour hard continually, only for rich men's gaines", and so "the task-masters are playing kept". The ploughman is "the Lands cheefe victualler".[18] All wealth is created by labourers but consumed by their masters:

> I need not plough, since what the stooping Hine
> Gets of my pregnant Land must all be mine . . .
>
> To digg for Wealth we weary not our Limbs,
> Gold, though the heavy'st Metall, hither swims;
> Ours is the Harvest where the *Indians* mowe,
> We plough the Deep, and reap what others Sowe.[19]

The interests of wealth are flatly opposed to those of the population at large: "our punie depopulators alledge for their doings the Kings and countreys good; and we will believe them, when they can perswade us that their private coffers are the Kings exchequer".[20] The wealthy man's "only glory [is] to

grow excessively rich . . . by making poor people sell their
labour to them at their own prices".[21] Consequently labourers
are no more than "Beasts to the Rich":[22]

> our surly supercilious Lords,
> Bigge in their frownes and haughty in their words,
> Looke downe on those whose humble fruitfull paine
> Their proud and barren greatnesse must susteine.
> <div align="right">(<i>Coopers Hill</i>, 1642)</div>

To assail the evils of enclosure is to take on the bulk of the
ruling class, as Laud found to his cost; "the revenue of too
many of the court consisted principally in enclosures, and
improvements of that nature, which he still opposed passion-
ately except they were founded upon law . . . And so he did a
little too much countenance the Commission for Depopulation".[23] It is generally assumed by contemporary writers that
rural wealth and oppression are synonymous. Vaughan thanks
God for his poverty; had he been rich

> I should perhaps eate Orphans, and sucke up
> A dozen distrest widowes in one Cup.

Thomas Jordan assumes that it is impossible to go to the
country and

> Perswade some great Corne-master . . . to refraine
> That thrifty course, and give his Country *Graine*.[24]

John Abbott praises ants because

> They hoard up corn, but not as Farmers doe
> And Covetous Curmudgions, that undoe
> The poore and country, to bring out again
> And dearly sell it in a dearth of graine.[25]

Edward Buckler speaks for the general experience of man-
kind:

> Why doth the Land-lord rack? the Us'rer bite?
> Why doth the Judge with bribes his conscience stain. . .
> Here I am poore: my daily drops of sweat

> Will not maintain my full-stock'd family:
> A dozen hungrie children crie for meat
> And I have none . . .
> Here the oppressour with his griping claws
> Sits on my Skirts: my racking land-lord rears
> Both tent and fine; with potent looks he aws
> Me from mine own.[26]

"Drinking the sweat of others" is only a conceited way of saying that others work to provide one's income; in the same way

> The toyling Craftsman drinketh his own sweat,
> And out hard iron hammereth his meat.[27]

Economically it is perfectly true that "the rich eat the Poor like bread".[28] "Bad owners of inclosed grounds" are denounced for having

> rob'd the earth of her increase,
> Stor'd up that fading treasure, and spoke peace
> Unto your wretched thoughts;[29]

but every landowner lives by storing the produce of his private estate, excluding strangers and commanding their labour in peace. All estates are the result of enclosure and, in a period when rents rise disproportionately everywhere, all landlords are rackers.[30]

Poets are thus divided, loyal to their traditional role as moralists against oppression but more immediately loyal to their patrons and their property. They try to reconcile themselves in several ways: they may suggest that the crimes of wealth are only committed by political enemies, the parliamentary *nouveaux riches*;[31] or they may try to separate the effect of enclosure from its cause and so mythologize the landscape. Corbett gives a realistic view of the scene he finds so delightful on his travels:

> Nature is wanton there, and the Highway
> Seem'd to be private, though it open lay:
> As if some Swelling Lawyer for his health

Or frantic Usurer to tame his wealth
Had chosen out ten miles by *Trent*, to trye
Two great effects of Art and Industry.

(*Iter Boreale*)

Few poets are quite as frank. Their ideal landscape is private
and well-defended, but this is ascribed to wild and fragrant
Nature rather than frantic wealth. For Fanshawe, the repulsive
state of primitive man is like a common field before
enclosure:

Before the Earth was held in severall
'Twas one great feild where all the creatures fedd
As in a common.

Nature herself is agonized by this—"what availes my store
Heapt in a common field"[32]—and is only satisfied when private enclosure is invented. Henry More imagines that he is
looking at the earth from a great height; its principal features
are "Fair Fields and rich Enclosures".[33] Milton's *Ludlow Mask*
assumes that the enclosure of the president's estate is "holier
ground", suitable for a spirit to inhabit; beyond lie wild forests
and "unharbour'd Heaths", the abode of demons and perver-
sions (lines 943 and 423). "Paradise" means enclosed ground;
when the angels appear to the shepherds in Joseph Beaumont's
Psyche (1648), their place becomes hallowed and "no more a
common Country Field" (p. 110). The "champain head" of
Milton's Paradise is crowned by an "enclosure green"
(IV.133–4); the two seem to be distinct areas but cannot in fact
be distinguished. Milton deliberately combines the best features of private land and primeval wilderness; Eden is an
"enclosure wild", which in the fallen world would be a contradiction in terms (IX.543). In other poets Paradise is either
diffused throughout the world or heavily gated and walled, an
"Inclosure" in the strictest sense. The garden is narrowly
defensive; in Joseph Beaumont's description of the expulsion,
for example,

poor *Adam* sees
The heavy Losse of his enclosed Home,
Finding in stead of blessed Flowres and Trees,

Thistles and Thorns all arm'd with pikes and pricks,
Amongst whose Crowd he vex'd and tatter'd sticks.

(*Psyche*, p. 94)

Even in the infancy of the world, enclosure is conceived as a rampart against an armed multitude.

The metaphorical associations of private property are often sweet or impressive, and those of common land repulsive. Jeremiah Wells congratulates a friend on her marriage:

Thus Barren Heaths are Wast and Common laid;
Eden it self was an Inclosure made.[34]

Rowland Watkyns advises chastity:

Make not thy self a Common; it is found,
There's better pasture in inclosed ground.[35]

But the same example could be used to advocate seduction; in the debate between the smiling cheeks and frowning forehead,

Alas! the fronts [Love's] common feild,
That often falow lyes untild;
But in the cheekes still flowry close
He pasture finds, and fatter grows.[36]

Such imagery is not only erotic. John Hall congratulates Samuel Harding because

th'hast *engross't* all wit, and set a *price*,
So *high*, that he's undone who ever *buyes*.[37]

Ralph Bathurst praises Selden's work as architect of the *mare clausum* policy:

Your hand inclos'd the watery plaines, and thus
Was no lesse fence to them, as they to us.[38]

In Quarles's eclogues enclosure always denotes correctness, diligence and godliness:

Amongst wise Shepheards is not often found
Costly inclosures, and a barren ground.

The corrupt French clergy complain that

> Our Hedge is broken, and our Pastures yeeld
> But slender profit: All's turn'd Common-field.

Arminianism is

> So poor a *Fense*, young Swain, that 'tis suppos'd
> Yee feed in Common, though yee seem enclos'd.[39]

Parliamentarians, according to Cowley, believe "noe things or places sacred. . . . But with ther God himselfe in Common Live."[40] William Cavendish uses enclosure to signify moral virtue, contrasting himself with a younger man

> Whose Minde yett hath no bounds settl'd att all,
> No Pale about him, Hedg, or Ditch, or wall.[41]

Martin Lluellin compares the king's enemies with enclosure-breakers, who seem in his mind to be like waters dammed up against the wall of private property; they "*streight* Prospect scorne, and *Private* view . . . and . . . to the *Rageing of their Sea*, they doe Let in the *Madnesse of the People* too".[42] We have now come full circle; private enclosure of common land, a traditional symbol of the overthrow of moral bulwarks by violent greed, is now equated with those very bulwarks.

Royalist country poets are amphibious creatures. They recognize aggression and injustice but their first concern is with themselves, their "estate" in life and the means to support it—"the *trinkets* of *self Interest*".[43] They did not share the reforming zeal of Hartlib and his circle, which appealed to the public good and denounced "a base privacy of spirit".[44] George Eliot described self-interest in a fascinating metaphor; the pattern of fine scratches on polished metal, she noticed, seemed to form a circle round a candle-flame though they were in fact randomly spread (*Middlemarch*, ch. 27). Our poets sort the good and the evil of seventeenth-century society into such a pattern. They must seem to enjoy a kindly light amidst the encircling gloom of faction and oppression—to inhabit a local paradise in the wild wood.

.   .   .

Satire is a beam to penetrate the dark forest of finance and power. The satirist is allowed to attack the possession of wealth itself—provided he does so in terms of individual morality. The conventional ogre-landlord merges into the conventional millionaire:

> Let the extorting Us'rer carp and care,
> And pinch his guts his god to spare,
> And let him unknown wayes invent
> To raise or else to rack his rent . . .[45]

Avarice leaves great scars on the landscape itself:

> The wicked rips Earth's bowels to find
> Treasures to fil his mind.[46]

Restless self-destructive avarice made the fog which spoils Denham's view from Cooper's hill and the ruin which culminates it. Drayton is Denham's master here; avarice inspired the "sacrilege" which destroyed Glastonbury, betrayed the ideal state of ancient Britain to the Romans, and is now destroying the country's balance of payments and forests. Drayton never tires of denouncing "caitifes . . . who having sold our woods, doe lastly sell our soyle";[47] the huckstering of land is inseparable from its destruction.

What is offered as an antidote? To celebrate the life of a country gentleman, poets feel it necessary to exorcise the demon of wealth:

> Nor are thy daily and devout affaires
>   Attended with those desp'rate cares,
> Th'industrious Merchant has; who for to find
>   Gold runneth to the Western Inde,
> And back again (tortur'd with fears) doth fly,
>   Untaught to suffer Poverty . . .
>
> Let that goe heape a masse of wretched wealth,
>   Purchas'd by rapine, worse then stealth,
> And brooding o're it sit, with broadest eyes,
>   Not doing good scarce when he dyes . . .
>
> Let others sit and brood upon that Ore
> Which they've collected from the Indian shore . . .[48]

Denham confronts the rabid finance of the City with the quality of his own retired life and the river-landscape where it takes place:

> Sweet Thames, the eldest and the noblest sonne
> Of old Oceanus, doth swiftly runne . . .
> And though his clearer sand no golden veynes
> Like *Tagus* and *Pactolus* streames containes,
> His genuine and less guilty wealth t'explore
> Search not his bottome, but behold his shore.
>
> (Coopers Hill, 1642)

Panegyric topography shows us a form of wealth redeemed, by its purity, from the usual horrors that wealth brings. Edmund Elys's wit is "no gold stream" but flows with milk and honey.[49] Thomas Vaughan can "*levie* . . . harmless *Contributions*" from the river Usk since its clarity and steadfastness teach him moral lessons.[50] Tagus itself now has (metaphorical) "*Silver* waters", which give it greater credit than its former "*Golden Sands*".[51] Cowley uses the image of two rivers to maintain 'that a pleasant poverty is to bee preferred before discontented riches', in the ode of that name:

> Why o doth gaudy *Tagus* ravish thee,
>   Though *Neptune's* treasurehouse it be?
> Why doth *Pactolus* thee bewitch,
> Infected yet with *Midas'* glorious Itch?

Gold is the cause of both extremes, restlessness and stagnation:

> Their dull and sleepy streams are not at all
>   Like other Flouds, Poeticall;
>   They have no dance, noe wanton sport,
> No gentle murmur, the lov'd shore to court . . .
> No fish inhabite the adulterate floud.

Coal-mining is praised in the same terms in Thomas Winnard's *News from Newcastle* (1651):

> Who'd dote on Gold! a thing so strange and od?
> 'Tis most contemptible when made a God.
> All sins and mischifs thence have rise and swell:

> One *Indies* more would make another Hell.
> Our *Mines* are Innocent (p. 1).

Innocent wealth sustains a moderate and loving society; guilty wealth destroys it:

> The mod'rate value of our guiltlesse *Oare*
> Makes no man Ath'ist, nor no Woman Whore.
> . . . Our *Mine's* a common Good, a Joy
> Not made to ruine, but inrich our *Troy* (ibid., pp. 2–3).

Innocent commerce is embodied in a Georgic vision of the happy farming community; high finance "doth in hel the Harvest home proclaim".[52] The husbandman by the Thames is set against the City merchant, simple natives against brutal imperialists:

> Whilst yet our world was new,
> When not discover'd by the old;
> Ere beggar'd slaves we grew,
> For having silver hills, and strands of gold . . .
> When none did riches wish,
> And none rich by bus'ness made;
> When all did hunt or fish,
> And sport was all our labour and our trade,
>   We danc'd and we sung,
>   And lookt ever young,
>   And from restraints were free.[53]

These lines are sung by the Incas; division into black and white becomes complete when guilty avariee can be identified with a national enemy.

Since Elizabethan times there had been two conflicting colonial policies in England. The contemporary imagination was deeply affected by the spoils of exploration—we can hardly open a volume of poems without finding some reference to the two Indies of spice and mine.

> The two Iberian nations had fixed their eyes upon tropical lands as alone worth exploiting, and had established in these their principal seats. Vast territories within the temperate zone in both hemispheres lay therefore unoccupied, in part, indeed,

undiscovered. Not only might England win wealth from these lands . . . but their acquisition would put her on more equal terms territorially with Spain.[54]

This policy, formulated by John Dee and the elder Hackluyt among others, was upheld by "the small farmers and cultivators to whom land was more precious than gold";[55] they were critical of the royal craze for bullion. Drayton's ode on the Virginian voyage captures this sense of an earthly paradise of fertile soil and ends with a message of blessing to Hackluyt the younger, who continued the insistence on "innocent" wealth in temperate colonies. The usual moral disparagement of gold takes on a specific political sense:

> England's a perfect *World*! has *Indies* too!
> Correct your *Maps: New-Castle* is *Peru*.
> Let th'haughty *Spanyard* triumph, till 'tis told
> Our *sootie-Min'rals* purifie his *Gold*.
>> (*News from Newcastle*, p. 1)

Topographical poetry makes fullest use of this topos, ironically, when the place described is of major economic importance—the Newcastle coal-industry in Winnard's poem, or the market-gardens of the Thames valley in *Coopers Hill*. Samuel Danforth, an early colonist, applies it to New England:

> Iron and Lead are found,
> Better than Peru's gold or Mexico's
> Which cannot weapon us against our foes
> Nor make us howes, nor siths, nor plough-shares mend:
> Without which tools mens honest lives would end.
> Some silver-mine, if any here do wish,
> They it may find i'th'bellyes of our fish . . .[56]

In his historical poem *King Henry the Second* (1633) Thomas May elaborates the innocent wealth of Ireland:

> Though from the wounded entrailes of her ground
> No gold be digg'd, no pretious pearles be found
> Within these lakes, nor from the glistering rockes
> 'Rich diamonds gather'd, plentious are her flockes

> And graine. She wants the meanes of those sad crimes
> That doe infest the gawdy Easterne clymes;
> She brings no poysons, such as guilty gold
> And cups of choicest gemmes so often hold (f.G7).

This recitation is designed to inspire a colonial invasion. Marvell and Waller both celebrate the natural wealth of Bermuda as a sign of its blessedness, and associate the behaviour of England's colonial rivals with impiety. The Spanish fleet, in Marvell's *On the Victory Obtained by Blake*, is

> Frayted with acted Guilt, and Guilt to come . . .
> The new Worlds wounded Intrails they had tore
> For wealth wherewith to wound the old once more.

Britain, on the other hand, protects the Canaries, a land

> not curst with Gold,
> With fatal Gold, for still where that does grow
> Neither the Soyl nor People quiet know.
> Which troubles men to raise it when 'tis Ore,
> And when 'tis raised does trouble them much more.

Spanish colonial policy perverts the land, according to Waller:

> Of Nature's bounty men forbore to taste,
> And the best portion of the Earth lay waste.
> (*Upon a War with Spain*)

Cromwell attacks it out of moral outrage and not financial greed:

> When *Britain* looking with a just disdain
> Upon this gilded Majesty of *Spain*,
> And knowing well that Empire must decline,
> Whose chief support and sinews are of coin,
> Our nations sollid vertue did oppose
> To the rich troublers of the worlds repose (*ibid.*)

This is just as well, for Blake's splendid victory at Santa Cruz brought back no prize-money at all. Marvell's poem is a skilful consolation for that loss.

Rural financial satire is based on the distinction between true wealth and false:

> The world's false riches, and the plentyest store,
> Breed but in man the coveting of more,
> Not satisfie; true riches is content.[57]

Gold is a breeder of extremes, of violent greed and torpid corruption; content, normally represented by the self-contained life of a country gentleman, is always moderate:

> Who measures poverty by Nature's rules,
> And frames his mind to what he hath, is rich.[58]

True wealth is equated with country simplicity and this is by definition natural; it is the opposite of "superfluities", foreign goods, violent desires and impious experiments. The mower attacks gardens in precisely these terms; they are guilty, feverish and stagnant at the same time, hubristic, adulterate—"'tis all enforc'd". False guilty wealth corresponds to everything harsh, mercantile and colonial—cash, jewels and spices, extracted by terrifying labour in the worst and furthest places. True innocent wealth is represented by landed estates, homely green "self-renewing vegetable bliss".[59] One is soft, the other hard; one living, one dead:

> Consider pray, *Gold* hath no life therein
> And *Life* in *Nature* is the richest thing.[60]

Rural poetry defends an imaginary England, green and pleasant, from which all hardness and extortion has been banished. The ideal landscape is thus living proof of innocence in financial affairs, a stick to beat one's enemies, whether they are city merchants or Spanish admirals. Just as *Appleton House* disarms warfare by its garden and meadow imagery, so the innocent country assimilates the world of wealth and violence:

> Go, let the diving *Negro* seek
> For Gemmes hid in some forlorne creeke:
>   We all Pearles scorne,
>   Save what the dewy morne

Congeals upon each little spire of grass;
Which careless shepeards beat down as they pass;
    And gold ne're here appears,
    Save what the yellow Ceres beares . . .[61]

Where only in Sheep-sheering Time
The *Rich* the *Poor* do seem to *Fleece*,
And of oppression all their crime
Is only whilst they make their *Cheese* . . .[62]

Being defined as the opposite of gold, the ideal countryside can
be a repository for all other qualities so defined—the "true
wealth" of contentment, religion or the Muse.

The distinction of true and false wealth is quite illusory.
Rural poetry "always confuses the shamefulness of *huckstering
the land* with the perfectly rational consequence, inevitable and
desirable within the realm of private property, of the *huckstering of private property* in land".[63] Wealth in land only makes
sense when converted into cash and is just as much a product of hard labour. Urban satirists attack it just as ve-
hemently:

    yee groveling *Muck-worms*, yee that build
Like *Ants* in Mole-hills; and tye field to field . . .

Content ne'er dwells 'mong dirty land; who sells it
Parts with a deal of care, and Scurvy toil;
Men never are ingenious that are clogg'd with it.[64]

The early American settlers, for all their godly professions,
have "insatiate minds for meadow":

With little goods, but many words, aboord comes one and sayes
"I long to see my feet on shore, where cloudy pillar stayes;"
As high as clouds he darts his words, but it is earth he wants.[65]

Landscapes and fine gardens

                    shew how art of men
            Can purchase Nature at a price
            Would stock old Paradise agen.[66]

The extravagant courtier is a walking landscape:

> That Cloake to No'hs Ark well you may compare:
> For every living beast he had lies there.
> His hose and dublet like that mighty Flood
> Hath dround each Field and over-whelm'd each wood.
> A lease with divers Coppie-holds doth ride
> In an Impropriation by his side.[67]

The countryside is an object of capital investment and conspicuous consumption, as Brian Fairfax's *The Vocal Oak* makes clear. He laments the felling of Nun Appleton woods for cash, juxtaposing the "innocent Toyes" of London life with the real landscape destroyed to buy them:

> How many stately Oks must bye a Fan;
> What Lands a dish from China or Japan.
> How many Acres of this flowry mead
> Must bye a flowred Satin for a Bed,
> What Mannors Morgagd to supply a feast,
> What Trees and Houses eaten by a Guest,
> Till all's reduc'd at last to what we see,
> Painted in Landskips and in Tapistry.[68]

Fairfax's irony destroys the false correspondence between land and "Landskips" in order to show more clearly their true relationship. True and false wealth are not distinct and opposed, but are simply subjective categories—"the names . . . of the same Formes misliked".[69] But this dichotomy is essential to the transformation of topography into ideal landscape. It should not be exposed as mere poetic fiction. Analysis is dangerous; the purpose of panegyric topography is to make it unthinkable.

In Richard Fanshawe's *Progress of Learning* the sinister figure of Craft makes a penetrating observation; he argues against those who "Gold contemne" but

> Only in boasting writings did Condemne
> The thing which in their hearts they most desire,
> Which poets ev'n denying had confest,
> Styling the *Golden Age* what they would have *The best*.[70]

His suspicions are confirmed by contemporary topographical poetry; the green and innocent landscape is everywhere depicted in hard financial terms. Sunlight in a wood "Seem'd to have brought the Gold-smiths World againe."[71] Since the Middle Ages nature had been conceived in richly jewelled metaphors, as a type of the heavenly city. Now, however, such imagery becomes secular and mercantile. The landscape is a royal exchange

> Where prodig' Nature sets abroad her booth
> Of richest beauties.[72]

"Flowers and plants combine" like early capitalists,

> That in those sweet Exchecquers they
> May that stock of spices lay,
> Which (like Easterne winds) thy breath
> Does to'th perfum'd ayre bequeath.[73]

Once again we see Nature submitting to the laws of investment and consumption:

> The *factour-wind* from far shall bring
> The *Odours* of the *Scatter'd* Spring,
> And *loaden* with the rich *Arreare*
> *Spend* it in *Spicie whispers* there.[74]

We are instructed to "charge a *Subsidie* oth' Spring, let May bring in her *Levies*";[75] Herrick's 'Pray and prosper' allows us to imagine the result:

> Butter of *Amber, Cream*, and *Wine*, and *Oile*
> Shall run, as rivers, all throughout thy soyl.
> Wod'st thou to sincere-silver turn thy mold?
> Pray once, twice pray; and turn thy ground to gold.

Earth is everywhere turned to gold; every meadow is enamelled or embroidered, every grove is a richly-furnished palace, rivers always run on pearls and dew forms "silver drops . . . t'enrich the lowly plain".[76] John Eliot, in 'a New-years Gift to the Marchioness of Winchester', promises

> Your private walks and Arbours I would pave
> With orient Pearl;[77]

instead she is to accept his poem. The problem is that poets want to honour the land but cannot conceive of honour apart from the jewels, masquing costumes and tapestries of the court. One wishes they had not taken Sidney so literally: "Nature hath not set forth the earth in so rich a tapestry as poets have done. Her world is brazen; the poets only deliver a golden."

This imagery may sometimes be appropriate or keenly observed but on the whole the effect is lurid and absurd: Nature has an enamelled wardrobe, the "smooth enamel'd green" receives footprints and quaint enamelled eyes are thrown, like the flowers which "milde *Zephyrus* threw downe to paint the walkes"; lovers meet in bowers "bedeck'd with pearls, and strew'd about with love" and tread where

> The flowrie Floore's embelished
> With Cloris's painted Tapsterie.[78]

The notion of "natural wealth" establishes a poetic licence for all kinds of vulgarities and contradictions. Cowley, for example, attacks the "gaudy *Tagus*" with its corrupt "added beauty", but in the same poem "fish enrich the Brooke with silver scales" and

> *Dasyes* the first borne of the teeming Spring,
> On each side their embrodery bring.

What is this if not added beauty? He disparages "Painted flowers" and "thou Tulip, who thy stock in paint dost wast" but in

> My garden painted ore
> With natures hand, not arts,
> A suddaine paint adornes the trees,
> And all those divers ornaments abound,
> That variously may paint the gawdy ground.[79]

We see here a paradox which Fanshawe's Craft would find

amusing; the natural and innocent countryside, an antidote to wealth, was depicted as the folly of a Baroque millionaire.

Craft is the villain of Fanshawe's poem; the aureate style of natural description would not have seemed contradictory. The wealth of nature is by definition natural; by not being violent, it is free from exploitation and decay. The metaphorical silver, gold and embroidery of the *locus amoenus* are "riches that can never fade".[80] The velvet and jewels of Aramantha's grove, in Lovelace's *Pastorall*, are "supply'd still with a self-recruit"; the satitist attacks opulence because the earth's resources are squandered to maintain it, but in "Nature" this problem is magically resolved. In the earthly paradise, in fact, "innocent" and "guilty" wealth are reconciled. Lucrative and expensive tropical products were associated, in poetical tradition, with avarice and guilt; every stage of their acquisition and sale was violent in some way. Yet the topographical poetry of Denham and Waller tries to assimilate this process to the "natural" world of simple husbandry. *Coopers Hill* attacks the "guilty wealth" of Tagus and Pactolus and the money-crazed City of London, but he glorifies the Thames for being the vehicle of colonial trade:

> Spices he brings, and treasures from the West;
> Find wealth where 'tis, and gives it where it wants,
> Cities in Desarts, woods in Cities plants.

Denham praises in "natural" metaphor what he earlier claimed to abhor; he proposes a similar reconciliation in the state. Locke's earliest writing shows the same tendency to naturalize mercantilism, without losing sight of the paradox.[81] In *The Battell of the Summer Islands* Waller traces this paradox to its source in the colonies themselves; Bermuda is presented as a place where the usual opposition of plutocracy and rural poverty vanishes. Wealth is still defined as the possession of expensive colonial goods, and still equated with happiness; but here it is "naturally" abundant. Since pearls, tobacco, cedarwood and ambergris are common as dirt, the people must be supremely happy. The poet tries to turn his metaphor into evidence for a state of blessedness, where wealth really is natural and its hostilities are transcended.

.　　　.　　　.

Landed wealth, as we have seen, is transformed into the "natural" wealth of landscape. The behaviour of those who possess it is correspondingly naturalized, and all sense of arrogance and violence removed.

The traditional justification of wealth was charity. Samuel Daniel expresses this doctrine in his usual thoughtful way, in his address to Sir Thomas Bodley. Wealth does not guarantee peace:

> The grounds, the lands, which now thou callest thine,
> Have had a thousand lords that term'd them theirs,
> And will be soon again pent from thy line
> By some concussion, change, or wastefull heires.

This is not just a *memento mori* but a theory of vicissitude which anticipates Pope's *Moral Epistles*. All violent things are self-destructive in time:

> For well we see how private heapes (which care
> And greedy toyle provides for her owne endes)
> Doe speede with her succeeders, and what share
> Is left of all that store, for which it spendes
> It selfe, not having what it hath in use,
> And no good t'others nor it selfe conferres.

Wealth must be "in use"—referring not, as it often does, to usury but to acts of charity for the common good.

> Fortune mocking our abuse
> Would teach us that it is not ours but hers
> That which we leave: and if we make it not
> The good of many, she will take that paine,
> And re-dispers th'inclosed parcelles, got
> From many hands, t'in-common them againe.

Private enclosure is set against public good. We must communicate our goods,

> And not, like beasts of prey, draw all to our Den
> T'inglut our selves and our owne progenie

Daniel is greatly influenced by Roman moralists. Horace

complains of the encroachment of great landlords and the
decay of the ideals of Romulus and Cato; "small private
wealth, large communal property—so ran the rule then" (Ode
15, Book II). But though nationalization of the land was an
early Roman ideal, it was flatly against the English system;
indeed Harrington was to propose something like the reverse.
Instead the public was to benefit by charitable institutions,
offshoots of private wealth. Daniel's poem celebrates one such
scheme, the Bodleian library—

> an everlasting Granery
> Of Artes, the universall State to feede . . .
> Happy erected walles whose reverent piles
> Harbour all commers, feede the multitude:
> Not like the prowd-built pallace that beguiles
> The hungry soule with empty solitude;
> Or onely raisde for private luxurie
> Stands as an open marke for Envies view.

Daniel praises the public library in the terms Jonson applies to
Penshurst or Carew to Wrest; its happy walls and hospitable
fare are contrasted with the tight and invidious house of pride.
Charity is a mediator between private estate and public wel-
fare. The poor are brought into the warm and the rich seem
charming for the use to which they put their wealth, not let-
ting it stagnate.

The central act of charity, according to this panegyric tradition, is feeding. It was difficult to praise a patron *without*
wishing "happinesse to hospitalitie, or a hearty wish to good
house-keeping" (the title of a poem of Herrick's). Wrest is "a
house for hospitalitie"; Belvoir is built by Humility and has
Bounty as the Porter;[82] Appleton house is designed by Humility and adorned by "a Stately *Frontispiece of Poor*"; Bretby
displays greater hospitality than any household in recorded
history.[83] Roger Twysden is lamented by "his men and tenants" because

> His house was rightly termed Hall,
> Whose bread and beef were ready;
> It was a very hospital
> And refuge for the needy.[84]

General Hastings "setts ope his boundless bounties" at Ashby castle,[85] and Captain Dover's

> drinke from *Wickham* reaches to the *Hill*,
> Runns night and day, carouse may all their fill.[86]

Every patron aspires to be "the open free hearted and free handed Landlord . . . Mr Generous . . . the sole surviving sonne Of long since banisht Hospitality".[87]

These words are significant; Mr Generous is the *sole* surviving exponent of *long since* vanished bounty, and the speaker must disavow "flattery". The death of hospitality was already a standard theme in Elizabethan satire and "Mock-Beggar Hall" was hated wherever ballads were sold. Henry Hallhead sees new households everywhere failing to make customary provision for the poor; he writes partly from tradition and partly from direct observation.[88] It is doubtful whether open house hospitality was ever much practised; almsgivers preferred safer investments.[89] Robert Sidney impoverished himself by it at Penshurst.[90] Herrick's hero Lewis Pemberton died in debt, though he seems to have tried to solve his financial problems by promising judgments on the same land to two different people.[91] William Cavendish was temporarily ruined by lavish public feasting at Bolsover and Welbeck; Clarendon hated this expense "which (God be thanked) . . . no man ever after imitated".[92] The poet's task was to make an isolated and dwindling practice into a universal ideal.

Traditional society is embalmed in the warm fluid of charity:

> at large Tables fill'd with wholesome meates
> The servant, Tennant, and kind neighbour eates.
> Some of that ranke, spun of a finer thred,
> Are with the Women, Steward, and Chaplaine fed
> With daintier cates; Others of better note
> Whom wealth, parts, office, or the Heralds coate
> Have sever'd from the common, freely sit
> At the Lords Table, whose spread sides admit
> A large accesse of friends to fill those seates
> Of his capacious circle, fill'd with meates
> Of choycest rellish, till his Oaken back
> Under the load of pil'd-up dishes crack.
>
> (Carew, *To my friend G.N. from Wrest*).

The public meals of the great house display the benevolence of the lord but also reduce the lower orders to simply physical creatures whose entire world is consummated by a joint of beef. There is a peculiar and slightly grotesque heartiness about hospitality-poems, a smell of gravy that is absent from the usual decorous verse of the period. The act of feeding, as the poets present it, reinforces the divisions in society by rendering them benign, harmonious and apparently natural to the species. But the country house poem depicts an inverted world. We have already seen how wealth and leisure is recognized as the creation of the labouring poor. The hospitable patron and the ghoulish oppressor must not be seen to be parallel; it is therefore suggested that wealth flows first from the landlord and not from the labourers and tenants he commands. At Penshurst

> all come in, the farmer and the clowne:
> And no one empty-handed, to salute
> Thy lord, and lady, though they have no sute . . .
> But what can this (more than expresse their love)
> Adde to thy free provisions, farre above
> The neede of such?

Jonson's poem may be compared with Peter Hausted's *Ad Populum* of 1644, which laments the destruction of that world by a hostile and greedy army. Before the war the farmer was prosperous and happy, but now he is reduced to begging from insolent soldiers with the same degree

> Of Cringeing and sordid Idolatry
> Ye used in the former dayes to fall
> Prostrate unto your Land-Lord in his Hall,
> Where with low Leggs, and in an humble guise
> Ye offer'd up a Capon-Sacrifice
> Upon his Worship at a New-yeares Tide:
> For which i'th Buttery having stuff'd your hide
> With store of Drinke, as heartlesse as 'twas cold . . .
> Ye took your leave.[93]

These two accounts of country hospitality differ only in glamour. *To Penshurst, From Wrest* or *To Pemberton* are triumphs of the literary imagination. To a severer conscience they might seem less worthy. Winstanley denounces the hypocrisy of glamourizing poverty.[94] Joseph Beaumont questions his own intentions:

> Art sure th'ast given so much to the Poor?
> Was't not thy meaning to bestow
> Part on thine own Vain-glory?[95]

George Wither glorifies the charitable Westrow family and denounces in contrast those who starve orphans

> And have, with what their *Servants* blood did buy,
> Inlarg'd their *Fields*, and rais'd their *houses* high.

But such an utterance in verse was already associated with hypocrisy; he feels he must disavow rhetoric, and points out that his praise *"is real truth*; and no *poetick strain"*[96], referred to on p. 187 below.

These feasts were in any case strictly seasonal—isolated outbursts of potlatch to accompany a royal visit or a country festival. Both were rare. On these few days of the year the ordered state of things is ritually reversed; their significance derives from their contrast with normal life:

> The rout of rurall folke come thronging in
> (Their rudenesse then is thought no sinne).
> (Jonson, *To Sir Robert Wroth*)

We are reminded of the feast of Misrule, or of Maundy Thursday, when the monarch would wash the feet of selected paupers. This contrast was clear to both rulers and ruled, as we learn from the Christmas Carol that Wither wrote as a countryman:

> And those that hardly all the yeare
> Had Bread to eat, or Raggs to weare,
> Will have both Clothes and daintie fare:
> And all the day be merry.[97]

The bitterness of the working year is recalled throughout the poem and gives resonance to the sounds of deliberate merri-

ment. Even those who lament the suppression of sports cannot
conceal this bitterness:

> the merry Gambolls, dances and friscolls, [with] which the
> toyling Plowswaine, and Labourer, once a year were wont to be
> recreated, and their spirits and hopes reviv'd for a whole 12
> month, are now extinct.[98]

Thomas Salusbury's *Knowsley Masque* makes entertainment
out of the end of Christmas:

> the dull clowne o'th Country
> Shall whistle to his teame most dolefullie
> And under everie hedge in every Corner
> Shall grunt a groane till teare stand in his eyes
> For loathness to depart with Christmas pyes.[99]

The fasting days, scrawny ghosts whose breaths smell of
infection and stale debauchery, rush onto the stage and carry
off the fat "gambolls" who represent Christmas; this makes
the second antimasque.

These isolated freedoms clearly functioned as safety-valves;
they exorcised the "spirits of revenge"[100] and set the seal of
licence on the social order. Complete impropriation of the
crop is legitimized by the harvest supper, the command to
labour by occasional sports.[101] The enclosure of common land
may be alleviated by open days; at Appleton house, between
the mowing and the floating of the meadows,

> The Villagers in common chase
> Their Cattle (st.57).

In this stanza Marvell hints that the usual problems of enclosure and oppression have been solved by generous comprom-
ise—"Levellers" are no threat. In Marvell social doctrine is
typically unobtrusive; the significance of festive concessions is
normally spelled out:

> Who durst assemble such a Troope as hee
> But might of Insurrection charged bee;
> His Souldiers, though they every one discent,

In mindes, in manners, yet his *Merriment*
Ones them; *Lords, Knights, Swaines, Shepheards, Churles* agree,
To crowne his sports, *Discords* makes *Harmony*.[102]

The festival is thus a device for procuring charm, a transcendent power which abolishes the struggle of opposites. This poet assumes that the normal state of society is dissent, just as the normal life of the swarthy shepherds is unmitigated sweat. As part of the celebration of freedom, the authorities take the precaution of speaking directly to the rustics about their obligations:

Back Shepherds, back, enough your play,
Till next Sun-shine holiday . . .

Give end unto your rudeness: Know at length
Whose time and patience you have urg'd, the *Kings*!
Whose single watch defendeth all your sleepes!
Whose labours are your rests! Whose thoughts and cares
Breed your delights! whose bus'nesse all your leasures . . .

Shepheards rejoyce, tis hee shall make you free.[103]

These propositions are deft reversals of the accepted truth. The people's labours are the ruler's rests, their thoughts and cares breed his delights, their business is his leisure. The very essence of nobility is power over the life-work of others; *they* make *him* free. Gatherings always gave a chance to teach the poor their duties and at festivals the pill is sweetened by the general atmosphere of joy. On these days-upside-down the doctrine is suitably roundabout; the life of the poor—their work, their leisure, and even the productivity of the land they till—is not theirs at all but emanates from their Landlord's goodwill.

George Wither's *Haleluiah* (1641) includes hymns for country festivities throughout the year. Their purpose is to replace the "rude jollities used in some places" with more pious celebration, without losing the occasion to crown the labour of the day and foster the sense of community. They are written in strong, simple phrases, supposedly suited to a gathering of labourers:

> For that which we in hope have sown,
>   And till'd with costly pain,
> We, by *Gods* grace, have Reap'd and Mown,
>   With likelihood of gain . . .
> The *Fruits* for which we delv'd and plough'd
>   And toyled long with care
> In Barnes and Stacks are hous'd and mow'd,
>   Of which right glad we are (p. 67).

It is hard to determine what "we" means. The rubric of 'At Seed-time' is addressed exclusively to the employer; the hymn is supposed to be uttered ("not . . . without profit") when "*Husbandmen* . . . have . . . their *seed-Cake*, or some other extraordinary Allowance". "Our Labour" is an ambiguous phrase; it repudiates the fellow-feeling it seems to evoke by claiming the harvest as the farmer's work. This exclusivity becomes clear in the final prayer of 'When Harvest is Come Home':

> As when thy *Manna* downe did fall,
>   So be it also now:
> Let them whose gath'rings are but small,
>   Confesse they have enow:
> Blesse thou our Basket and our Store,
>   And, when refresh't we be,
> Let us distribute to the poore
>   The portion due to thee.
> But let us chiefly mind their need
>   Whose Labours were employ'd
> To *Till* what *them* and *us* must feed,
>   And what is now injoy'd (ibid. p. 68).

Not only is the labourer excluded from the circle of celebrants—his wages are described as alms.

The language of these occasional poems shows a mixture of callousness and affection. Mildmay Fane's 'My Hock-Cart, or Reaping Day', like Wither's hymns, is written in the first person plural, and seems to call for collective effort; after describing the fine morning, the poet reminds himself of his duties:

> Yet there will more goe to't:
> Words will not do't
> But hands employd must bee,
> And sickles used.[104]

Fane employs "words" in one sense and "hands" in another—the very opposite, since his power to employ farm-hands means he will never use his own. He describes his workers as fully-automatic reaping machines:

> hands employd must bee
> And sickles used with rakes and furmety
> And binders too be gott
> With the black Jack and flagon pott
> That whilst with working each doe sweate
> Those may allay and temper heate.
>   And for to add to thes
>   The bacon peass
> The sith and pitching forke
> Must all in season too be sett a work
> Nor the browne Lusty lass
> In her straw hatt must here unmentioned pas
> But every one in their Compartments Come
> And reape and binde and loade my Hock Cart home.

It requires some effort to arrest this soft and sliding language and separate its meanings. "Rakes and furmety and binders" are spoken of together; people and tools are equally "employd ... used ... gott ... sett a worke". But three quite different things are meant—wielding pitchforks, supervising workers and pumping bacon and peas into them, cynically enough, to produce more work; the harvesters themselves could not possibly conflate them. Nor would they miss the changing meaning of "must" in the last lines quoted. It would be unfair to accuse Fane of cruelty or dishonesty. 'My Hock Cart' is a private, mild, spontaneous poem; it goes on to describe the beautiful colour of the reapers in the field ("White wast Coates mixt with petty Coates of red") and to encourage their games and ceremonies. Fane would not have made a conscious mental effort to reduce his work-force to picturesque machinery; anything else would be unthinkable for him.

Herrick's 'The Hock-cart, or Harvest Home' may have suggested Fane's poem,[105] and uses the same revealing shifts of language. The opening lines seem to share the experience of the harvesters:

> Come Sons of Summer, by whose toile
> We are the Lords of Wine and Oile:
> By whose tough labours, and rough hands,
> We rip up first, then reap our lands . . .

Herrick is not usually successful in longer poems but here we find a unity and fatness of tone which reminds us of the original meaning of satire—*rus saturum laudere*. The poem is peasant music; its sounds are warm and ringing and the line tends to resolve into heavy beats. Salusbury gives a similar metre to August in the *Knowsley Masque*. Inversion and enjambement serve not to propel an argument but to imitate the movement of the cart and the spring of feet, in swaying syncopated rhythms:

> Crown'd with the eares of corne, now come . . .
> The Harvest Swaines, and Wenches bound
> For joy, to see the *Hock-cart* crown'd . . .
> Some crosse the Fill-horse; some with great
> Devotion, stroak the home-borne wheat . . .
> Ye shall see first the large and cheefe
> Foundation of your Feast, Fat Beefe . . .
> If smirking Wine be wanting here,
> There's that, which drowns all care, stout Beere.

This voice is carefully evolved to match the occasion. Herrick is the master of ceremonies, standing at the door of the hall. He calls the lord to the threshhold to see the cart and its leaders and hear the crowd hidden behind, which he describes in more detail than Fane can command from where he stands; but he is also able to speak directly to the workers and moralize the feast he ushers them towards. The whole poem is designed to represent the sharing of the emotion of harvest and to suggest a close and benevolent relationship between the classes.

But its content is severely divisive. The communion of

experience is only apparent; "We" only plough and reap by reducing men to instruments of our power. The harvesters are reminded that their own roughness is a mark of their separation from "us". Later in the poem they are invited to drink to "the rough Sickle, and crookt Sythe"—terms they could hardly associate with the elegant gleaming tools they have just hung up. A sickle is not rough to the hand, and a scythe is not "crooked" but subtly curved to allow the mower's back to remain straight. Herrick may have known this, but if so he clearly did not feel his experience was relevant at this point. The occasion of the poem demanded a different set of associations, more suitable for its didactic purpose. Labourers are—or should be—roughened and bent by toil, and their identities should be derived entirely from their labour; epithets can therefore be transferred from man to implement. The cameraderie of 'The Hock Cart' is used to teach distance, and the poem's vocabulary is carefully selected to this end. He speaks to Fane of "harvest swains", "rural younglings" and "rustics", but addresses them as "Sons of Summer", "brave boys" or "frolic boys". He invites the men to drown their cares in beer but in the final lines he claims

> that this pleasure is like raine,
> Not sent ye for to drowne your paine,
> But for to make it spring againe.

How can sorrow be drowned and not drowned? The distinction rests, like everything else in the poem, on the difference between the experience of the common man and that of the landlord. "Care", in the jovial heart of the poem, is something we would all wish away; the tone is sympathetic. "Pain", in the harsh didactic conclusion, can only mean "the responsibility to labour with skill". The former irradiates the latter and makes it seem natural to accept another man's assessment of your value and purpose—even when he thinks you are a sickle. Only in such a yielding state of mind could the poem's chief lesson seem just: "Feed him ye must, whose food fils you." The harvest of 1647 gave Fane about £5,750 in rent and over £1000 worth of grain; each labourer that year received five pounds and a dinner:[106]

It did not do to look beneath the surface. Laura's father . . . used to say that the farmer paid his men starvation wages all the year and thought he made it up to them by giving that one good meal. The farmer did not think so, because he did not think at all, and the men did not think either on that day; they were too busy enjoying the food and the fun (*Lark Rise*, ch. 25).

If we look beneath the surface, it is not just to raise indignation in the manner of a nineteenth-century liberal historian, but to show the conditions in which the imagination worked; the more glaring is the inequality, the more the poet has to clothe naked ideology in an august and impenetrable robe. The depiction of charity in rural verse has a reassuring purpose—to give extreme wealth a sweet aspect or sensation of legitimacy.

6

The Vanishing Swain

Literary depictions of rural labour

Me thought I was i'th'countrey,
*   where poore men take great paines,*
And labour hard continually,
*   onely for rich men's gaines:*
Like th'Israelites in Egypt,
*   the poore are kept in thrall;*
The task-masters are playing kept,
*   But poore men pay for all.*

(Ballad: 'The Poore Man Payes for All')

For the governing classes of seventeenth-century England property was the sole basis of identity. Landless tenants and labourers were seen only as adjuncts of their labour and their tools; "I have brought my properties with me," as Notch says in Jonson's *Masque of Augures*, "to expresse what I am." They are instruments of pain, as Herrick and Fane assume when they describe the harvest. They are shadows in an antemasque, either violent or non-existent; in both cases they are against Nature.

By a curious turn of logic, Nature is defined so as to exclude most members of the human race. "The originall of King-doms," writes one political theorist, "is of three sorts, to wit, Naturall, (which we may also call civill), Violent, (or if you will, Martiall), or mixt of these two"; "our Moderne King-domes" allow violence as a protection against the misman-agement of other states, though not against one's own.[1] Har-rington's political theory depends on a similarly chauvinistic definition of Nature. Power must be vested in the landowners, otherwise the state is "not natural, but violent".[2] The natural state must be determined by laws which put an end to the alienation of land; innovation is "a violence, and removing landmarks".[3] The state thus established may increase its powers by planting colonies, either within its borders, or in conquered provinces. It is just and natural to subdue other lands by violence, provided they are subjected totally; "the ballance of Forraign or Provincial Empire is of a contrary nature" to that at home. The owners of colonial estates should be "least admitted to the Government abroad: for men, like flowers or roots, being transplanted take after the soyl wherein they grow". For Harrington the national boundary is all-important, determining whether to apply the laws of Nature or their precise opposite. He even describes ancient Roman history in terms of an unhistorical Italian nation-state:

> the Common-wealth of *Rome*, by planting *Colonies* of her Citizens within the bound of *Italy*, took the best way of propagating her self, and naturalizing the Country; whereas if she had planted such Colonies without the bounds of Italy, it would have alien'd the Citizens, and given a root unto liberty abroad, that might have sprung up forraign or savage and hostile to her; wherefore she never made any such dispersion of herself and her strength, till she was under the yoke of her *Emperours*.

Here we see the doctrine of nature in action; naturalization is opposed to alienation. The same laws that establish the natural state maintain a "Forraign Empire" in violation of all its principles. The subject or foreign population need not even be geographically remote. In Venice, for example, only three thousand people had the vote. For Harrington only this oligarchy can be called "native"; all the rest of the population, and all the outskirts and allied towns, are *"Provinces"*. In this way Venice manages to avoid "diffusing the Common-wealth throughout her Territories". The implications of this are astonishing; the bulk of the people are conquered foreigners, "naturally" devoid of power even in the country they farm and maintain. Since the commonwealth *is* the home farm in Harrington's ideal Britain, it follows that the tenants and labourers of the estate are no more than alien objects of dominion:

> a man may as well say that it is unlawfull for him who hath made a fair and honest purchase to have tenants, as for a Government that hath made a just progresse, and inlargement of it self, to have Provinces.

The land they work is equally alien—null, barbarous or hostile, like the wilderness of Comus.

Harrington was not alone in describing the landless as aliens and enemies. Thomas Vaughan equates doing good to the poor with "*charity* unto my *Foes*".[4] In the Putney debates it was agreed that "you have five to one in this Kingdome that have noe permanent interest",[5] but Ireton still argues that they are "extraneous", and equates them with foreign visitors who must obey our laws though they have no say in them. Sexby exclaims, acutely, that by this argument "wee were meere mercinarie souldiers". Rainborough sees that "the one parte shall make hewers of wood and drawers of water of the other five, and soe the greatest parte of the Nation bee enslav'd". But the levellers' outrage rests on the same principle as the complacency of the vast majority of writers.[6] Wage-labourers are "slaves or vassals born, in the tenure and occupation of another inheriting Lord";[7] they have no proper existence. "Servants and labourers . . . are included in their masters."[8] Though Hobbes proposes the equality of all men under the sovereign power, the servant has no part in it:

> the Master of the Servant, is Master also of all that he hath; and may exact the use thereof. . . . For he holdeth his life of his Master, by the covenant of obedience; that is, of owning, and authorising whatsoever the Master shall do. And in case the Master, if he refuse, kill him, or cast him into bonds, or otherwise punish him for his disobedience, he is himself the author of the same; and cannot accuse him of injury.[9]

Hobbes explains quite clearly that the master rules by "Dominion acquired by Conquest, or Victory in war";[10] the labourer is a defeated enemy.

The 1630s and 40s were dominated by the fear of class war. Perez Zagorin maintains that we cannot discuss seventeenth-century society in terms of classes;[11] but it is clear even from his own examples that both sides saw the conflict as economic, and recognized that status depended on the means of producing wealth. The gentry are "those that live plentifully and at ease upon their rents";[12] "we eat and drink and rise up to play and this is to live like a gentleman, for what is a gentleman but his pleasures?"[13] The interests of rich and poor are fundamentally opposed; Felltham assumes that it is almost impossible to

> Erect a Centre, where the fervent Love
> Of Lord and Labourer together move
> And meet.[14]

As colonel Rich explained,

> if the master and servant shall bee equall Electors, then clearlie
> those that have noe interest in the Kingedome will make itt their
> interest to chuse those that have noe interest. Itt may happen,
> that the majority may by law, nott in a confusion, destroy
> propertie.[15]

More violent means were at hand; one 'Digger Song' advises
the people to rise up "with spades and hoes and plowes",

> seeing Cavaliers are bold
> To kill you if they could, and rights from you to hold.[16]

These threats were not confined to small groups of Diggers.
'The Armies Message or Declaration' reminded parliament
that

> You call us servants, but shall see
> We shortly will your masters bee.[17]

The Putney debates revolved around the question of votes for
the propertyless, as Sexby pointed out:

> they cannot settle upon any other untill this bee done. Itt was the
> ground that wee tooke uppe armes, and itt is the ground which
> wee shall maintaine.[18]

Sexby's experience seems to contradict Zagorin's—the war,
he feels, was fought between economically-determined
groups. The poor were equally clear that "the gentrye" were
their collective enemy,[19] profiting from their abjection—

> My landlord's riches doe increase,
> but poore men pay for all,

as the ballad says. Radical and popular literature sees quite
clearly how "great Men . . . doe the poor devour":[20] "the

Poore are now the rich-mans prey . . . We know that *Cain* is still alive in all the great Landlords . . . These are all striving to get into a body againe, that they may set up a new Norman slaverie over us".[21] Class war could hardly be more clearly defined.

Threat became action; armed invasions of private property were increasingly widespread, frequent and organized.[22] Though these were only sporadic, they filled the minds of landlords with "continual anxiety".[23] Robert Coster claims, quite accurately, that

> The Gentry are
> fil'd with the like care,
> How they shall their Power maintaine,
> For they know
> If Tyranny goe
> They must pack to *France* or to *Spaine*.[24]

The spectre of agrarian revolt was often invoked; "the poore will breake downe our hedges, and we shall have the least part of the fruit":[25]

> The Hammer and the Spade shall think that they
> Could without King or Kesar the land sway . . .
>
> *Fools*, Clownes, and very dunghill things,
> Shall act the part of *Lords* and *Kings* . . .
>
> The Countrey up against us rise,
> Making our goods their lawfull prise . . .[26]

Every effort was made to associate the Parliamentary opposition with communist revolution, incongruous as that now seems. They are a "muddy throng of Earth-borne Traitors", led by "a *Jack Cade*, or a *Wat Tyler*".[27] In *The Distracted State* (1651) Tatham shows a riot of "the People casting up their Caps, crying Liberty, Liberty" (p. 25)—they are misled by local republicans. In his *Scots Figgaries* (1652) the discontented peasantry take to the stage with pitchforks (pp. 23–4). Tatham's purpose is to show how Scots agitators "bewitch" the people into expressing hatred for priests, church organs, tithes and bishops (pp. 16–18); but in the actual scene of their rising these topical issues are not mentioned. Instead they demand the right to "break the Cords of our slavery" and work unmolested:

> for my part Neighbours, Ile work hard, earn my bread with the sweat of my browes, none shall eat away the fruit of my labour, but I will sit down when it is done, and laugh in dispight of all the Kasars in the World.

Despite his obvious bias, Tatham gives this peasant army a political momentum of its own.

In this conflict the land is both setting and cause. It is a continuous reminder of the power of labourers to transform the wilderness, and a monument to their exclusion from its benefits. Landscape, the artistic treatment of the land, must exalt the result and conceal the process. *Topographia*, as I showed in Chapter 5, allows the poet to imagine an innocent and perpetually happy form of wealth, though gold is traditionally the essence of violence—"*Saturnian* Metals forc't by sweltring Gnoffes"[28] and breeding avarice and war. It allows him also to propound a naturally harmonious State, though he saw "meere oppugnancie" all around him, and the issue decided by the public sword. The rural population, forced like the Israelites to do hard labour for their enemies, were a continual threat to public order—"a hotchpotch of the rabble, a mechanick sorded state composed of those under *Kettes* Oke of *Reformation*,

> Of Countrey gnoffes, Hob, Dick and Hick,
>   with Clubs and clouted shoon."[29]

They too must be transformed to become innocent and perpetually happy.

The country labourer might be forgiven for thinking that this transformation was overdue. Margaret Cavendish, smarting under the confiscations of parliament, described society under Charles I as "all happy, even to the Peasantry"; but it is widely recognized that the condition of the rural poor was more terrible in the years 1620–50 than at any other time.[30] Enclosures led to mass evictions and vagabondage. The response of the State, as Adam Moore noted, was "to make continuall Massacres of them".[31] Moore proposes state-sponsored labouring schemes; but for those in work an average wage of sixpence a day "will but halfe buy bread, for they have little else to eate".[32] Wages were officially fixed below the cost of subsistence;[33] 'All Things be Dear but Poor Mens Labour', as the ballad of that name recognizes:

> Beef and Mutton is so dear
> a mans weeks wages cannot buy it . . .
> A loaf of sixpence is but small . . .
> Sixpence a day, is now the pay
> for a days work, and held a favour:
> This must maintain Wife and Babes.

In 1650 the diggers of Wellingborough say "our lives are a burden to us, divers of us having five, six, seven, eight, nine in family; and we cannot get bread for one of them by our labour".[34] As early as 1611 Arthur Standish had seen that food was "more deere in price within these last six yeares than in twentie yeares before: and if the dearth of victuals shall happen to increase but a few yeares to come . . . the poore man by his labours shall not get wherewith to relieve himselfe and family".[35] The catastrophe was increased by bad harvests, plundering armies and the brutality of property-owners. "Great men are apt to eat out the poor and forget their promises and ingagements. . . . The rich eat the Poor like bread."[36] The trickery and violence of landowners is recorded in detail.[37] The condition of the poor was as appalling as that of the Victorian factory-worker or the mediaeval serf; "their condition is still the same or worse . . . they see the dirt of their own ditches Lord it over them, and the body of them (perhaps) more despised than ever".[38] Contempt for the labouring poor was virulent and deep-rooted:

> It makes my very heart to ake
> to hear poor people thus complaining,
> For all their care and pains they take
> rich men are still the poor distaining.
>   ('All Things be Dear but Poor Mens Labour')

Even in radical religious communities those with social pre-
tensions would hate and shun "base" members, as Ralph
Austen repeatedly complains. God, however, is "not rigorous
and severe, as some earthly Masters are".[39]

This "continuall Massacre" of the poor is clearly at odds
with traditional moral teaching. Christianity upheld the blessedness of the poor, and the responsibility of the rich; all men
are equal before God, who has created inequality in order that
the rich may exercise compassion. In law, too, men are supposed to be equal:

> In Justice let the *Poor* man be
> As precious as the *Peer*.[40]

Corn-hoarding and enclosures were attacked in statutes and
proclamations, as well as in literary satire; the depopulating
landlord hates the poor because they are "the justices intel-
ligencers".[41] The superior happiness of country life inspired
official proclamations as well as odes and pastorals. Both
attitudes, reverence and disgust, are sincerely felt; only a tortuous mythology could reconcile them. The literary imagination tries to create a satisfactory version of the countryside,
recognizable but cleaned of threats. This "country" appears
complete in all its scenes and relationships; closer examina-
tion shows it to be subtly dissociated from contemporary
reality.

This dissociation is sometimes explicit and sometimes by
omission.

Patrick Hannay, for example, describes the Surrey countryside as if it were divided into opposing areas, one beautiful, the
other hideous. The meadows are populated by fairies, muses
and nymphs, but in the other place

> those who there inhabit suting well
> With such a place doe either *Nigro's* seeme,
> Or harbingers for *Pluto* Prince of hell,
> Or his fire-beaters one might rightly deeme;
> Their sight would make a soule of hell to dreame,
> Besmeard with sut, and breathing pitchie smoake,
> Which (save themselves) a living wight would choke.

Croydon and the Thames valley are not merely contrasted, but opposed—as the behaviour of their inhabitants makes clear:

> These with the demi-gods still disagreeing,
> (As vice with vertue ever is at jarre)
> With all who in the pleasant wood have being
> Doe undertake an everlasting warre,
> Cut downe their groves, and often doe them skarre,
> And in a close-pent fire their arbours burne,
> While as the *Muses* can doe nought but mourne.[42]

Since these monsters are local charcoal-makers, "nymphs" and "demi-gods" must refer to the gentry and courtiers who take their pleasure in estates near to Town. The colliers work to produce essential fuel; but their land is stigmatized as barren, and they are given no purpose in life except to assault the sylvan deities of Twickenham and Richmond. Both sides are equally dissociated from their actual relationship with the land. Productive labour is presented as motiveless violence, while the title and occupation of the gentry is made to seem sacred and primeval.

The "natural" inhabitants of the country are credited with supernatural powers; Fanshawe's address to the gentry in his 'Ode' recalls Marx's comments on "the perversion of concepts in political economy, which turns the fertility of the land into an attribute of the landlord":[43]

> The country too ev'n chopps [i.e. gasps] for raine:
> You that exhale it by your power
> Lett the fatt dropps fall downe againe
> > In a full showre.

The mistress is allotted an equivalent power in her own realm, the flower-garden—

> She the prime and chiefest flow'r
> In all the Garden by her pow'r
> And only life-inspiring breath
> Like the warm Sun redeems from death
> Their drooping heads, and bids them live
> To tel us Shee their sweets did give.[44]

This is not merely Baroque extravagance; the magic has a consistent purpose. William Basse, for example, imagines that the trees near Boarstall uproot themselves and travel the countryside; thanks to his Muse,

> Musique joyn'd with love performes a deede
> That seem'd a hundred pioners to neede.

In the moral of the poem these Orphic powers are explained as

> Sweete motions that enlive
> All good affections, teaching payne to please,
> Make wonder feizible, and labour ease.[45]

The essence of this magic is the replacement of "a hundred pioneers" [i.e. labourers]; to "make labour ease" the labour-force must be dissolved away. This poetic fiction is "feizable" because it corresponds to a political assumption—that the production of crops is in the landowner's power, and those who do the work are "included in" him. It is all the easier therefore to associate him with the supernatural:

> *Fauns* and *Faryes* do the Meadows till,
> More by their presence than their skill.
> ('The Mower against Gardens')

Nature and the landlord enter a pact to exclude middle-men—all those who treat the raw material of the fields for the use of others. The inert defeat the strenuous. Nature, instead of man, "labours hard".[46] Planting, gathering, manufacture, sale and transport are spirited away, and those who do this dirty work are singled out for special abuse. The "aliens" of rural satire belong to this middle ground; clowns and profiteers are both absent from the ideal landscape, where

> the pregnant Earth unplow'd
> Her fruitful store supplies,[47]

and

> The willing Oxe of himselfe came
> Home to the slaughter with the Lambe,

Fig. 6 Vaclav Hollar, *Albury*, four of a set of eight prints (British Museum)

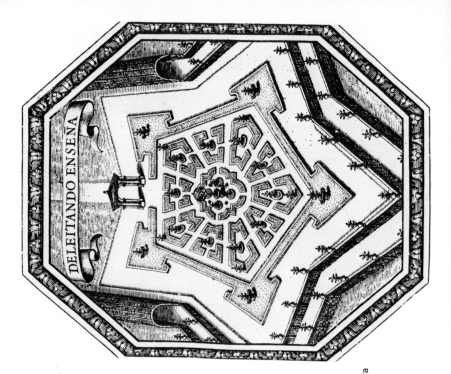

Fig. 7 *(left)* Jan Amos Comenius, *Orbis Sensualium Pictus* (Nuremberg, 1658) p. 286 (Bodleian Library)

Fig. 8 *(right)* Diego Saavedra de Fajardo, *Idea Principis Christiano-Politici* (Brussels, 1649) p. 31 (photo: Liverpool University)

Fig. 9 Giovanni Merlo and
Jacopo Pecini, *Trophaeum
Vitae Solitariae* (Venice,
c. 1605) pl. 24 (Bodleian
Library)

Fig. 10 *(left)* Justus Sadelaer et al., *Solitudo, sive Vitae Foeminarum Anachoritarum* (Venice, 1621) pl. 2, detail (Bodleian Library)

Fig. 11 *(right)* Marcus Sadelaer et al., *Sylvae Sacrae: Monumenta Sacrioris* (Venice, c.1605) pl. 24, detail (Bodleian Library)

> And every beast did thither bring
> Himselfe to be an offering.
>
> > (Carew, 'To Saxham')

Agricultural improvement and mercantile power cannot be wholly suppressed when they are the dominant concerns of society; instead they become tokens of the earthly paradise:

> The taste of hot *Arabia's* Spice we know,
> Free from the scorching sun that makes it grow;
> Without the Worm in *Persian* Silks we shine,
> And without Planting Drink of every Vine;
> To digg for Wealth we weary not our Limbs,
> Gold, though the heavy'st Metall, hither swims;
> Ours is the Harvest where the *Indians* mowe,
> We plough the Deep, and reap what others Sowe.
>
> > (Waller, *A Panegyrick*)

Here we see conceit and reality side by side; Waller says quite openly that "we reap what others Sowe", but gold "swims" and the sea pays "Tribute" (*ibid.*) In both cases the labour of others is whole-heartedly consumed.

In this magic economy the real labourer has no place. The poet's landscape resembles the depopulated regions described with horror by those who campaigned against enclosures—"nothing remaines but a champant wildernesse for sheepe, with a Cote, a pastorall boy, his dogge, a crooke and a pipe".[48] The pastoral and sylvan scene is glorified, though the history of the countryside taught that this most "natural" scenery is the result of the most vicious repression, the mediaeval forest laws and Tudor pastoral enclosures. Camden's *Britannia* provides a classic account of the cruel forest laws, but in the same passage he idealizes the Windsor landscape that Denham was to describe: "behind it arise hils every-where, neither rough nor over high, attired, as it were, with woods and even dedicated as one would say by nature to hunting game". It does not occur to him that his "nature" and the hunting laws are the same thing. The poet's favourite scenery "did seem inclosed, though it open lay";[49] they discredit enclosures in conventional satire, but celebrate their effect in *topographia*. Henry Hallhead, by contrast, attacks enclosure because "it hardens mens hearts one against another";[50] "in common fields they live like loving neighbours together for the most part. . . . You are all incorporate, and become as one body, and so do use your Common as an inseperable spouse."[51] This aspect of rural society is seldom treated in literature. Wye Saltonstall recognizes that "a poore Village . . . proves that man is *animall politicum*, that delights in neighbourhood, and would not live in a Wilderness".[52] Casimir Sarbiewski praises rural community spirit:

> Nor passe we by as the least good,
> A *peacefull, loving neighbourhood.*[53]

But such tributes are rare in Caroline poetry. Nature is depicted as a bustling and co-operative society of creatures, but actual people appear only here and there, as conventional and anonymous staffage. The parts of the landscape are proudly catalogued, but "Damon" "Dick" and "Clott" scarcely have names. Their gatherings are assumed to be drunken or seditious except on the occasional sports-day. Peasants and labourers are never shown to form a natural community.

Such are the omissions which qualify and transform the rural world. Raymond Williams traces their effect in *To Penshurst*, and links them, quite rightly, to the Biblical conception of labour as the curse of Adam; "this magical extraction of the curse of labour is achieved by a simple extraction of the existence of labourers".[54] But is it a simple process? As Alastair Fowler notes,[55] waiters and cheese-makers are not abstracted from *To Penshurst*; nor are sturdy farm girls and grateful farmers. This mental liquidation is guided by a selective principle. The poet aims to preserve the natural and expunge the violent. Mining, as we have seen, is presented as savage and impious; metals can only trouble the peace of the countryside, whether as gold or as "the rough sickle and crookt scythe", wounding the earth. He will admit only primitive and wholesome technology, "guiltless of fire" like Adam and Eve's. Cheesemaking is acceptably innocent, because it involves no fire or metal:

> And of oppression all their crime
> Is only whilst they make their *Cheese.*[56]

Unfortunately there are very few activities to which this applies. Poets often blame the invention of metal for destroying the Golden Age; but the real countryside around them was to a large extent created by the steel and cutting-tool industry.

It takes some effort to appreciate what has been censored from the ideal landscape. There is virtually no mention of land-clearance, tree-felling, pruning, chopping, digging, hoeing, weeding, branding, gelding, slaughtering, salting, tanning, brewing, boiling, smelting, forging, milling, thatching, fencing and hurdle-making, hedging, road-mending and haulage. Almost everything which anybody *does* in the countryside is taboo. We miss the confidence and appetite for detail which Drayton shows in his praise of the English tool-industry.[57] Edward Buckler catches this tone momentarily:

> Look we a little on this land of ours . . .
> Ours is a land of barly and of wheat:
> Our stones are iron, and our hills yield brasse.
> A land wherein th'inhabitants do eat
> Bread without scarcenesse . . .[58]

More significantly, it is found in the verse of American settlers, less inclined to despise the labour of clearing the land. One passage from *Good News from New-England* (1648) stands out in particular; it is almost unique in showing a full working landscape:

> Give eare I pray unto the praise set on a new Plantation,
> "First for the medow sirs" says one, "I have found such a station,
> Where grasse doth grow as high as I, round stalkes and very thicke,
> No hassocks but a bottom plain, Carts cannot therein stick.
> Salt hay and fresh there thousands are of acres I do deeme,
> A gallant harbour there's for ships the best that yet is seene.
> Boates may come up unto our doors, the Creeks convenient lye,
> Fish plenty taken in them are, plains plowable hard by.
> No bush nor roots to hinder them, yet stately timber is,
> In every swamp, yea uplands too, most clapboard trees I wis.
> Clay there for bricke and tile, pot-earth with ease, and store,
> Some men suppose black lead is there, silver and copper ore.

> Carry but guns, and wild fowle will be brought unto your
> dishes,
> Venison and Moose you there may catch according to your
> wishes.
> All creatures thrive exceeding well, Goats, Swine, and sheep for
> meat,
> Horse, Cows, and Calves encrease as well, ther's store of
> English wheat".[59]

But these are exceptions that prove the rule; the English
gentleman-poet despises practicality and resourcefulness.

These things have their uses, however; labourers and their
tools are so evil and contemptible that they are evoked to
discredit an enemy, to depict extreme malignancy or despair,
or to embellish the landscape of horror. This is the function of
Hannay's charcoal-burners and the blacksmith's forges in
Henry More's valley of despair.[60] The mill is an instrument of
torture;[61] Volpone is proud that he owns "no mills for yron,
Oyle, corne or men, to grinde 'hem into poulder". Marvell
burlesques the "mad labour" of the Dutch, calling them
dung-beetles and their leader *"King of Spades"* ('The Character
of Holland'). Except in the verse of professional travellers like
John Taylor, roads and transportation are also "base" topics:

> The saucie Dust checkt into mud and mire
> Merits no mention; our reports are higher . . .[62]

Richard II uses "the Kings high-way, Some way of common
trade" to evoke a particular horror (III.iii). Croydon has filthy
lanes, but in the adjoining paradise roads are not mentioned at
all. Corbett is relieved to find a stretch of road which seemed
like a private estate.[63] Waller congratulates the British for
dominating the sea so thoroughly:

> Others may use the Ocean as their Road,
> Only the *English* make it their aboad.[64]

Since roads are the opposite of homes they are assumed to be
alien, violent places; people who inhabit them are thus doubly
vile. Henry Tubbe attacks Cromwellians as "Shifting Vaga-
bonds, that make the Earth their Thoroughfaire and their

Home too".[65] John Marsh dismisses his opponents as "Gipsies, fickle fortune tellers."[66] The nuns in *Appleton House* behave "like Gipsies that a child hath stoln" (st.34). A ceremonial avenue, on the other hand, is something splendid—

> Where the two Woods have made a Lane;
> While, like a *Guard* on either side,
> The Trees before their *Lord* divide (st.78).

No one could accuse it of being devoted to menial necessities.

Cutting-tools are used to elicit a cold thrill of horror—"but ah the Sickle! Golden Eares are Cropt. . . ."[67] Some poets try to distinguish the "innocent wounds" of ploughing from real malice and warfare;[68] others are less rational. Agricultural tools, the means of life, are associated with lurking violence and death. "The rude Ax with heaved stroke"[69] denotes the senseless violation of nature rather than the cheerful sound of new building. Thomas Weaver describes how agriculture flourishes in the Isle of Man free from fear of "th'Sequestrators sickle".[70] The sickle of death in Edward Buckler's poem destroys the laughing and singing valleys of corn.[71] Mathew Stevenson threatens his coy mistress:

> When Autumne hath possess'd your own fair Field . . .
> Pray do but feel
> The stone-cold steel.[72]

"Iron" in Marvell denotes painful separation. Joseph Beaumont uses ploughing to depict the most hideous grief, when Mary sees Christ being tortured,[73] or when his own daughter dies:

> But ah! the flattering treacherous Year
> Which rose and shin'd till now so cleer;
> With sudden frowns plough'd up his brow,
> And violently study'd how
> To mock my Joy's precocitie.[74]

Ploughing is the initiation of a year of growth, but Beaumont associates it with the wanton destruction of growth, with storms and the breaking of buds. This hatred is strengthened by the feeling that tools could become weapons, as Tatham suggests in his scenes of peasant rebellion—"'tis dangerous medling with edge-tooles".[75] Once again the rule is tested by a significant exception. The carving of names in trees is a "liberal" use of cutting-tools—pure recreation without a taint of labour. It is therefore an acceptable ornament in the landscape of pleasure.[76]

This obliteration of country-life is not confined to tools and their users; it extends to the whole machinery of their control, to mentions of rent, tenure, eviction and the enforcement of game and trespass laws, the work of the pinder, game-keeper and bailiff. In the chap-book *Pinder of Wakefield* Robin Hood and his men go "tearing downe of hedges, making new pathes over the Corne, cutting downe of stiles, carrying long staves on their shoulders, breaking all the good orders that George had made";[77] from reading poetry one would hardly know that such things exist. We glimpse them here and there, in flippant and fantastic moments. Cowley addresses the grasshopper in terms he would not dare use to a patron, however hungry for praise:

> All the *Fields* which thou dost see,
> All the *Plants* belong to *Thee* . . .
> Man for thee does sow and plow;
> *Farmer He*, and *Land-Lord Thou*!
>
> (*Anacreontiques*)

During the flood at Appleton eels bellow in the ox, horses kick in panic at leeches, and

> *Salmons* trespassing are found;
> And Pikes are taken in the Pound (st.60);

beneath the conceit is a vivid reminder of the roughness of an ordinary day on the farm. In the tropical paradise of Bermuda Waller discovers a place where fantasy becomes reality:

> Tobacco is their worst of things which they
> To English landlords as their tribute pay:
> Such is the mould, that the blest tenant feeds
> On pretious fruits, and payes his rent in weeds.
>
> (*The Battell of the Summer Islands*)

Waller's wit would have no point unless this position were normally reversed. Rent can only be a proper object of wit in a world-upside-down. The gentry overwhelmed by the Peasants Revolt "were becomming tenants at will, in Villeinage, to their vassals".[78] In revolutionary London

> *Princes* and *Nobles* are still
> Not *tenants* for *life*, but at *will*,
> And the giddy-brain'd *rout* is their *Lord*.[79]

"Rents, labour, trade, and tillage"[80] are the foundations of seventeenth-century society; only when it is inverted do they come into view.

To read early Augustan poetry, as Paul Fussell says, "is to enter a new world sustained by ideas of property, boundaries, rents, and upkeep".[81] The Caroline poet assumes that these things breed violence, and does his best to disarm them. *Topographia* is thus a system of innocent land-relationships, where natural magic does the work of production, and "green Thought" replaces contentious reason. Its poets subscribe to a sort of rough Platonism, in which the noble is the essential and the rest superfluous. If a mixture is "raised" or sublimated the gross matter vanishes and the pure elements recombine; seen from the proper mental height the grosser part of society evaporates too:

> the business and the crowd
> Seem at this distance but a darker cloud:
> And is to him who rightly things esteems
> No other in effect than what it seems.
>   (*Coopers Hill*, 1655)

In this "right perspective" the mental idea or effect is superior to the physical reality. A metaphor may be "nobler" than its vehicle if it depicts something more in keeping with a noble way of life:

> I need not plough, since what the stooping Hine
> Gets of my pregnant Land must all be mine;
> But in this nobler Tillage 'tis not so . . .
>   (Waller, 'In answer to Sir John Sucking's verses')

In the ideal landscape everything made by "base" human effort is annihilated "to a green Thought in a green Shade". 'The Garden' is a witty attempt to imagine a world with only one person in it. In general, topographical poetry represents not innocent personal solipsism but the solipsism of class and party. It represents an attempt to create,

>   transcending these,
>   Far other Worlds,

populated entirely by royalist country gentlemen.

A taboo, in the strict sense, marks an area of real fascination; remove it, and there should be a fervent use of the very themes which have been suppressed. This seems to be true of those areas of literature where reality is inverted. Seventeenth-century metaphors are crowded with references to rent and tillage—an intrusive feature of metaphysical wit. Raymond Williams remarks that we learn more about country life from Lovelace's 'Elinda's Glove' than from most retirement-poems.[82] Margaret Cavendish's 'Mine of *Wit*' is a very informative account of mining, unusual in English verse.[83] Such metaphors can be applied to every subject, including poetry itself. Joseph Beaumont rests like a "tired plowman".[84] Vaughan's genius creates poets,

>   And they, like *Tenants* better'd by their *land*,
>   Should pay thee *Rent* for what they understand.[85]

William Hammond uses the imagery of wealth to avoid having to explain his real financial position:

>   If Summes and Terrars I must bring,
>   Nor may my Inventory hide,
>   Know I am richer than the King
>   Who gilt Pactolus yellow Tide,
>   For Love is our Philosophers stone . . .[86]

Hammond feels his love to be like a field crumbled under the rollers; Cowley describes how the "estate" of his love is gradually devoured by weeds. Lovers are tenants and farmers of Elysium, engross or monopolize blessings, and pay rent in kisses. Rober Fletcher is "Lord of the Mannor" of his mistress's waist.[87] A tricky affair is like a hard journey.[88] "Sighs" in John Quarles's romance, "made way For words (like Pyoneers)".[89] Randolph describes sex as grafting, though the usual metaphor is ploughing or thrusting in the sickle.[90] We should remember, as Waller points out, that seduction is "nobler Tillage".

Estate-business provides a model for the discussion of political events. Here too the metaphor turns up a realistic and often cruel image of country life. Quarles describes the Puritan takeover of government as a series of brutal evictions.[91] Habington depicts the horror of war in terms which the poor labourer might find familiar:

> A foreign enemy gathers the fruit
> The sweat and labour of your subjects planted:
> In the cool shadow of the vine we prun'd
> [War] wantonly lies down, and roughly bids
> The owner press the grape.[92]

'Jack the plough-lad' laments in Thomas Robins's poem:

> we fall
> To the Plough and Cart with a heavy heart,
> To stir up our ground, and to save our Grain;
> So small is our share that fals to our part,
> Would God that our Master would come home again.[93]

The absent master is Charles II and the whole poem is a royalist allegory, but it is no less vivid. Metaphor and reality combine in Abiezer Coppe's denunciation of the rich:

> the plague of God is in your purses, barns, houses, horses, murrain will take your hogs (O ye fat swine of the earth) who shall shortly go to the knife, and be hung up i'th roof. . . .[94]

Caroline poets idealized the countryside to suppress the spectre of violence; here it comes into the open.

Since the work-taboo is a way of reinforcing the grandeur and idealism of the land-owner, it is only logical for that to be reversed when the poet contemplates the divine power which

in turn is above him. He imagines life from below. Joseph
Beaumont, for example, rebukes himself for bullying his servant with the thought that

> I have a Master too: nor is
>   My Servant bound to my
> Commands so much as I to His.[95]

The poet conceives the life of the lower orders entirely in
terms of hardships and obligations; that is why he expunges
them from his landscape. Consequently devotional verse is
full of images of hardship—rough roads, hard digging, stony
ground, sharp knives pruning the soul, and landlords demand-
ing rent. Poets were capable of observing husbandry in detail
when the genre required it. The devout man in Christopher
Wyvill's *Thoughts* must

> Stub-up the thornes, un-pave the soyle, and make
> The well-injected seed deep rooting take.[96]

In William Denny's allegory the Farm is welcomed for its
fertility and joy, and not scorned for its dirt and boorishness.[97]
"The *Plough* and *Spade*, *Dung*, *Dust*, and *Miery-clay*" are emblems of true humility.[98] This creates a localized insight into the
lower depths of society:

> the Shepheard's fat enough
> That owns the flock; I doe but dresse his vine,
> And treade the Presse; 'tis he that drinks the wine . . .
> There's nothing cheaper now than poor men's sweat.
> We are poor Tenants, Swain; the *Pound's* not ours,
> The *Pound* belongs to you; The Lordship's yours.[99]

We learn of "Gods Skullions" and tenants-at-will, of villeinage, ejections and the burning of cottages, mortgages, seisins
and the sequestration and alienation of land; of the innumer-
able diseases of livestock, the variety of crops, and the complicated equipment of farm work; of the problems of wandering
the roads in search of work and having to eat a wretched
mixture of grain and sand, gleaned from a sodden field in

winter;[100] and of the simple joy of seeing one's own village in the distance:

> I kenn my home; and it affords some ease
> To see far off the smoking Villages.
> (Herrick, 'To his ever-loving God')

In all Herrick's country-verse there is nothing which captures so well an actual moment of country life; it took the contemplation of heaven to release this from his memory. Labour on earth is servile, and freedom is synonymous with leisured wealth. But as God's "service is perfect freedom", devotional poetry gives a natural sanction for the depiction of rural labour.

I have dealt so far with the attempt to avoid and discredit the peasant labourer, and to create a landscape which replaces him. Literature provides several opportunities to depict him more directly—the pastoral shepherd, the Horatian happy man, the "County-Virgins" and "painful Husbandman" who decorate the ideal landscape,[101] or the hideous villein of burlesque, familiar from Sidney and Spenser. All these have an element of acknowledged unreality. Pastoral, in particular, insists that its "shepherds" bear no relation to actual shepherds.[102] No other genre insists so absolutely on a basic contradiction. The reader of the epic may with a little effort imagine himself a heroic prince; the georgic might be put into practice by giving orders, if not by manual work; but every schoolboy knew from the moment he opened Virgil that pastoral poetry is a guise, an exercise, a way of announcing one's début or discussing weightier affairs. Indeed, people who believe the pastoral to be literally true are forever excluded from seeing its point. Deny it—as Margaret Cavendish did and Dr Johnson was to do in his review of *Lycidas*—and the cultured poet meets the peasant face to face, bristling with disgust.

The separation of styles and genres allows contradictory attitudes even in the same author. Idealization and virulent contempt can therefore exist side by side; Arcadia borders on the sterile wilderness of the Helots. John Eliot presents himself as a woodland poet and champion of the country poor; but his description of "a coy country Lass" with stinking breath and lurid cheeks evokes a Swiftian disgust without Swift's redeeming humanism.[103] In Laurence Price's 'Two Jeering Lovers' the city girl loathes the dribbling mouth, twisted features and stinking breeches of her country suitor.[104] George Wharton has "Diggon" praise "Madge" for

> Thy dried thighes, the which do stand
> Asunder like two blasted Oakes,
> Or like to neer adjoining Rocks.[105]

Margaret Cavendish's 'Description of *Shepherds*, and *Shepherdesses*' is a protest against the pastoral convention:

> The *Shepherdesses* which great Flocks doe keep
> Are dabl'd high with dew, following their Sheep;
> Milking their Ewes their hands doe dirty make,
> For, being wet, dirt from their Duggs doe take.
> The Sun doth scorch the skin, it yellow growes;
> Their eyes are red, lips dry with wind that blowes.[106]

She describes the leathery skin, harsh voice, lazy snoring, dull brains and childish crafts of the shepherd, and begs her fellow-writers never to use such revolting beings as a vehicle for romantic fiction:

> Those that are nicely bred fine cloaths still love;
> A white hand sluttish seemes in dirty Glove.

Elsewhere, like any "nicely bred" poet, she idealizes country poverty and the cottage life.[107] Richard Flecknoe is proud to live in an age so free of snobbishness,

> poverty being as honorable now
> As twas when *Cincinattus* held the Plow,
> *Senators* sow'd and reap't, and who had been
> In Carr of Triumph fetcht the Harvest in.[108]

But a few pages earlier, in 'An execration of the Small Poxe', he shows a more cavalier attitude. He wishes the epidemic would spare his well-bred friends, and confine itself instead to

```
      some Country wench
Nature, and worser breeding, gave a face
Could not be much more ugly than it was;
Or Hob-nayl Clown, with whom (when most profuse
Of its ill-favour'd favours) 'twas no news
T'have's face for lasting studded like his shooes.
On whose foule features, tan'd complexion
(Fit home-spun stuff for it t'embroyder on)
No matter . . .¹⁰⁹
```

The double standard of seventeenth-century poets could hardly be more clearly or hideously illustrated.

Rural society is equally hideous in the poets' eyes. The devil in George Wharton's *Grand Pluto's Progresse* (1647) explains that when he visited England he reckoned to make little headway in country districts:

```
I'de thought their plaine rigid Rusticitie
Had furnisht them with such simplicitie
That they were void of those crimes cleave to them
Who a man only as his clothes esteeme.¹¹⁰
```

He is delighted to find poor labourers and rich farmers alike viciously competitive, setting traps for their neighbours' sheep and maiming their horses when they stray. The country was famous for its tedium even more than for its villainy. The dullness of country life was a set theme for the practising wit,¹¹¹ especially among poets of country retirement. Habington expresses his distaste in typically "moderate" terms; he loves the beauty and fertility of the countryside and thinks it is a good place for dim-witted paupers to retire to,

```
But hate that he who's warme with holy fire
Of any knowledge, and 'mong us may feast
On Nectar'd wit, should turne himself t'a beast,
And graze ith' Country. Why did nature wrong
So much her paines as to give you a tongue
And fluent language, If converse you hold
With Oxen in the stall, and sheepe ith' fold?¹¹²
```

Though he scorns the "City Dame" for thinking that beyond Brentford "there's no land but *Barbary*", he makes exactly the same assumption himself. Alexander Brome, who sets himself up as "a *Rustick*" in praise of the country life, shows the same contempt for country people:

> Here, if we mix with *company*, 'tis such
> As can say *nothing* though they talk too *much*.
> Here we learn *georgicks*, here the *Bucolicks*,
> Which buildings cheapest, *timber*, *stone*, or *bricks*.
> Here *Adams* natural Sons, all made of *Earth*—
> *Earth's* their *Religion*, their *discourse*, their *mirth*. [113]

Vaughan writes 'to his retired friend, an Invitation to Brecknock':

> Come! leave this sullen state, and let not Wine
> And precious Witt lye dead for want of thine;
> Shall the dull *Market-land-lord* with his *Rout*
> Of sneaking Tenants durtily swill out
> This harmlesse liquor? shall they knock and beat
> For sack, only to talk of *Rye* and *Wheat*?

William Hammond spends a "night of rurall contemplation" in the absence of his friend Thomas Stanley; "all the reason I encounter", he concludes, "can Scarse win beliefe a rustick is a man". [114]

In each case the assumption is the same; the farmer, because he works on the land, is not a human being at all but a mass of soil, hobnails and manure:

> thou horrid Lumpe
> Of leather, coarse wooll, ignorance and husbandry,
> Most pitifully compounded, thou that
> Hast liv'd so long a dunghill, till the weeds
> Had over-grown thee, and but ten yards off
> Cosen'd a horse that came to graze upon thee. [115]

The landlord derived his title from his estates in every sense— his status, his freedom to consume and command, and sometime even his name. By a grim parodic application of this rule, peasants and labourers *are* what they live by. The daughter of a "dunghil-raker" is sarcastically "noble" because

Her fathers Castle freed her from the Law,
Being wal'd with mud, thatch't with a trusse of straw.
'Twas seven foot in height, judge you the strength:
Six foot in breadth, but ful nine foot in length.[116]

The lower orders are conceived as simple adjuncts of their
physical circumstances, their diet, the tools they wield, or the
ugliest features of the landscape around them:

> *Dean-Bourn*, farewell; I never look to see
> *Deane*, or thy warty incivility.
> Thy rockie bottome, that doth teare thy streams
> And makes them frantick ev'n to all extreames,
> To my content I never sho'd behold
> Were thy streames silver, or thy rocks all gold.
> Rockie thou art; and rockie we discover
> Thy men; and rockie are thy wayes all over.
> O men, O manners; Now and ever knowne
> To be *A Rockie Generation*!
> A people currish; churlish as the Seas;
> And rude (almost) as rudest Salvages.
>   (Herrick, 'To *Dean-bourn*')

'To *Dean-bourn*' is a ghastly reversal of *Coopers Hill*.

The treatment of rural workers need not be hostile, but
writers are overridingly aware of labour and the status it
confers. However impressive and sympathetic the description, working men and women are always mere embodiments
of toil. Benlowes sees the mower in terms of his "big-swoln
Veins", his "crooked Sythe" and the "strain" of his work.[117]
Marvell's mowers work and argue with passionate directness,
but they are never far from being walking emblems.[118] They
are inextricable from the process of mowing, just as the
salmon-fishers are entangled with their boats. Sympathy is
qualified by the exercise of wit; even at rest, trying to escape from his labour, the worker is pursued by reminders of
work:

> When the laborious *Plow-man* hath by *day*
> Worri'd *himself*, and *Earth*, and water'd it
> With his own sweat, cool *night* his head doth lay

> Safe on his Bed, and teach him to forget
> His toilesome work; whilst soft and gentle sleep
> Yeilds him a crop of pleasant dreams to reap.[119]

The hour of repose is a congenial theme because the poet can share the relief of finishing work without having to imagine that the worker has any experience beyond it:

> But, hark, 'tis late; the *Whislers* knock from Plough;
> The droyling *Swineheards* Drum beats now;
> *Maids* have their *Cursies* made to th'spungy-teated Cow.
> *Larks* roosted are, the folded *Flocks* are pent
> In hurdled Grates, the tir'd *Ox* sent
> In loose Trace home . . .[120]

The emotional conflict of Arcadianism and disgust is temporarily suspended.

Panegyric magnifies the actions of great men and multiplies their virtues; the praise of country workers reduces them to emblems of a single virtue, and obliterates some vital dimension of their life. Mildmay Fane's 'Upon William Sharp a Colliers ploughing the moulhil or sandy bank neer Apthorp bridg'[121] is amusing, loftily sympathetic and keenly detailed; but we are never allowed to forget the poet's efforts to get the subject in perspective. Sharp is in turn a parody of the landed gentleman, a satirical stick to beat the fashionable life, an adjunct of soil and tools, an emblem of rural content and self-sufficiency, and a burlesque figure whose only "Cattle" are fleas. The wit in each case hinges on the notion of littleness. For all his fascination with William Sharp's endeavour, Fane can only give him a reduced form of humanity. Richard James's *Iter Lancastrense* is a delightful poem, full of humane and intelligent observation; but he still feels that he must justify his descriptions of rural work and moralize the simple life it supports:

> Ladyes of Courte and Cittie dames, not fleere [i.e. "do not mock"],
> Because I praise my virgins for this gheere.

He proceeds to expound the traditional rude health and happi-

ness of dairy life, and to pour scorn on sickly city ways. These
are contented workers, completely absorbed in their work; the
poet's imagination reduces people to automata, and then congratulates them on their virtuous self-limitation. The ancient
fisherman on the beach at North Meols casts himself in such a
role:

> you gentlemen at ease,
> Whoe money have and goe where ere you please,
> Are never quiett; wearye of the daye,
> You now comme hither to drive time away:
> Must time be driven? longest day with us
> Shutts in too soone, as never tedious
> Unto our buisnesse; making, mending nett,
> Preparing hooks and baits, wherewith to gett
> Cod, whiting, place, uppon the sandie shelvs,
> Where with to feede the markett and our selvs.[122]

Thomas Jordan gives 'Mr. *Bushel's* Miners in *Devonshire*' a
beautiful and dignified song, but he makes them express an
outsider's view of themselves:

> *Ladies* of Love and Leisure,
>   Where is your *Greatness* gone?
> What sudden high displeasure
>   Hath forc'd you from your own?
> Whilest we live here obscurely
>   In *Cottages* unknown,
>   No *Cares* or *fears*
>   We ever think upon.
> Our Wals are highest *Mountains*
>   For we live in a *Coomb*;
> We *drink* of flowing *Fountains*,
>   Our *Dwelling* is our *Tomb*.[123]

They are *personae*; even though their song is filled with realistic
details it cannot be taken literally. It is written in the first
person, but cannot be read as a dramatization of subjective
experience. Miners' cottages are not presumably "unknown"
to their inmates, who would hardly want to see them as their
"*Tomb*". Their professed ignorance of war does not prevent
them from explaining how silver causes it. They describe their

innocent provincial lives as an urbane stranger would, in terms of national public opinion. Herrick's 'The Country Life' is a fascinating description of the small farmer's daily round; but it is framed between sentences which make nonsense of the very idea that country people can be happy:

> Sweet Country life, to such unknown
> Whose lives are others, not their own!
>
> Oh happy life! if that their good
> The Husbandmen but understood!

Dissociation could hardly go further. Country people are reduced to a state of not even knowing whether they are happy or miserable; their happiness is a property of the poet instead.[124]

Rural poetry reduces country people to a few simple qualities, and then expropriates them. Its sympathy is of a specialized kind, more akin to magic than to humane understanding; the poet tries to acquire by imitation the qualities admired. He "recreates himself" by celebrating sturdiness—

> *Jone* takes her neat-rub'd paile, and now
> She trips to milk the Sand-red *Cow*;
> Where, for some sturdy foot-ball *Swaine*,
> *Jone* strokes a *sillibub* or twaine—

hearty sensuality—

> The maid, (and thereby hangs a tale,
> For such a maid no Whitson-ale
>   Could ever yet produce)
> No Grape that's kindly ripe, could be
> So round, so plump, so soft as she,
>   Nor half so full of Juyce—

wholesomeness—

> There from the tree
> Wee'l cherries plucke, and pick the strawbery,
>   And every day
> Go see the wholesome Country Girles make hay—

or unselfconsciousness—

> I am for the lasse that doth pisse on the grasse
> Though the Courtiers unworthy esteeme her.[125]

The poet cannot easily share the experience of country life, except as pure entertainment. He is unwilling to "own the Village Life a life of pain"—perhaps because its hardship actually repelled him. Elizabeth Bracknell, for example, presents the plight of four country people in an antemasque:

> Hen   I have lost my melch Cow.
> Pratt   And I have lost my Sow.
> Rye   And for my Corne I cannot keepe.
> Hay   Neither can I my pritty sheepe.
> Hen   And I have lost fowre dozen of Eggs
> Pratt   My Pigs are gone, and all their Heads . . .
> Hay   And our Purses, they are empty.[126]

We are meant to roar with laughter. The poet must see the peasants as an art-form, and they must not; this is the essence of the pastoral, the *beatus ille* convention and the antemasque. The griefs of Marvell's mowers cannot deserve the seriousness with which they are sometimes taken; they are clearly announced as theatre. Sympathy may never expand beyond this frame.

Secular poetry tends to make the labourer a marginal isolated figure. In Christian homiletic verse the converse is true; he is a central example of proper humility, and society is seen to bear upon him. Truth must not be sought in great men's houses:

> You'l sooner find her in some poor mans Cottage,
> Whose low-pric'd labour hardly will sustain
> His house with bread, and free his bed from rain.[127]

In praising the blessed privilege of poverty Jordan reveals how monstrous it is. Joseph Beaumont teaches the necessity of submission in adversity; to make his message sterner he gives an astonishingly direct account of a poor man's life:

> Is *Poverty* thy Lot? Then look to be
> The helplesse Butt of *Wrong* and of *Disgrace*:
> Thy joints must buckle to hard *Industrie*;
> Continuall *Sweat* must reak upon thy face;
> Yet wanting what should fill and hide thy skin,
> Thou shalt *without* be *naked*, and *within*.[128]

George Wither writes hymns for employers to give to their
workers, designed to cheer them up without making them
rebellious (*Haleluiah*, 1641). He allows "a Labourer" to
remind the rich of their proper attitudes:

> You that enjoy both goods and lands,
>   And are not forc'd by sweat
> And by the labour of your hands
>   To earn the Food you eat;
> Give thanks for this your easie lot
>   And do not us disdain
> Whose Bread and Raiment must be got
>   By taking daily pains (p. 434).

He recognizes the massive power of the employer and the
discontent it breeds:

> Discourage not thy self, my Soul,
> Nor murmur, though compel'd we be
> To live subjected to controule,
> When many others may be free:
> For, though the pride of some disdains
> Our mean and much dispised Lot,
> We shall not lose our honest pains,
> Nor shall our suff'rance be forgot (p. 366).

This beautiful hymn is written, as Wither explains, "that
Servants may be . . . stirred up to discharge their duties with
cheerfulnesse and singlenesse of heart". These poems are
addressed directly to the subject people; their starkness and
clarity are markedly different from the usual Cavalier entertainment.

The paradox of homiletic teaching is well illustrated in the
poems of Edward Calver. In order to enforce the duty of
discretion and meekness he creates the figure of Passion, who

passes through the various states of poverty and wealth and youth and age; Discretion rebukes him at each stage. *Passion in Want* is the traditional lament of a poor labourer, Lazarus addressing Dives. His deprivation is so intense that daylight is an instrument of torture:

> Sun, rise not yet then, let me rest a while,
> For when thou risest I must fall to toyle;
> The day, which gives to other men delight,
> That is my Mill to grind in till tis night.
> (*Passion and Discretion in Youth and Age* (1641) p. 89).

He longs to be able to rest like an animal when darkness comes, but his children are hungry:

> Why was I made an instrument to breed you,
> And not made able, being bred, to feed you? . . .
> Some feed on dainties, and I fed with drosse;
> They take no paines, I labour like a horse . . .
> Their Fragments are too good for me; tis well
> If I can be partaker of the smell (pp. 90–1).

The corn-hoarding landlord laughs to hear his children's cries. All his painful exertion is to create wealth for others, and none for himself— "I plow, and sow, but others reape the fruite" (p.92). He compares himself to a beast in the collar, under the whip of a prejudiced law:

> Tis my offence that onely doth offend,
> Or my offence that onely is discern'd (p. 88).

To complain of injustice is to bring further vengeance on his head:

> What helpelesse then? yea hopelesse too, indeed,
> For I must suffer, 'tis by Law decreed.
> I must submit to each insulting checke;
> The burden still must lye upon my necke (p. 89).

It is pointless to try to be good or wise, since

> Thy grandest vice is nothing in esteeme;
> My greatest Vertues less than nothing seeme (p. 91).

He sees a completely divided society; education and employment is guaranteed only to the rich. Even his birth was miserable:

> My silly Parents sighing for reliefe,
> One cryd for help, the other wept for griefe.
>
> (*Divine Passions* (1643) p. 6).

The world is

> unto the great
> A flattering Syren, but unto the small
> A very savage cruell Caniball . . .
> And if poor *Lazarus* seeks to be imploy'd
> Or sues for aide, he is by thee deny'd;
> Thou only cry'st "he doth my honour blemish,
> Correct the rascall, let the vermine famish" (*ibid.*, p. 8).

This, of course, is the unthinkable and seditious blasphemy of Passion. Discretion corrects him; true wealth is heavenly, and this suffering is all part of God's meticulous plan. But in doing so he carries the analysis still further:

> Tis true, tis hard, I know, to humane nature
> To yeeld subjection to a fellow creature,
> That the same mould, same workmanship and all
> Should downe unto the self-same creature fall . . .
> What though the man thou stoup'st unto be vaine,
> Or one that doth requite thee with disdaine?
> Or one that shuns thee as he walkes the streete,
> As if thou shouldst infect him when you meete.
> Or one that takes thee for a varmine, which
> Doth live upon the substance of the rich,
> And thereupon, in safeguard of his store,
> Doth keepe a dogge to keepe thee from his doore . . .
> Or hast thou food, it must be of the worst,
> And, ere thou hast it, thou must earne it first;
> Thou must consume thy body into sweate
> Before thou canst refresh the same with meate.
> Which being fed, tis but (as fed in vaine)
> To make it fit to be consum'd againe:
> Or as the Galley slave is with the Turke,
> Thou dost but eate to make thee strong to worke.
>
> (*Passion and Discretion*, pp. 93–5)

Such is the curse of Adam.

Calver is writing a religious tract, but he has provided a remarkable secular analysis of economic exploitation. It consumes the victim and poisons even the experience of daylight and sleep. He is forced to live on what the rich throw away, and even that is granted so that he stays alive to work; yet he knows that he has produced what they consume. He sees that every opportunity and form of life is taken from him with material wealth. He must suffer brutal mutilation, and the universal presumption of guilt; he has no redress against the insults and gloatings of his masters, nor against the crowning accusation of parasitism. Lazarus is reduced to a minimal existence by the assaults of Dives.

Seventeenth-century literature has lost any sense of the countryside as a "field full of folk". Virgilian pastoral thrives, but true Georgics are hard to find. The world of work is no longer thought fit for poetry, except in eccentric and popular verse.[129] Like a new colony, the land is cleared of its troublesome natives and planted with a new and more loyal population—hilarious bumpkins, contented morons, fauns, fairies and demigods. The "organic" society of nature is made to oppose human society rather than to confirm it. Landscape becomes a defence against the violent world of men:

> It is my comfort to escape the rude
> And sluttish trouble of the multitude:
> Flowers, rivers, woods, the pleasant air and wind,
> With sacred thoughts do feed my serious mind.[130]

Conclusion
Beginning theory

. . . you will uncode all landscapes . . .
(Seamus Heaney, 'The Peninsular')

This will be a conclusion in which nothing is concluded. I would certainly like to make good after my labours, to landscape the ground I have chosen to build in. It would be satisfying to tie up loose ends, to make a decent closure or frame, to emphasize the relaxed orderliness of the argument, the depth of the perspective and the comprehensiveness of the material. That is exactly how *topographia* works, as I showed in Chapter 2. I would then be reproducing its effects, creating a world; my conclusion would have the pleasant task of making dissent unthinkable.

Instead I will offer a disclosure. The literary text is always both product and process, and my trick in this book is to force a wedge between the two in order to clarify their connection. It is a beautifully finished product, rounded-off and sealed in a form of words which later readers may ignore but cannot change, irreducable to any message; but it is also a process of interpreting and changing the world, of assimilating thoughts and influences, of adapting the writer's career and voice to the varying demands of historical situations, and of smoothing over contradictions. Literature is *in use*. One cannot reduce one aspect to the other, nor pursue either in isolation; they are dialectically linked. Hence, taking landscape as a product, I ask what are the particular "green" thought-processes that create it—but immediately I am asking how landscape influences and operates on existing physics and sociology. To reveal the process is to see how its traces make the product distinctive. I should therefore give some account of the influences and assumptions that have worked on this book, and of the contradictions it has attempted to conceal. This may clear the ground for a theory of rural literature.

E. R. Curtius's *European Literature and the Latin Middle Ages* was an important influence. It encouraged me to dream of a science of literature, objective and transindividual. Nothing should be taken literally or personally; my work was to be an exhaustive catalogue of the serried ranks of *topoi* in which literature simultaneously reflected and excluded the world. Curtius's scholarship rests on a feeble and reactionary theory, however; he asks us to see literature as a recrystallization of forms throughout history, but also as a guarantee of a civilization once flourishing but now in Spenglerean decline. Ernst Auerbach's *Mimesis* provided a necessary counterbalance; a paragraph from any text could be tenderly dissected to reveal a three-dimensional world of historical change and class-consciousness. He shows how the "separation of styles" is confirmed by the separation of classes in society, and how certain kinds of existence (peasantry, labour, bodily functions) could only be treated in a way which seals them off from full seriousness. A proper theory of rural literature would account for these invisible bulkheads which allow the co-existence, even in the same volume of verse, of praise and revulsion, idealism and materialism, radical social criticism and Arcadian complacency. I have located but not explained them. The work of Curtius and Auerbach, and the concepts of *topos, genre* and *decorum*, should be a starting-point.

The problem, then, was to determine the social meaning of literature without losing sight of its specificity, to combine the insights of formalism and historicism without falling into either error.[1] Literature is not "pure" form, but neither is it pure evidence in a documentary study of public opinion. It displays two kinds of "attitude". Any poem, any sentence in literature, can be uttered either as a statement or as a specimen of aesthetic gesture, as content or as form. George Wither recognizes this on several occasions, protesting that his social philosophy is uttered "not alone in show, but truly such", that it is "*real truth*, and no *poetick strain*" (pp. 122 and 145 above). We can assume, since he felt it necessary to protest, that any topic discussed in poetry could have been placed in a distinct epistemological category, "poetic truth" rather than truth itself. Wither asserts the contrary in verse, of course. Likewise the author of 'The Poore Man Payes for All'—penetrating social criticism from the worker's point of view—declares in his epigraph that

> This is but a dreame which here shall insue,
> But the Author wishes his words were not true.

He refers to the dream-vision form of his ballad, but his words could equally apply to any depiction of real social issues in literature. Poetry is simultaneously a vision of the highest truth, interpreting and changing the world, and an aesthete's dream; it is impossible to resolve it fully into one or the other. A poem like *Coopers Hill* puts this uncertainty to good use, presenting ideological statements as aesthetic masterpieces, incontrovertible not because of the soundness of their arguments but because controversy is not appropriate in the first place; other poets of Denham's circle took a more defensive line, maintaining the purity of their poetry against those who argue that it contributes directly to political agitation, that "*Parnassus* calv'd *Edge-hill*". Only "Levellers of *Wit, Delvers* in Poetry" would try "to make *Parnassus* a *St Georges Hill*".[2] The theorist tempted by formalism should never lose sight of the possibility that Parnassus might have calved Edge Hill, or *Coopers Hill* prevented it. My practice tends to veer in the opposite direction; sometimes I use texts as dissociated artefacts, sometimes as direct statements, my choice often guided more by the requirements of polemic than of theory.

This book took shape under the influence of two concepts, two models of how literature might operate in society—*mythology* and *ideology*. Both of them are useful, but neither is entirely adequate. My notions of mythology came from Lévi-Strauss and Barthes. Reading Lévi-Strauss suggested to me that images should be considered as "goods to think with", that they formed rigorous structures of meaning extending far beyond and above the schemes of rational thought, and that this "logic of myth" could be discovered by the exhaustive mapping of texts. But neither his method nor his material is directly relevant to this study; he seems to abstract a structure from the Amazonian myths he collects, and to pay little attention either to their surface form or to the political circumstances in which they might be used.[3] Roland Barthes, on the other hand, deals with his own immediate surroundings as myth, guided by three different meanings of the term—plausible lies to be unmasked, the ulterior meanings of things revealed by semiology, and political ideology operating under the guise of "naturalness" and "the decorative display of *what-goes-without-saying*" which "gives an historical intention a natural justification". "Bourgeois ideology", like myth itself, "transforms . . . History into Nature".[4] The demonstration of the historicity of "Nature", and its covertly propagandist use, is the backbone of my work; indeed I extend the analysis to show how the political concept "Violence" is made to work simultaneously as an inversion of Nature and as a part of it. Barthes's work was congenial also because it seemed to show that the whole material and cultural world could be uncoded, and its social meaning revealed:

> A tree is a tree. Yes, of course. But a tree as expressed by Minou Douret is no longer quite a tree; it is a tree which is decorated, adapted to a certain type of consumption, laden with literary self-indulgence, revolt, images, in short with a type of social *usage* which is added to pure matter.[5]

The same could be said of a rural scene by Milton or Mildmay Fane; there is, in short, a politics of landscape. The images of myth appear moreover "rich, fully experienced, spontaneous, innocent, *indisputable*";[6] I say the same of *Coopers Hill*.

Barthes's conception of ideology, like his example of the tree, derives from the early work of Marx and Engels. The *Economic and Philosophical Manuscripts of 1844* and *The German Ideology*, though not much to do with literary theory,[7] provide a clear and powerful account of ideology:

> We set out from real, active men, and on the basis of their real life-process we demonstrate the development of the ideological reflexes and echoes of this life-process. The phantoms formed in the human brain are also, necessarily, sublimates of their material life-process, which is empirically verifiable and bound to material premises. Morality, religion, metaphysics, all the rest of ideology and their corresponding forms of consciousness, thus no longer retain the semblance of independence.

"In all ideology men and their circumstances appear upside-down as in a *camera obscura*"; in a class-society this inversion is done by presenting real economic relationships as pure ideas and eternal essences:

> The ideas of the ruling class are in every epoch the ruling ideas. [These] are nothing more than the ideal expression of the dominant material relationships.[8]

I was able to see the whole system of aesthetic *topographia*, and the myths that accompany it, as a superstructure founded on the relationships engendered by "rents, labour, trade and tillage"; Barthes's semiology seemed abstract by comparison. Rural literature is ideological, then, if it persuades its readers that the landowner's partial point of view is the only natural one. It is obvious that in this sense of false doctrine—which I use almost exclusively in this book—literature can certainly not be reduced to ideology, and Raymond Williams is right to castigate old-fashioned Marxism for doing so.[9] But recent Marxists have denounced this narrow use of "ideology" as non-materialist and non-dialectical, and replaced it by a more generous and all-pervasive concept—"the lived relation between men and their world, or a reflected form of this unconscious relation". In this developed form, ideology does not simply refer to *ideas* but to values and feelings, ways of conceiving and acting out social roles, invisible structures, unconscious assumptions, images and even the forms of art and literature; it is not necessarily false, but may be coherent and logical, including "elements of knowledge" and offering many and various ways of access to the reality of its time.[10] In my opinion, the concept as now defined is too large to be of any practical use in critical analysis and thus tends towards "pure" theory, something which Marxism is dedicated to unmask—as ideology.

I occupy a theoretically ill-defined middle ground between the two definitions, early and late. I agree with Terry Eagleton that the critic's task "is to understand the complex indirect relations between [literary] works and the ideological worlds they inhabit", but do not see why "ideology is not in the first place a set of doctrines" nor "a simple reflection of a ruling

class's ideas".[11] Complexity enters when ideology is naturalized through literature—never a simple reflection. The rentier,
peasant and proto-capitalist ideologies of seventeenth-century
literature are not complex, but they operate throughout the
text in multifarious ways. Ideologies in literature may be
entirely overt ("Feed him ye must, whose food fils you") or
barely hinted; they may even be experienced as a suppression
of mention, a conspiracy of silence. Ideology may shroud itself
in "natural" imagery, or it may confer a logical, scientific
colour on whimsical analogies. When hostile and contradictory social views are so widely current as to be unavoidable (in
the propaganda battles of the Civil War, for example, or in the
enclosure-controversy) the poet's imagination has the task of
"clothing naked ideology in an august and impenetrable
robe". Or it can provide vivid and realistic access to counter-
ideologies while keeping them strictly localized or encapsu-
lated in figures of speech or specialized modes; Edward
Calver's depiction of poverty is a good example. Literature
can impose aesthetic integration on heterogeneous matter
("one perfect peece it grows"), separate what is dialectically
linked, and join in harmony what is profoundly antagonistic.
Traditional *topoi* may be adjusted to form structural hom-
ologies or congruities with current political situations, sometimes direct and sometimes inverted. "Flowers, rivers,
woods" enable the poet "to escape the rude and sluttish trouble of the multitude"; the *locus amoenus* becomes an exact
counterpart to the political and economic power of London, or
the pastoral swain to the actual shepherd. Dorothy Osborne's
encounter with the village-girls (Chapter 6, note 124) shows
how such images can be experienced as real even in the presence of the object they replace; such cases confirm Marx's
image of ideology as an inverting lens. A poem like *Coopers
Hill* can thus "offer a way of coping with the collapse of a
political world" by creating an equivalent but opposite image
that seems to replace it. Literature can "anchor" ideology by
translating it into apparently concrete terms—by *embodying* it;
or it may disembody the concrete by divorcing it from its
material cause, as in the "removal" of labour from the landscape. It has various ways of hindering analytical thought by
substituting diffuse but sensational images. It can propagate

illusory distinctions like "natural" and "guilty" wealth, and blur epistemological categories by making two things aesthetically equivalent, and then injecting sufficient logical vocabulary to make dissolution seem like resolution. In short, it does most of those things which Eagleton reproves us for thinking it does—expressing, reflecting, deflecting, realizing, concretizing, bringing alive, enacting.[12] In each of these operations a specifically literary device combines with a specific ideology at a historical moment. I cannot see how I could identify these concrete social practices without in some way abstracting an ideological content from the literary form.

To begin a theory of the social meaning of literature we must go beyond "mere content". This is often done by recasting the question as a problem of form, on the grounds that since literature is fully described in the content-form duality, then to isolate the precise ideological function of form is to discover the same of literature in general. Thus Pierre Macherey points out that

> ideology only enters the literary work inasmuch as it is confronted by or opposed to specifically literary devices; so we must formulate the problem of *putting into form (il faut donc poser le problème de la mise en forme).*[13]

And Terry Eagleton asserts that "the true bearers of ideology in art are the very forms, rather than abstractable content, of the work itself".[14] It is a mistake to solve any literary critical problem simply in terms of form and content, however. In the first place, "form" and "content" are analytical devices, not essences. It is a matter of interpretative strategy whether a text is read as content or as form; like "product" and "process" they can only be understood as a dialectical unity. Macherey and Eagleton[15] grasp this, of course, but they do not fully recognize that the specificity of literature is not a product of the text at all; neither its form nor its content need be distinguishable from reportage, philosophy or any other kind of discourse, but it may still be as different from these as a boxing-match is from a street fight. What kind of meaning to expect, what criteria to apply, what is to be regarded as *thinkable*—these are determined by pre-existing concepts, norms and regulations which together make up the social institution of Literature. (We call this an institution—seventeenth-century writers called it *Parnassus*). The mode of literary production and the role of the author are both located in the institution, and need have no effect on form or content. The institution forms the immediate context which combines with the content-in-form of the text to create meaning in literature. Only this irreducable triad can be fully ideological. The content of a poem often corresponds to ideology in the narrow sense, but the institution may intervene to depoliticize it, insisting that we read it as form, that we emphasize the sea-change that statements suffer when translated into poetry. On the other hand, form is not in itself ideological. Brecht made the mistake of assuming that ruptures in the form of his plays would correspond directly to the revolutionary break with old forms of society; he failed to allow for the *institution* of bourgeois theatre, which has of course accepted his plays into the canon without a tremor.[16] Terry Eagleton argues that form is ideological, but most of the examples he brings forward, inasmuch as they can be assigned to "form" or "content" at all, belong to the latter.[17] *Genres* and *modes* may loosely be called "forms", but that does not make them opposed to content; most genres are in fact defined by their subject-matter, like the pastoral, the social-comment-novel, or the fantastic. Genre, style and rhetorical figures can only be understood as institutionally-determined[18] couplings of certain contents with certain forms. This makes us see them as coherent units, properties of the writer—"proprieties", in seventeenth-century English. Within the boundaries of each genre and each commonplace (*locus, topos*) special rules apply; form is given significance inasmuch as it is proper to the content, and vice versa. Eagleton claims that "the fissuring of organic form is a progressive act" in the late nineteenth century,[19] but he does not ask why people should have read a certain form as significantly "organic" in the first place—a reading determined in the institution and not a property of the text. Macherey, on the other hand, believes that form is not in itself ideological—indeed it may "combat" ideology—but being material it allows ideology to be seen whole, with all its gaps and jagged edges.[20] This argument leads him to overemphasize the brokenness of form itself, by which he seems to mean the things it leaves unsaid, its concealments and silences; he does not realize that the fissures he discovers are in fact those "invisible bulkheads" installed by the institution. I would ask, rather, how does the artificial "closure" of literary form come to be read sometimes as evidence for the wholeness and rightness of its content, and sometimes as an instruction to disregard it? The question is begged by assuming that form is intrinsically ideological. And Macherey, by assuming that epistemological breaks are generated by the form and not the institution, seems to fall into the same error.

My sketch of a theory would begin by determining the nature of this institution, its material base in Literary Modes of Production and its superstructure of Aesthetic Ideology, to use Eagleton's terms. I would expect to find that neither level was ideological *per se*, but only inasmuch as it shared in General Ideology and Mode of Production. So for example the notion of a Muse is neutral except when it is used to insult a working-class poet:

> who'd expect a *Poeme* from a wight
> Nurs'd up with Beanes and Butter-milke, or, on
> Festivall dayes, stale Bisket and *Poore John*?
> Strange dyet to traine up a *Muse* . . .[21]

It would never have been suggested that a gentleman-poet wrote well because he could afford good food; materialist criteria belong exclusively to the low. Stylistic decorum here cooperates with the immediate political need to crush James Strong, who had written in praise of a regiment of women taking up arms for Parliament. "Base Poets", similarly, are attacked because their efforts to join the institution, expressed in metaphors of owning Parnassus, are not backed up by real ownership of land:

> Base Poets think their Title doth high sound,
> Though they doe only own *Parnassus* ground.[22]

But the same conceit applied to social equals yields an entirely different formula; "wealth poetical", the symbolic possession of Parnassus or the imaginary possession-by-description of an actual landscape, becomes a morally superior *substitute* for the real estate it both emulates and reviles:

> While you a spot of Earth possess with care
> Below the notice of the Geographer,
>   I by the freedom of my soul
>   Possess, nay more, enjoy the whole . . .
> I can enjoy what's yours much more than you.
>   Your meadow's beauty I survey
>   Which you prize only for its hay.
>   There can I sit beneath a tree
>   And write an ode or elegy.
> What to you care does to me pleasure bring;
> You own the cage, I in it sit and sing.[23]

We see this also in the passage from Emerson quoted at the head of this book:

> The charming landscape which I saw this morning is indubitably made up of some twenty or thirty farms. Miller owns this field, Locke that, and Manning the woodland beyond. But none of them owns the landscape. There is a property in the horizon which no man has but he whose eye can integrate all the parts, that is, the poet.

Here is the central ideological fact of rural literature: it succeeds as description the more it approaches identity with the world of rural production, but it is meaningful *as literature* precisely because it is not that world, because it triumphs over and obliterates it.

Notes

I have silently modernized punctuation (and occasionally spelling) when the original would have seriously distracted the reader. My D.Phil. dissertation ("*Topographia* and Topographical Poetry in English 1640–1660", Oxford 1976) should be consulted for more faithful transcriptions and fully corroborative evidence.

The place of publication has been omitted when it is in the British Isles.

Preface

1. Originally *La Poétique de l'Espace*; I have used Maria Jolas's translation (Boston Mass., 1969 ed.) Bachelard's reflections on topographical themes in 20th-century French literature could be applied to my material—for example, the lamp in the dark wood (pp. 33–7), the way "the human experience of the house transcends geometry" and so is expressed as a swelling of its walls (pp. 47–51), while conversely our imagination turns the landscape into a house (cp. *Upon Appleton House*).
2. *Critical Quarterly* X (1968) p. 277—an early draft of Chapter 3 of *The Country and the City*.

Introduction

1. Cp. R. H. Perkinson, *ELH* III (1936) p. 70+ and T. Miles, *RES* XVIII (1942) p. 428+.
2. Charles Cotton, *The Wonders of the Peake* II. 29–31.
3. See H. V. S. and M. S. Ogden, *English Taste in Landscape in the Seventeenth Century* (Ann Arbor, 1955), and cp. the craze for the world "landscape" 1600–60, shown in *OED*.
4. Cowley, 'The Encrease'.
5. Richard Elton, *The Compleat Body of the Art Military* (1650) f. §4.
6. Henry Peacham, qu. in Ogden and Ogden, op. cit. (n. 3 above) p. 5.
7. Cowley, 'For Hope'.

Chapter 1

1. *A Relation of a Journey* (1615) p. 154.
2. Cp. H. V. S. and M. S. Ogden, *English Taste in Landscape in the Seventeenth Century* (Ann Arbor, 1955) pp. 6–7.
3. *Arcadia* tr. R. Nash (Detroit, 1966) pp. 42–4.
4. *Diana* tr. B. Yonge (1598) p. 152; *Arcadia* (*Works* ed. Feuillerat I) p. 91.
5. *Landscape in Poetry from Spenser to Milton* (Oxford B. Litt. thesis 1964) p. 4+.
6. E. W.'s *Thameseidos* (1600), for example, has a "Land-shaft" which represents the Thames valley (f.A3). Edward Norgate explains that landscape was invented when a Flemish painter captured in a single canvas a rambling spoken description of a holiday in the Ardennes (*Miniatura* ed. M. Hardie (1919) pp. 45–6).
7. Ogden and Ogden, *Taste in Landscape*, p. 5.
8. Ibid. p. 1 (from an anonymous MS).
9. Ibid. pp. 6 and 8.
10. Ibid. p. 172 (edited from Norgate's manuscript of 1629).
11. *Miniatura* (1649) ed. M. Hardie (1919) p. 52.
12. *Icon Animorum* (1614) tr. Thomas May (1631) p. 37; cp. Sidney, *Works* ed. Feuillerat II.24: a wood "sett in so perfet an order, that everie waye the eye being full, yet no way was stopped".
13. *Reliquiae* (1651) p. 204.
14. *Poems etc.* (1645) pp. 164–5; Suckling in fact wrote half of this poem. It anticipates Pope's *Epistle to Burlington* by applying an Augustan theory of landscape to moral issues.
15. Joshuah Sylvester, *Complete Works* ed. Grosart (1880) I.83.
16. *Britannia's Pastorals* I (1613) p. 42.
17. *Iter Boreale* in *Poems* ed. J. A. W. Bennett and H. R. Trevor-Roper (1955) p. 38. This became a famous passage—cp. P. J., *A Scottish Journie* ed. C. H. Firth in *Miscellanies of the Scottish History Society* II (1904) pp. 279, 281.
18. *Complete Poems* ed. Grosart (1878) p. 68.
19. *Poems* ed. G. Thorn-Drury (1929) p. 27.
20. *Norm and Form* (2nd ed., 1971) p. 119.
21. Sanderson, *Graphice* (1659) p. 25.
22. Joseph Beaumont, *Psyche* (1648) p. 191, where they decorate an elegant but morally suspect house.
23. Davenant, *Dramatic Works* III (1873) p. 259.
24. *Barbados* (1657) f.a1v–2 (dated 1653).
25. Wotton, *Reliquiae* (1651) p. 204.

26. Jonson, ed. Herford and Simpsons VII. 170—referring to a "lantschap".
27. *Poems* ed. J. H. McDonald and N. P. Brown (1967) p. 41.
28. *Landscape, Portrait, Still Life* (1949) p. 19.
29. *Poems and Fancies* (1653) p. "159" i.e. f.Cc4.
30. *Works* ed. Martin (2nd ed., 1957) p. 617.
31. John Evelyn, qu. by H. V. S. Ogden in his valuable article 'The principles of variety and contrast in seventeenth-century aesthetics, and Milton's poetry', *JHI* X (1949) p. 175.
32. 'The Author's Preface' to *Gondibert* ed. D. F. Gladish (1971) p. 4.
33. *Poems and Fancies* (1653) p. 118.
34. *Poems* ed. C. H. Wilkinson (1930) p. 181; cp. Anne Kemp's broadside 'Contemplation on Bassets-down Hill' (1658)—the prospect would provide Apelles with "a picture of Elizium".
35. *Poems* (1657) p. 29. There is no flower painter of the time named Maes, but several general artists or landscapists—Adriaan, Aert, Gerrit or even the famous Nicolaes.
36. Ibid. p. 27.
37. Ibid. pp. 30–1. Revett does not appear to be in the *NCBEL*, despite a modern selection by D. M. Friedman (1966), who has no comment on this poem. He contents himself with saying (page xix), "his pastorals and landscapes reveal no markedly individual response to the countryside; they are simply exercises in familiar Latin and Renaissance 'kinds' ".
38. See n.31 above.
39. Norgate gives some interesting information about painting shadows. Though Pink (a fine green pigment) may be mixed in to heighten *flesh* tones (*Miniatura* (1649) ed. M. Hardie (1919) p. 14), shadows in landscape are always brown (Umber and Cologne Earth, p. 15, and a mixture of English Ochre and Indigo, pp. 13 and 23).
40. 'On a Drop of Dew' line 40—the most drastic form of movement-into-the-light.
41. *Works* (Columbia ed.) XVIII.377.
42. L. Lerner, *The Uses of Nostalgia* (1972) p. 203.
43. Ed. and tr. W. Kirkconnell in *The Celestial Cycle* (Toronto, 1952) p. 98+.
44. *L'Adamo* (Milan, 1613) p. 66+.
45. *Poems* ed. Grosart (1876) p. 78.
46. IV.243, 342, 538; V.125, 203; VII.458; VIII.261–2, 275; IX. 115–6. Water is often given a central position in these "single-

line landscapes"; in his marginalia on William Browne, Milton picked out examples of "the power of water".

47. Richard Flecknoe, 'Mr Muley's Kinta' in *Ten Years Travell* (1656) p. 52; *Upon Appleton House* st. 95.
48. Eldred Revett, see p. 19 above.
49. *The Picturesque* (1927, 2nd ed. 1967) p. 22; *Milton, Mannerism and Baroque* (Toronto, 1963) p. 89; 'Symbolic Landscape in *Paradise Lost*', *Milton Studies* II (1970) p. 40; *A Reading of Paradise Lost* (1965) p. 79, and cp. J. H. Hagstrum, *The Sister Arts* (Chicago, 1958) p. 126. Cp. on the other hand the work of H. D. Demaray (*Gardens and Culture* (Beirut, 1969) p. 136+).
50. *PMLA* XLII (1927) p. 149.
51. Op cit. p. 252+; *Mnemosyne* (1970) p. 12; *Heroic Nature: Ideal Landscape in English Poetry from Marvell to Thomson* (Evanston Ill., 1973) p. 21 (English poets "began to be aware of painted landscapes . . . in the later seventeenth century"). Cp. also J. D. Hunt, *The Figure in the Landscape* (1976) pp. 225–6, where the influence of landscape painting is again denied.
52. *Icon Animorum* tr. Thomas May (1631) p. 41.
53. Edmund Borlase in *Elegies on Horatio Veere* (1642) f. E5.
54. Edward Norgate, *Miniatura* (1649 version) ed. M. Hardie (1919) p. 52 and 1629 version ed. Ogden and Ogden in *Taste in Landscape* (Ann Arbor, 1955) p. 172.
55. *Philosophical Fancies* (1653) p. 91.

Chapter 2

1. e.g. Burton, *Anatomy of Melancholy* ed. A. H. Bullen (1903) II.79; H.A., *Parthenia Sacra* ed. I. Fletcher (1950) p. 227.
2. Cowley on Falkland, in *Poems* ed. A. R. Waller (1905) p. 19.
3. Cp. William Habington, *Poems* ed. K. Allott (1948) pp. 142–3.
4. *The Progresse of Learning* in *Shorter Poems and Translations* ed. N. W. Bawcutt (1964) pp. 20–1. The passage is discussed more fully in Chapter 4.
5. *Poems* ed. C. H. Wilkinson (1930 ed.) p. 181; cp. Joseph Beaumont, 'The Garden' in *Minor Poems* ed. E. Robinson (1914) p. 450.
6. John Harrington, *Polindor and Flostella* (1652) p. 60—a late survival of the "compacted" taste.
7. Margaret Cavendish, *Poems and Fancies* (1653) p. "177" i.e. 117.
8. William Habington, *Poems* ed. K. Allott (1948) p. 93.
9. *Poems* ed. Grosart (1878) I.161–2.

10. Ibid. p. 174.
11. Ibid. p. 175
12. Cowley, 'The Despair'.
13. Jane Cavendish, MS. Bodl. Rawl. poet 16, p. 65. The whole Cavendish family indulged in such melancholy landscape—cp. William's *Phansey's* ed. D. Grant (1956) p. 87 and Margaret's *Poems and Fancies* (1653) pp. 79, 107, 158–160 (i.e. ff.Cc3v–4v).
14. '*Landscape* and the "art prospective" in England 1584–1660', *JWCI* (forthcoming).
15. *A Ternary of Paradoxes* (1650) f.B3, p. 108, p. 69.
16. *Il Pastor Fido* (1647) f.A4; he has just illustrated the idea by describing an anamorphic or trick picture which varies with the light—another instance of the interchangeability of the different meanings of "prospective".
17. *Britannia's Pastorals* II (1616) p. 23.
18. *Campo-Musae* (1643) p. 25; cp. Baxter, *Poetical Fragments* (1681) p. 17—"Maps, and Landskips of the Holy Land".
19. Samuel Daniel, *Works* ed. Grosart (1885) I.244.
20. Martin Lluelyn, *Men-Miracles* (1646) p. 102; Thomas Wincoll, *Plantagenets Tragicall Story* (1649) p. 100; Robert Waring in Cartwright, *Comedies, Tragi-Comedies with Other Poems* (1651) f.*7. Cp. also Edward Sherburne, *Poems and Translations* ed. F. J. van Beeck (Assen, 1961) p. 93 (on a new grammar) and Southwell's 'Vale of Teares', which is both "streight" and "vast", and so doubly distressing.
21. *Philosophical Poems* ed. G. Bullough (1931) p. 63.
22. All examples from *OED*.
23. John Quarles, *Dimagoras* (1658) p. 60.
24. *Irene* in *Works* (1711) p. 168.
25. *Flowers of Sion* in *Poems* (1656) p. 104; cp. William Hammond "our life is but a painted perspective; Greif the false light, that doth the distance give" *Poems* (1655) p. 72.

Chapter 3

1. See my 'The Matter of Britain: Topographical Poetry in English 1600–1660', *N&Q*, forthcoming 1978.
2. J. M .Wallace, in *Critical Inquiry* I (1974) p. 287. According to Wallace, Denham's two works are not parallel but consecutive. *Coopers Hill* is a defence of parliamentary royalism, written in

the wake of the King's departure for Scotland in August 1641; *The Sophy* continues the political discussion, as Denham becomes more critical of Charles. How all this takes place "within the limits set by his increasing royalism", and why both works are published on the eve of civil war, remains for Wallace a "serious critical problem". Since the play deals with the perils of fear and jealousy, and since "Fears and Jealousies" were a catch-phrase of political pamphleteering in 1642, then it follows that the entire play is a political pamphlet, with Charles as its central figure. It may be objected that England did not have a senile King, a simple-minded and militaristic prince, a sensitive and strong-minded princess, and a grandson ready to take command; or that the "fears" of 1642 were overstated in order to justify aggression, while those in the play are insufficiently heeded. Wallace replies that the features of Charles are *distributed* between "the good prince and the tyrannical emperor".

3. *De Quattuor Virtutibus* (c. 1520 ed.) f. A7: "Quid prodest varios stellarum inquirere cursus? Quid res et causas noscere, inepte, petis? Quid cupis innumeras discendo amplectier artes? Et toto veros orbe te ferre situs?" The emendation from "disendo" was suggested by Francis Cairns.

4. Denham, *Poetical Works*, ed. T. H. Banks (2nd ed., Hamden Conn., 1969) p. 193 (my emphasis). Another "scientific" aspect of *Coopers Hill* is suggested by J. W. Foster ('The Measure of Paradise: Topography in Eighteenth-Century Poetry', *ECS* IX (1975–6) pp. 240–3) who relates it to contemporary surveying.

5. William Peaps, *Love in it's Extasie* (1649) f. D2. For the emblems of Diego de Saavedra see Henkel and Schöne, *Emblemata* (Stuttgart, 1967).

6. Samuel Daniel, *Complete Works* ed. Grosart (1885) I.273.

7. Crashaw, *Poems* ed. Martin (2nd ed., 1957) p. 410.

8. (1647) f. A4v.

9. Ibid. f. A3v. Jean-François Nicéron devotes the whole of the last book of his *La Perspective Curieuse* (Paris, 1638) to this device, and claims it to be as important as the microscope and the telescope; like Fanshawe, he deduces a serious political message from its optical trickery (pp. 173–4, 189, and plates 48–9). See my letter in *Art Bulletin* LIX (1977) p. 659.

10. *Complete Works* ed. Grosart (1885) I. 204.

11. R. Nevo, *The Dial of Virtue* (Princeton, 1963) p. 18; J. M. Wallace, *ELH* XLI (1974) p. 497. Cp. ibid. p. 500—"not a party poet"—and J. W. Foster, *ECS* IX (1975–6) p. 237.

12. By C.I. (Jan. 1642); cp. esp. f.A2v. The fog of error was used in London pageantry—e.g. Middleton's *Triumphs of Truth* (1613).

13. *Midsummers Prognostication of Pacification and Unity* (June 1642) p. 1.

14. *Poems* ed. J. Craigie II (1958) p. 188. Ironically, the far left also attacked Magna Carta (e.g. P. Zagorin, *Political Thought in the English Revolution* (1954) pp. 11, 23, 27, 51).

15. E.g. Drayton, *Poly-Olbion* ed. J. W. Hebel (1961 ed.) p. 337; Edward Herbert's *Life*; Howell, *Poems* (1664) p. 14; Lovelace, *Poems* ed. C. H. Wilkinson (1930 ed.) p. 182.

16. E.g. *Poems* ed. Grosart (1878) I.170.

17. *Theatre of the Empire of Great Britaine* (1611) p. 11; *Occasionall Meditations* (1630) p. 192; *Upon Appleton House* st. 27.

18. Cp. the play *Edward III*, Prynne's *Sovereigne Power of Parliaments* (1643) II.55, and J. M. Wallace, *ELH* XLI (1974) pp. 501–2, (but Denham does not blame Edward, merely regrets that history prevented him from knowing about Charles I).

19. Ff.F2v, F4v, K2–v.

20. Ff.C2v–3 are particularly like Denham; he quotes *Hosea* 5.10, which may well be a source of the threatening element in Denham's flood-imagery, and insists on mutual boundaries and respect of law.

21. I refer to Charles's pronouncements by date only, where possible; cp. 7 *May*, 14 *May* f.A2v.

22. J. M. Wallace quotes such an example (*ELH* XLI (1974) p. 507) yet he continues to believe Denham a moderate "parliamentary royalist". Wallace's case rests on giving *Coopers Hill* an early date; he claims that its themes and images belong uniquely to August 1641, and the aftermath of the Anglo-Scots treaty and the King's departure for Scotland. There is no internal evidence for such a date, and O Hehir recognizes that the poem belongs to the crisis year of 1642. Wallace tells us repeatedly what Denham was thinking and doing in the Autumn of 1641, but in fact those months of the poet's life are curiously undocumented. Nor do they provide a unique theme. Scotland is not a dominant topic of the poem. The idea that wise kings wage foreign wars is a commonplace, and not special to that August. He explains Denham's threatening flood-imagery by suggesting that in the summer of 1641 there was a general fear of the King's returning at the head of an army; but such alarms were greater in the following year, after he had left London. His interpretation of the landscape is equally constricted. He compares the double "visit" of the Thames with Charles's double

farewell to Parliament before he left for Scotland; but such an interpretation is unnecessary—Denham refers to home and colonial produce, the one brought downstream and the other upstream on the tide. And he discovers August 1641 in the hanging woods above Runnymede, which Denham compares, conventionally enough, to great lords frowning on the humble folk below. Apparently these "were the lords of the privy council" responsible for collecting ship-money; the poet, to put his true subject beyond doubt, "makes the hill an intrinsically Scottish mountain, not a Surrey hillock" (p. 516 and note).

23. E.g. *Eikon Basilike* Chapter 4, answered by Milton (Columbia ed. V. 125), paraphrased by Stanley (*Poems and Translations* ed. G. M. Crump (1962) p. 277), and echoed in the anonymous *Stipendariae Lacrymae* (Hague, 1654) p. 29.

24. Cp. Charles's publications: *2 Mar, 21 Mar* p. 10+, *28 Mar, 3 June* p. 1, *17 June* p. 5, *16 July* p. 8, *12 Aug* f.C3; for Parliament's denial that there was any violence, except from the King's men, see their *Declaration or Remonstrance of 19 May* pp. 8–9, and for their pleading, cp. esp. *Horrible Newes* f.A2. Henry Glapthorne's topographical poem *White-Hall* ("Written 1642") centres on this episode.

25. B. O Hehir, op. cit. p. 113.

26. *14 Feb* p. 4; *April 18th; April 28th* p. 5; *Answer to a Book of 19 May* p. 29; *27 May; 3 June* p. 4; *14 June; 16 June* pp. 6–7; *18 June; 20th June; Answer to a Paper of 21 June* p. 7; *Answer to 16 July* p. 18.

27. George Wither, *Vox Pacifica* (1645) p. 203.

28. *Poetical Works* ed. T. H. Banks (2nd ed., Hamden Conn., 1969) p. 143.

29. Written 1641, edited by C. H. Firth in *Miscellanies of the Scottish Historical Society* II (1904).

30. This account of *Coopers Hill* should be compared with W. B. Carnochan, *Confinement and Flight: an Essay on English Literature of the Eighteenth Century* (1977) pp. 108–17. His version of the poem is incompatible with mine. He makes no reference to its politics. Denham grapples with the problems, not of Puritan and Royalist, but of how to defeat gravity, how to get to the top of Cooper's hill, and how to see *through* St. Anne's hill. He looks *up* at Cooper's hill, and is embarrassed by the physical act of climbing it; he therefore replaces the view from the summit with a bird's-eye or god's-eye view of the landscape. We are told that the poet's eye might not have seen St. Paul's at all, and then that it roams the vault of air in all directions and floats

freely around the cathedral dome, together with the readers of the poem. But in turning to the denunciation of Henry VIII "the poet comes back to himself" (p. 117). A critic is entitled to select only those aspects of a "seminal" work which affect his subject—but in this case the features selected do not exist.

31. *E in C* XXII (1972) p. 48+.

32. According to Henry Wotton (*Reliquiae* (1651) p. 204) the ideal prospect should give "lordship" both to the eye and to the foot.

33. C. Molesworth in *SEL* XIII (1973) p. 159; R. Colie, *My Eccho-ing Song* (Princeton, 1970) p. 217.

34. I presume Marvell describes the small tributary, now silted up but evident from the stone bridge to the NW of the house, which runs southward into the Wharfe at Nun Appleton. This would also account for the intimate scale of the description in st. 79-80 (the Wharfe is not serpentine, but forms a larger curve) and the plural "Floods" in st. 10; the "limpid Brook" of st. 88 is more apt as a metaphor for Maria if we realize that it is about to enter a bigger river.

35. Heywood, quoted in K. Scoular, *Natural Magic* (1965) p. 9.

36. D. Foskett, *Cooper and His Contemporaries* (1974) p. 46. The identity of the sitter has been doubted, but it shows a marked resemblance to known portraits of the Fairfaxes, and to later society portraits of Mary herself.

37. *Last Instructions to a Painter*, line 892.

38. Denham, *The Sophy* (1642) p. 11; cp. Carew *From Wrest*, where innocent hunting ("th'embleme of warre") in the home counties is contrasted with real war in the North.

39. This identification is not certain, but the first lord (Marvell's patron's grandfather) is most likely to have fought in *"Poland"*—perhaps in the cause of Protestant Sweden.

40. Marvell, 'The Mower to the Glo-Worms'; this, together with Camerarius's emblem of the nightingale's music-lesson (Henkel and Schöne, column 872), makes me believe the nightingale in *Ap. House* to be *primarily* a didactic image, not erotic.

41. 'Marvell's Warlike Studies,' *Essays in Criticism* (forthcoming).

42. Milton asks why he retired, and tries several answers (*Defensio Secunda*, Columbia ed. VIII. 218); so does Samuel Colvile (his poem transcribed by Charles Fairfax in *Analecta Fairfaxiana* uncatalogued manuscript in Brotherton Collection, University of Leeds, p. 131).

43. *Answer to the Petition of June 17th*, pp. 2–3.

44. Milton, loc. cit.; cp. John Favour on Ferdinando, "self-conquerour first, He grew more expert thence To fight abroad

by home-experience" (BL Add. MS. 11743, f. 20). But Fairfax will not fight.

45. As Edward Calver described him in a poem of the same name (1648), upholding his wisdom and "innocency" (p. 7).

46. *Scoticlassicum* (1650) p. 8, very sarcastic about Fairfax.

47. E.g. *Cromwell's Conspiracy* 1659) f.E3; cp. the *Villiers Ode* attributed to Marvell—"long-deceived *Fairfax*".

48. *An Elegie on the Most Barbarous, Unparallel'd, Unsouldiery Murder of Lucas and Lisle* (1648) p. 4.

49. Henry King, *Elegy on Lucas and Lisle* in *Poems* ed. M. Crum (1965) p. 107. Cp. John Ashmore, *Odes of Horace* (1621) p. 65 'To the famous Martialist, Captaine *William Ferfax*'—"nor from thy Name dost thou degenerate . . .".

50. Mildmay Fane, *Fugitive Poetry* (Harvard f.MS. Eng. 645) f.Av. Fairfax is "black Tom" and the two, riding in a closed carriage to give themselves an air of grandeur, look like "the Lobster Lady and her mate" (ibid. f.A). Fairfax is attacked also in Ibid. pp. 25 and 89, but there is nothing to support Eleanor Withington's fascinating conjecture (*HLB* XI (1957), p. 61), that Fane accused Fairfax of being a "cold niggardly opportunist . . . trying by his very aloofness to reserve through his one child the real balance of power".

51. *The Fairfax Correspondence* ed. G. W. Johnson (1848) I.cviii.

52. BL Eg. MS. 2146, p. 81.

53. In a letter to Milton of June 2nd 1654 Marvell compares the *Defensio Secunda* first to a "scale" leading "to the Height of the Roman Eloquence" and then to the spiralling Trajan's column "when I consider how equally it turnes and rises with so many figures".

54. Marvell, *Poems* ed. H. M. Margoliouth (3rd ed., 1971) pp. 94, 93, 429, 113 and 139.

55. *The Taking of Leicester* (1646) p. 7.

56. St.6; cp. Marvell's letter to Cromwell (July 28th 1653) describing the educative atmosphere in the Oxenbridge family "whose Doctrine and Example are like a Book and a Map, not onely instructing the Eare but demonstrating to the Ey which way to travell".

57. There may also be a hint of another principle for organizing the landscape, the placing of high and low. Marvell seems to adopt various low styles before reaching his lofty conclusion—burlesque in the nunnery, pastoral in the meadow, and parody in the wood; if so, this adds to the explicit symbolism of height and lowness in stanzas 8, 65, and 89.

58. Cp. *Last Instructions* lines 14–15; in Chapman's *Middle Temple Masque* Indian feather-work contrasts "humbly" with the beauty of the courtiers' own costumes.

59. *Psyche* (1648) p. 42; Psyche is accompanied by a spiritual guide, who cures her by instruction.

60. *Works* ed. Feuillerat I.154.

61. Marvell, letter of 17th June 1661.

62. *Passion and Discretion in Youth and Age* (1641); in Marvell's adaptation this becomes the former age and the present—and he refers to himself as a "trifling *Youth*" in order to be more parallel with Maria.

63. Described in e.g. J. Baltrušaitis, *Anamorphic Art* (English translation 1977).

64. St.57. In fact the comparison is not straightforward. Davenant does not appear IN the hexameral picture described in *Gondibert*, though Marvell's lines seem to say so. I suggest that he means "Cows in a field remind me of that hilarious time when Davenant brought out a poem full of howlers—remember 'Universal Herd'?" The "painted world" is then the beau monde.

65. Quoted in C. H. C. Baker, *Lely and the Stuart Portrait Painters* (1912) II.132.

66. 'Answer to the Preface' (1651), in *Gondibert* ed. D. F. Gladish (1971) p. 55.

67. *Last Instructions*, lines 269+

68. John Favour on Ferdinando Fairfax (BL Add. MS. 11743, f.20v); cp. Milton, 'Sonnet X', on the virtue of a great man passing to his daughter.

69. Cp. Fane (Harvard f. MS. Eng. 645, p. 25) "Though thy pretences may for fair stand, Black Tom, the rest in Latine's fire brand, And soe I feare thou art who prict with fame Embroylst thy native country in a flame." For frequent (and complementary) anagrams on the family name, see *Analecta Fairfaxiana* (n.41 above) pp. 17–18, 36–7, 41, 57, 115 and 119. The two commonest ideas in these poems are the torch of Rome and flames on the altar of virtue. The latter is echoed in st.86, but the former is now obsolete; instead, the Fairfaxes should pursue the "Flames" of mutual wedded love (st.66).

70. Samuel Daniel, 'To the Ladie Anne Clifford' in *Complete Works* ed. Grosart (1885) I.216; the whole poem advises and praises the daughter of a great lord while she is yet young, and sums up "Such are your holy bounds, who must convay (If God so please) the honourable bloud Of *Clifford* and of *Russell* led aright To many worthy stems."

71. John Tempest on Ferdinando Fairfax, but referring to Maria's generation (BL Add. MS. 11743, f.16v).

72. See my 'Upon Appleton House', *N&Q* N.S. XXIV (1977) pp. 547–8.

73. Marvell is, I think, careful to distinguish this afternoon performance in five acts from the nocturnal private performance of a masque. G. E. Bentley describes the Second Blackfriars in *The Jacobean and Caroline Stage*; Marvell too has clamour from the gods (grasshoppers), seating near the stage in the pit, back-chat with the comic characters (Thestylis). The squeaking of the grasshoppers from on high *may* be a reference to the classical theatre; each tier of seats was designed to correspond to a note in the scale, in ascending order.

74. *De Architectura* III Chapter 3; cp. *Last Instructions* line 235—"Thick was the Morning, and the *House* was thin."

75. *De Architectura* II Chapter 8.

76. St.96. Squareness helps to organize the poem: each stanza has eight lines of eight syllables; the four elements of the estate provide the basis for the description; they are introduced at the end of st.10 and the beginning of st.11, and reiterated with much pomp in st.87 and st.88—eight times eleven.

77. Thomas Jordan, 'A Defence for Musicke' (1653) ed. R. C. Elsley (*Thomas Jordan* (Oxford B. Litt., 1956) I.191–2).

Chapter 4

1. Peter Heylin, *Cosmographie* (1652) I.263.

2. Cp. P. Zagorin, *Political Thought in the English Revolution* (1954) pp. 51, 56; C. Hill, *The World Turned Upside Down* (1975 ed.) p. 136.

3. *The Clarke Papers* ed. C. H. Firth I (1891) pp. 302 and 314.

4. *Poems* ed. J. Craigie II (1958) p. 180.

5. Qu. M. James, *Social Problems and Policy during the Puritan Revolution* (1930) p. 129.

6. *1844 Manuscripts* ed. D. J. Struik (New York, 1964) p. 101.

7. Qu. in P. Zagorin, *Political Thought* (1954) p. 22.

8. *Tenure of Kings and Magistrates* (Columbia ed. V.40).

9. George Wither, *Vox Pacifica* (1645) p. 184.

10. Aston Cokaine, *Small Poems* (1658) p. "141", i.e. 241.

11. *Poly-Olbion* ed. J. W. Hebel (1961 ed.) pp. 54–5.

12. *The Civil War* ed. A. Pritchard (1973) p. 95.

13. *Poly-Olbion* ed. cit. pp. 143–4.
14. *The Case of the Common-Wealth of England, Stated* (2nd ed., 1650) p. 79.
15. Falkland, qu. by J. Wallace in *ELH* XLI (1974) p. 532n.
16. John Quarles, *Fons Lachrymarum* (1648) p. 98.
17. *Appleton House* st.43.
18. Thomas Weaver, *The Isle of Man* in *Songs and Poems of Love and Drollery* (1654) p. 66.
19. John Abbot (alias Rivers), *The Fable of Philo* (1645) pp. 13–14.
20. *Social Problems* (1930) p. 61+.
21. Cp. P. Zagorin, *Political Thought* (1954) p. 48.
22. Casimir Sarbiewski, *Odes* tr. G. Hils (1646) p. 85. The idea of produce without labour is a commonplace; Shakespeare gives it to Gonzago in *The Tempest*.
23. *Natures Pictures* (1656) p. 92.
24. *Ad Populum* (1644) pp. 3–5; cp. p. 5 "ye then Were not enslav'd, but free-borne Englishmen; Your Stacks of Corne were then your own. . . ."
25. John Beaumont, *Poems* ed. Grosart (1869) p. 148, on the marriage of Charles and Henrietta Maria. Like later Stuart panegyrists, he echoes Virgil's Eclogue IV.
26. Robert Baron, *Ερoτoπαιγνιov* (1647) p. 88.
27. Joseph Beaumont, *Psyche* (1648) p. 316.
28. *Shorter Poems and Translations* ed. N. W. Bawcutt (1964) p. 93 (earlier version).
29. Ibid. pp. 20–1, 23.
30. *Complete Works* ed. Grosart (1881) III.276.
31. Hobbes, *Leviathan* ed. C. B. Macpherson (1968) p. 225; Hobbes considers it necessary to refute the argument point by point.
32. *Otia Sacra* (1648) pp. 135–6.
33. George D'Ouvilly, *The False Favourit* (1657) p. 110.
34. *Philosophical Poems* ed. G. Bullough (1931) p. 52.
35. Mildmay Fane, *Otia Sacra* (1648) p. 154.
36. Robert Waring in Cartwright, *Comedies . . . with other Poems* (1651) f.*7.
37. Cp. *Fortunes Tennis-ball* (1640); *The Clarke Papers* ed. C. H. Firth I (1891) pp. 325–6; *The In-Securitie of Princes* (1649) f.A2; Abiezer Coppe, qu. N. Cohn, *The Pursuit of the Millenium* (1957) p. 360; Anna Trapnel, *The Cry of a Stone* (1654) p. 20. Spenser's levelling giant uses topographical terms in *Faerie Queene* V.ii.st.38, and is answered in st.41 by the "ideal co-operation" of nature; this episode had a topical interest, for it

was reprinted in 1648 as *The Fairie Leveller* (J. Frank, *Hobbled Pegasus* (Albuquerque, 1968) p. 209).

38. John Quarles, *Regale Lectum Miseriae* (1649) p. 38.
39. Qu. in C. Leech's ed. of Fane's *Raguaillo D'Oceano and Candy Restored* (Louvain, 1938) p. 45.
40. *Poems* (1664) p. 125.
41. *Poetical Works* ed. R. W. Bond (1893) pp. 315+, 341.
42. Edward Sherburne, *Poems and Translations* ed. F. J. van Beeck (Assen, 1961) pp. 16 and 18; Thomas May, *Henry the Second* (1663) f.E3; Thomas Washbourne, *Poems* ed. Grosart (1868) p. 216; John Beaumont, *Poems* ed. Grosart (1869) p. 138; Fanshawe, 'On his Majesties Great Shippe'; Lovelace, 'Lucasta at the Bath'; Suckling, *Non-dramatic Works* ed. T. Clayton (1971) p. 28; *Irenodia Cantabrigiensis* (1641) f.K1; Hobbes, *De Mirabilibus Pecci* (dual-language ed., 1678) pp. 2–5; Cotton, *Poems* (1689) p. 508.
43. George Daniel, *Selected Poems* ed. T. B. Stroup (Lexington Ky., 1959) p. 169.
44. *Faerie Queene*, III.vi.st.44.
45. Harrington and Wither believed that a *lex agraria* would create a perpetually settled state (*Oceana* (1656) p. 5; *The Dark Lantern* (1653) pp. 61–3). In 1659 Milton and Wither made last-minute attempts to convert the people to their views, and so guarantee a never-failing settlement (Columbia ed. VI. 146; *Epistolium-Vagum* (1659) p. 19, where he claims that the state will "henceforth from Violence protected stand").
46. *Poems* ed. K. Allott (1948) pp. 63–4.
47. Thomas Philipott, *Poems* ed. Martin (1950) p. 26.
48. *Poems* ed. Grosart (1868) pp. 109, 108; Denham uses the same notion to suggest that the plots of the city merely form a cyclic pattern in *Coopers Hill*.
49. *Of Monarchy*, in *Works* ed. Grosart (1870) I.20. Denham resembles Greville in a number of points, but *Of Monarchy* was suppressed in Greville's published works of 1633 (J. Rees, *Fulke Greville* (1971) p. 134) and circulated as an underground manuscript.
50. *Monumentum Regale* (1649) p. 11.
51. *Anima Magica Abscondita* (1650) p. 54. Henry More reviews this poem, very scathingly, in his *Observations* on Vaughan's book (1650) pp. 84–6. Both writers assume, however, that the relationship between bank and stream can and should be moralized.
52. *Complete Poems* ed. Grosart (1878) p. 170.
53. Cowley, *Davideis* in *Poems* ed. A. R. Waller (1905) p. 243. The

equation of flood and rebellion is too common to need quotation.

54. Ed. A. Clifford in *Tixall Poetry* (1813) pp. 79–82. The poem resembles *Coopers Hill* in other ways too—in the "local Parnassus" conceit at the start, in the equation of style and the river's behaviour, and in the evocation of the celestial Eridanus.

55. E.g. Anne Weamys, *Arcadia* (1651) p. 142 "the sweet societie of Birds".

56. Henry More, *Philosophical Poems* ed. G. Bullough (1931) p. 73, referring to "Behirah", the land of the democratic left. In his notes More explains by contrast his idea of "the genuine society that should be among men . . . right society . . . divine communiality . . . not onely supplying friendly one another in the necessities of life, but mutually cherishing in one another the divine life of the soul, and maintaining an inviolable concord" (ibid., p. 212).

58. *Poems and Fancies* (1653) p. "177", i.e. 117.

59. John Harington, *Polindor and Flostella* (1652) p. 84; Mathew Stevenson, *Occasion's Off-spring* (1654) p. 66; Habington, *Poems* ed. K. Allott (1948) p. 146.

60. Robert Baron, *Pocula Castalia* (1650) p. 86; Herrick, 'Farewell Frost, or welcome the Spring'; Robert Chamberlain, 'To his honoured friend, Mr *Giles Balle* Merchant. On the Spring' in *Nocturnall Lucubrations* (1638) f.H1.

61. Henricus Accipiter, i.e. Hawkins, *Parthenia Sacra* (1633) ed. I. Fletcher (1950) pp. 5–6.

62. *Poems* (1657) p. 74; *Occasion's Off-spring* (1654) p. 61.

63. *Poems and Fancies* (1653) p. 120; this is a punishment for political apostacy, N.B.

64. *Tarquin Banished* (1655) pp. 7–10.

65. Habington, *Poems* ed. K. Allott (1948) pp. 14 and 81.

66. *Annalia Dubrensia* ed. Grosart (1877) p. 10.

67. Thomas Nabbe's elegy in Thomas Beedome's posthumous *Poems Divine and Humane* (1641) f.B2.

68. Thomas Beedome, op. cit. f.C6.

69. Ibid. f.C7.

70. *New English Canaan* (Amsterdam, 1637) pp. 60 (the original was printed as prose) and 10.

71. *Poems* ed. Martin (1950) p. 28. This echo is not noted in B. K. Lewalski's study of the influence of Donne's *Anniversaries* (1973).

72. Denham, *Poetical Works* ed. T. H. Banks p. 119.

73. Richard Goodridge in Cartwright, *Comedies . . . with other Poems* (1651), unsigned sigla following *, f.10v.

74. *Annalia Dubrensia* ed. Grosart (1877) p. 33.

75. John Quarles, *Englands Complaint* in *Fons Lachrymarum* (1648) pp. 6 and 11.

76. See p. 103 above.

77. Milton, *In Quintum Novembris*; George Daniel, *Poems* ed. Grosart (1878) I.172; John Hepwith, *The Calidonian Forrest* (1641) p. 19; Henry Glapthorne, *White-Hall* (1643) *passim*; Henry More, *Philosophical Poems* ed. G. Bullough (1931) pp. 84–8; Margaret Cavendish, *Poems and Fancies* (1653) pp. 116–20.

78. William Davenant and Inigo Jones, *Salamacida Spolia* (1640) f.D3v.

79. The villain of Tatham's *Distracted State* says to his sword "it is not birth, or blood, but thou, dear instrument, That can defend, offend, raise, or dis-seat High Potentates, and make a beggar great" (*Dramatic Works* (1879) p. 106); but this belief is widespread, and not confined to Hobbes and the devil (P. Zagorin, *Political Thought in the English Revolution* (1954) p. 63+).

Chapter 5

1. William Cavendish, 'The Philosophers Complaint', in Margaret Cavendish, *Natures Pictures* (1656) p. 97.

2. Owen Felltham, *Poems* ed. T.-L. Pebworth and C. J. Summers (University Park Pa., 1973) p. 70.

3. Margaret Cavendish, 'Of Poverty', in *Poems and Fancies* (1653) p. 95; she was living in Rubens's magnificent house in Antwerp at the time (Douglas Grant, *Margaret the First* (1957) pp. 89–109). For the House of Pride and its freedom from opulence and oppression cp. also Vaughan's 'The Shepheards', Herrick's 'Panegerick to Sir *Lewis Pemberton*', Alexander Brome, *Songs and other Poems* (1661) p. 109.

4. *Otia Sacra* (1648) p. 139.

5. Margaret Cavendish, op. cit. p. 78.

6. *Works* ed. Grosart (1885) I.6 and 209.

7. *Poems* ed. K. Allott (1948) pp. 128 and 110.

8. *Natures Pictures* (1656) p. 38; (1659) I.149–50.

9. *A Collection of Emblemes* ed. R. Freeman and C. S. Hensley (Columbia S.C., 1975) p. 222—on the tortoise.

10. Chamberlayne, *Pharonnida* (1659) II, i.e. second pagination, pp. 49–53; this episode contrasts with a neighbouring valley where contented country folk live "each in his own unrack'd inheritance" (Ibid. p. 40+).

11. A compilation of John Collop, *Poems* ed. C. Hilberry (Madison, 1962) p. 71; Vaughan, 'To the pious memorie of *C. W. Esquire*'; Thomas Philipott, *Poems* ed. Martin (1950) p. 4; Richard Brome, *The Jovial Crew*, in *Dramatic Works* (1873) III.355–6.

12. George Wither, *Salt upon Salt* (1659) p. 54.

13. *The Revolt in the Provinces* (1960) p. 34.

14. Op. cit. pp. 355, 358 and 352; after heavy spending he still has a balance of £12,000.

15. *Poems* ed. K. Allott (1948) p. 86; cp. Drayton's praise of the Cheshire yeoman who only spent "their owne" estates (*Poly-Olbion*, ed. J. W. Hebel (1961 ed.) p. 219).

16. *Coopers Hill* (1642); the Machiavellian influence on Denham has not been discussed, nor the similarity of these lines to the end of Marvell's *Horatian Ode*.

17. Henry Norman et. al., *Declaration of the Poor of Iver* (1650) ed. K. Thomas, *Past and Present* XLII (1966) pp. 62–3; P. Zagorin, *Political Thought in the English Revolution* (1954) pp. 33 and 31; Winstanley, qu. C. Hill, *The World Turned Upside Down* (1975 ed.) p. 101; Henry Hallhead, *Inclosure Thrown Open* (1650) p. 4.

18. Wye Saltonstall, *Picturae Loquentes* (1946 ed.) p. 28.

19. Waller, 'In answer to Sir John Sucklings verses' and *A Panegyrick*.

20. Thomas Fuller, *The Holy State* ed. M. G. Walten (New York, 1938) II.246.

21. Hobbes, *Behemoth*, qu. in *Leviathan* ed. C. B. Macpherson (1968) p. 52.

22. Davenant, *Gondibert* ed. D. F. Gladish (1971) p. 118.

23. Clarendon, qu. M. James, *Social Problems and Policy during the Puritan Revolution* (1930) p. 81.

24. Vaughan 'To Amoret Weeping' ("perhaps" refers to his doubt as to what area of exploitation he might have taken up—he is certain that he would have done evil); Jordan, *Loves Dialect* (1646) p. 32.

25. *The Fable of Philo* (1645) p. 21 (Abbott sometimes used the name Rivers).

26. *A Buckler against Death* (1640) ff.D2 (his speaker is in fact "MAN") and B5v.

27. Robert Baron, *Pocula Castalia* (1650) p. 10. For economic "eat-

ing" cp. Robert Farley, *Kalendarium Humanae Vitae* (1638) f.H1 (rich gourmets "devoure whole woods and lakes and seas"); James Shirley, *The Cardinal* in *Works* ed. Gifford and Dyce (1833) V.302 and *Cupid and Death* (Ibid. VI.352); Wye Saltonstall, *Picturae Loquentes* (1946 ed.) p. 38 ("a christian Canniball, that devoures men alive"); *Epulae Thyesteae* (1649) *passim*; Robert Wild, *Iter Boreale* (1661 ed.) pp. 13–14, and Marvell, *Last Instructions* lines 135–8.

28. Vaughan, 'The Bee'; cp. *Habbakuk* 3. 14.
29. By Shakerley Marmion in *Annalia Dubrensia* ed. Grosart (1877) p. 62.
30. J. Thirsk ed., *The Agrarian History of England and Wales* IV (1967) p. 292; cp. Benlowes's vicious racking, described in H. Jenkins, *Edward Benlowes* (1952) p. 240.
31. Cp. Samuel Pordage, *Poems* (1660) f.B3—"*Monsters* that Kings and Bishops Lands devour, Kept by extorted sums the Nation poor"; *A New Letany for these Times* (1659) associates "the Teares of *Orphans*, and poor Widowes Cries" with Puritan hypocrisy (p. 5).
32. *Shorter Poems and Translations* ed. N. W. Bawcutt (1964) pp. 93 and 21.
33. *Complete Poems* ed. Grosart (1878) p. 177.
34. *Poems* (1667) p. 41.
35. *Flamma Sine Fumo* ed. P. C. Davies (1968) p. 109.
36. In A. Clifford ed., *Tixall Poetry* (1813) p. 27.
37. In Harding's *Sicily and Naples* (1640) f.A3.
38. (1654w) in *Literary Remains* ed. T. Warton (1761) p. 292.
39. *Complete Works* ed. Grosart (1881) III.203, 204 and 217.
40. *The Civil War* ed. A. Pritchard (1973) p. 110.
41. *The Phanseys* ed. D. Grant (1956) p. 47; the metaphorical meaning of "pale" dates from late Middle English.
42. *Men-Miracles* (1646) p. 102.
43. Wither, *Westrow Revived* (1653) p. 55.
44. Walter Blith, *The English Improver* (1649) f.a2.
45. John Dancer, *Aminta* (1660) p. 133.
46. Thomas Washbourne, *Poems* ed. Grosart (1868) p. 85.
47. *Poly-Olbion* ed. J. W. Hebel (1961 ed.) pp. 57, 144, 322, 398; cp. attacks on deforestation *passim*.
48. Herrick, 'A Country life'; Jonson, 'To Sir Robert Wroth'; Thomas Philipott, *Poems* ed. Martin (1946) p. 5.
49. *Dia Poemata* (1655) f.A7.
50. *Anima Magica Abscondita* (1650) p. 57.
51. Richard Flecknoe, *Ten Years Travells* (1656) p. 51.

52. Henry Bold, *Wit a Sporting* (1657) p. 41.

53. Davenant, *The Cruelty of the Spaniards* in *Dramatic Works* IV (1873) p. 79.

54. E. G. R. Taylor, *Late Tudor and Early Stuart Geography* (1934) p. 2.

55. Ibid. p. 3.

56. H. T. Meserole ed., *Seventeenth-Century American Poetry* (Garden City N.Y., 1968) p. 419.

57. Katherine Thimelby, 'The Golden Meane' ed. A. Clifford in *Tixall Poetry* (1813) p. 296.

58. Thomas Urchard, *Epigrams* (1646) p. 4.

59. Edward Herbert, 'Upon the Groves near Merlow Castle', in *Poems* ed. G. C. M. Smith (1923) p. 54.

60. Margaret Cavendish, *Poems and Fancies* (1653) p. 212.

61. Henry Wotton, *Reliquiae* (1651) pp. "232"–"333" i.e. 532–3.

62. Richard Flecknoe, 'Ode in Praise of the Country Life', in *Ten Years Travells* (1656) p. 169.

63. Marx, *1844 Manuscripts* ed. D. J. Struick (New York, 1964) p. 100; Marx ascribes this confusion to "romanticism" (ibid.)

64. Robert Fletcher, *Poems and Translations* ed. D. H. Woodward (Gainesville, 1970) p. 228; John Tatham, *The Scotch Figgaries* in *Dramatic Works* (1879) p. 131.

65. *Good News from New–England* ed. H. T. Meserole in *Seventeenth-Century American Poetry* (Garden City N.Y., 1968) p. 167.

66. James Shirley, *Poems* (1646) p. 69.

67. John Eliot, *Poems* (1658) p. 15; this is a satirical commonplace—cp. Tourneur, *The Revengers Tragedy* II.i.213+.

68. BL MS. Eg. 2146, f.3 ("supply" is Fairfax's emendation of "maintaine").

69. Hobbes, *Leviathan* ed. C. B. Macpherson (1968) p. 340; Hobbes is objecting to the habit of basing political philosophy on meaningless emotive words.

70. *Shorter Poems and Translations* ed. N. W. Bawcutt (1964) p. 26.

71. William Drummond, *Poetical Works* ed. L. E. Kastner (1913) I.72.

72. Joshuah Sylvester, *Works* ed. Grosart (1880) I.104.

73. Thomas Philipott, *Poems* ed. Martin (1946) p. 32.

74. Vaughan, 'To the River Isca'.

75. Richard Paige in the anthology *Musarum Oxoniensium Ελαιοφορια* 1654) p. 68.

76. John Chalkhill in *Caroline Poets* ed. G. Saintsbury II (1906) p. 374.

77. *Poems* (1658) p. 5.
78. John Collop, *Poems* ed. C. Hilberry (Madison, 1962) p. 122; Milton, *Arcades* 84 and *Lycidas* 139; William Browne, *Britannia's Pastorals* I (1613) p. 107; William Bosworth, *Arcadius and Sepha* ed. G. Saintsbury (op. cit.) p. 572; Robert Baron, *Pocula Castalia* (1650) p. 56. Marvell is perhaps parodying these clumsy metaphors when he carelessly treads on real strawberries (*Appleton House* st.67).
79. *Complete Works* ed. Grosart (1881) I.29–30; 105 and 120; 26; 105; 18.
80. Edward Herbert, *Poems* ed. G. C. M. Smith (1923) p. 54.
81.   Our ships are now most beneficiall growne,
        Since they bring home no spoiles but what's their owne.
        Unto these branchless *Pines* our forward spring
        Owes better fruit than Autumn's wont to bring.
   (In *Musarum Oxoniensium Ελαιοφορια* (1654) p. 95).
82. Thomas Bancroft, *The Heroical Lover* (1658) p. 83; the prefatory material makes it clear that "Eutopia" is an allusion to Belvoir, or at least its memory.
83. Aston Cokaine, *A Masque* in *Small Poems* (1658) p. 118+.
84. (1640w), qu. A Everitt, *Change in the Provinces* (1969) p. 33.
85. Thomas Pestell, *Poems* ed. H. Buchan (1940) p. 80.
86. Nicholaus Wallington in *Annalia Dubrensia* ed. Grosart (1877) p. 34.
87. Joseph Lee, *A Vindication of the Considerations* (1654) p. 26; Thomas Heywood, *Lancashire Witches* in *Dramatic Works* (1874) IV.172.
88. *Inclosure Thrown Open* (1650) p. 4+.
89. Charitable activity and concern for the poor was high during the interregnum, as W. K. Jordan and Charles Webster show (*The Charities of Rural England* (1961) *passim; The Great Instauration* (1975) pp. 361–2); but it was mostly concerned with setting up institutions by monetary grant.
90. J. C. A. Rathmell, 'Jonson, Lord Isle, and Penshurst', *ELR* I (1971) esp. pp. 250 and 259.
91. *Calendar of the Committee for Advance of Money* ed. M. A. E. Green (1888) p. 348.
92. Jonson ed. Herford and Simpsons X.704; Flecknoe, however, praises these lavish feasts and hopes they will happen again (*Heroick Portraits* (1660) ff.E5v and E6v).
93. P. 5; the capon (cp. *To Penshurst*) is made to seem a trifling gift—but cp. Baxter, qu. G. E. Fussell, *The English Rural Labourer* (1949) p. 28: "if . . . their hennes breed Chickens, they

cannot afford to eate them, but must sell them to make their rent. They cannot afford to eat the eggs that their hennes lay. . . ."

94. Qu. C. Hill, *The World Turned Upside Down* (1975 ed.) p. 141.

95. *Minor Poems* ed. E. Robinson (1914) p. 452.

96. *Westrow Revived* (1653) pp. 23 and 30.

97. *Juvenilia* ed. Spenser Society (1871) p. 917.

98. John Taylor, qu. R. H. Deming, *Ceremony and Art* (Hague, 1974) p. 142; Taylor does not explain what these "hopes" are.

99. (1641w) ed. R. J. Broadbent in *Transactions of the Historic Society of Lancashire and Cheshire for the Year 1925* (1926) p. 8.

100. Michelet, qu. H. R. Trevor-Roper, *The European Witch-craze* (1969) p. 29—"rural poverty . . . naturally drives men to invoke" them.

101. Randolph notes that "some think not fit there should be any sport I'th Country, 'tis a dish proper to th'Court. Mirth not becomes 'em, let the Sawcy swain Eate Beef, and Bacon, and goe sweat again"; but labourers need recreation *to keep them strong* (*Poems* ed. G. Thorn-Drury (1929) pp. 119–120.

102. Nicholaus Wallington in *Annalia Dubrensia* ed. Grosart (1877) pp. 34–5.

103. *Ludlow Mask* lines 958–9; Jonson, *Entertainment at Welbeck*; Marmion in *Annalia Dubrensia* ed. cit. p. 62.

104. In *Fugitive Poetry* ed. E. Withington *HLB* IX (1955) p. 69; this editor finds the poem's date impossible to read, and conjectures "1647", but Fane clearly writes "Upon my reaping-Day the 28th of August 1648" (compare the figure 8 on p. 42 of the manuscript, Harvard f. MS. Eng. 645).

105. Herrick's other poems to Fane allude to the publication of verses, Herrick's on p. 40 (of *Works* ed. Martin) and Fane's on pp. 172–3; this suggests that Herrick writes during the gestation of *Otia Sacra*—perhaps for the harvest of 1647.

106. These figures are based on L. Stone, *The Crisis in the Aristocracy* (1965) pp. 175, 761 and Appendix 14A which tells us Fane's rental income in 1641 and 1650 and his household's consumption of grain products in 1649; the *Compounding Calendar* ed. M. A. E. Green (1889+) p. 832, which gives his assessment in 1643 (he was not sequestered since he took the Covenant); and J. Thirsk ed., *The Agrarian History of England and Wales* IV (1967) pp. 436, 610 and 815+, which gives a rough average wage for Midlands resident labourers (scaling down the Kent figures, and making them up again with harvest-bonuses). Fane's sale

of produce (cp. Thirsk pp. 675–6) was probably considerably more than his domestic consumption (£650-worth in 1649).

Chapter 6

1. John Spelman, *The Duties both of Prince and People* (1642) pp. 2–3.
2. *Oceana* (1656) p. 4; the following argument is contained on pp. 4–9.
3. Hyde, quoted in J. M Wallace, '*Coopers Hill . . .*', *ELH* XLI (1974) p. 507.
4. *Anima Magica Abscondita* (1650) p. 54.
5. *The Clarke Papers* ed. C. H. Firth I (1891) p. 315; the argument is continued on pp. 319–320 and 323.
6. Documented in great detail in C. Hill, *Change and Continuity* 1974) p. 233+.
7. Milton, *Tenure of Kings and Magistrates* (Columbia ed. V.40).
8. Maximilian Petty, in *Clarke Papers* ed. cit. p. 342.
9. *Leviathan* ed. C. B. Macpherson (1968) p. 256.
10. Ibid. p. 255.
11. *The Court and the Country* (1969) p. 19+; he proposes instead the concept of status.
12. Ibid. p. 22 and notes; cp. Ibid p. 27 (economic status overruling tradition) and p. 29.
13. Viscount Conway, qu. M. Walzer, *The Revolution of the Saints* (Cambridge Mass., 1965) p. 252.
14. *Poems* ed. T. -L. Pebworth and C. J. Summers (University Park Pa., 1973) p. 64.
15. *Clarke Papers* ed. C. H. Firth I (1891) p. 315; note "clearlie".
16. In Winstanley, *Works* ed. G. H. Sabine (Ithaca N.Y., 1941 p. 663.
17. *The Elders Dreame* (1647) p. 5
18. *Clarke Papers* ed. cit. p. 330.
19. Winstanley op. cit. p. 663 and *passim*.
20. Ibid. p. 667; this 'Diggers Christmass-Caroll' explains the civil war as a squabble between "great Men" who trick the poor by democratic promises into helping them—actually increasing their slavery in the process.
21. H. E. Rollins ed., *The Pack of Autolycus* (1927) p. 35; Henry Norman et. al., *Declaration of the Poor of Iver* ed. K. Thomas in *Past and Present* XLII (1969) p. 61; Winstanley op. cit. p. 330.

22. Cp Brian Manning, *The English People and the English Revolution* (1976). For actual class-based insurrections, see especially pp. 112–138, 174–193 and 215–27; for hatred of the rich, pp. 262–85; for fear of risings, *passim*.

23. C. Hill, ed. of Winstanley, *The Law of Freedom* (1973) p. 22; cp. J. S. Morrill, *The Revolt in the Provinces* (1960) p. 34.

24. *A Mite* in Winstanley, *Works* ed. cit. p. 660.

25. John Gerard, *Herball* (1597) p. 1275; the speaker is "envie".

26. From a prophesy of 1642 in J. Frank, *Hobbled Pegasus* (Albuquerque, 1968) p. 69; Wither, *Amygdala Britannica* (1647) p. 10; John Marsh, *Mickle Monument* (1645) p. 63.

27. Francis Finch in *Musarum Oxoniensium Επιβατηρια* f.B4v; Charles I, *Answer to the XIX Propositions* (1642) f.B2v.

28. Henry Jacob, *Philologiae* (1652) p. 48; a "gnoffe" is a brutish yokel.

29. John Cleveland, *The Insurrection of Wat Tyler* (1654) p. 43.

30. Cp. P. Zagorin, *Political Thought* (1954) p. 61 and *The Court and the Country* (1969) p. 350; C. Hill, ed. Winstanley, *The Law of Freedom* (1973) pp. 20–1; further authorities are cited in detail there.

31. *Bread for the Poor* (1653) p. 30.

32. John Cooke, *Unum Necessarium, or the Poore Man's Case* (1648) pp. 24–5. In some regions labourers' wages were a shilling a day, but Winstanley (*Law of Freedom* ed. C. Hill (1973) p. 201) makes it clear that they could be as low as 4d. Adam Moore's Utopian schemes would only provide 8d. a day (op. cit. p. 29) "to redeem them from their ever-pre-endured penury" (ibid. p. 34).

33. C. Hill, *Change and Continuity* (1974) p. 220; strikes were "liable to the terrible penalties of treason" (ibid. p. 187).

34. Qu. in C. Hill ed., Winstanley, *Law of Freedom* (1973) p. 25.

35. *The Commons Complaint* (1611) p. 15.

36. Walter Blith, *The English Improver Improved* (1652) f.e4v (and cp. f.c4v); Vaughan, 'The Bee'.

37. Cp. Robert Powell, *Depopulation Arraigned* (1636) pp. 7–8 and *passim*; John Moore Jr., *The Crying Sin of England* (1653) p. 7+; Daniel Noddell, *The Great Complaint of Epworth* (1654) *passim*; B. Manning, *The English People* (1976) p. 233. The Digger communities suffered almost continuous violence.

38. Cleveland, *Wat Tyler* (1654) p. 148—a striking anticipation of Marx "the earth which is estranged from man . . . confronts him in the shape of a few great lords" (*1844 Manuscripts* ed. D. J. Struik (New York, 1964) p. 100).

39. *The Spirituall Use of an Orchard* (2nd ed., 1657) *passim*, esp. p. 160.

40. Wither, *Haleluiah* (1641) p. 353.

41. Thomas Overbury, *Miscellaneous Works* ed. E. F. Rimbault (1890) p. 132; cp. John Eliot, *Poems* (1658) p. 14.

42. *The Nightingale* (1622) p. 243. Cp. the mediaeval and popular treatment of dirty labourers, often complaining about their noise and roughness, but assuming that they belong to the community (cp. 'The Roaring Blacksmith' in H. E. Rollins, ed., *Cavalier and Puritan* (New York, 1923) p. 459+).

43. *1844 Manuscripts* ed. D. J. Struik (New York, 1964) p. 93.

44. Robert Heath, *Clarastella* (1650) p. 43.

45. *Poetical Works* ed. R. W. Bond (1893) pp. 335 and 341.

46. Joseph Beaumont, *Psyche* (1648) p. 116; the original (in plural) refers to fruit-trees.

47. Thomas Stanley, *Poems and Translations* ed. G. M. Crump (1962) p. 123; the idea is a common-place (cp. esp. Sandys, *Poetical Works* ed. R. Hooper (1872) II.402 "without his toil The ever-flourishing and fruitful Soil Unpurchas'd Food produc'd", and Cowley, *Poems* ed. A. R. Waller (1905) p. 160 "there neither *Earth* nor *Sea* they *plow*, Nor ought to *Labour* ow For *Food*").

48. Robert Powell, *Depopulation Arraigned* (1636) p. 55.

49. Robert Baron, *Pocula Castalia* (1650) p. 2.

50. *Inclosure Thrown Open* (1650) p. 10.

51. John Moore Jr., *A Scripture-word* (1656) p. 12; Adam Moore, *Bread for the Poor* (1653) f."A"2, i.e. B2.

52. *Picturae Loquentes* (1946 ed.) p. 66.

53. Tr. in Vaughan, *Works* ed. Martin (2nd ed., 1957) p. 92.

54. *The Country and the City* (1973) p. 32.

55. 'The "Better Marks" of Jonson's *To Penshurst*', *RES* N.S. XXIV (1973) p. 275.

56. Richard Flecknoe, 'Ode in Praise of the Country Life' in *Ten Years Travells* (1656) p. 169. This theory of "innocence" explains the frequent mention of curds and cheesecakes in rural poetry; Robert Fletcher, for example, describes Hyde Park covered in "curds and cream", like a starry night (*Poems and Translations* ed. D. H. Woodward (Gainesville, 1970) p. 197).

57. *Poly-Olbion* ed. J. W. Hebel (1961 ed.) pp. 365, 380.

58. *A Buckler agaynst the Feare of Death* (1640) f.D7v.

59. In H. T. Meserole ed., *17th-Century American Poetry* (Garden City N.Y., 1968) pp. 166–7.

60. *Philosophical Poems* ed. G. Bullough (1931) p. 83.

61. Edward Calver's description of the peasant's life, p. 183 above; the allusion is to the torture of Samson.
62. Mathew Stevenson, *Occasion's Off-spring* (1654) p. 67.
63. *Iter Boreale* in *Poems* ed. J. A. W. Bennett and H. R. Trevor-Roper (1955) p. 38.
64. *Poems etc.* (3rd ed., 1668) p. 194.
65. *Henry Tubbe* ed. G. C. M. Smith (1915) p. 91.
66. *Mickle Monument* (1645) p. 20.
67. Lovelace, 'The Grasse-hopper'.
68. E.g. "here . . . wounds are never found, Save what the *Plow-share* gives the ground" in Henry Wotton, *Reliquiae* (1651) p. 232.
69. *Il Penseroso* line 136.
70. *Songs and Poems of Love and Drollery* (1654) p. 66.
71. *A Buckler* (1640) f.B3.
72. *Occasion's Off-spring* (1654) p. 3.
73. *Psyche* (1648) p. 242.
74. *Minor Poems* ed. E. Robinson (1914) p. 394.
75. *The Scots Figgaries* (1652) p. 23; cp. *Psyche* (1648) p. "201", i.e. 210, where thorned plants are described as "armed Neighbours".
76. E.g., Virgil, Eclogue 10 lines 53–4; Carew, *The Rapture* line 122; Habington, *Poems* ed. K. Allott (1948) pp. 13 and 145; Herrick, *Poetical Works* ed. Martin (1956) pp. 160, 169 and 192; Waller, *Poems etc.* (1645) pp. 27 and 41; the theme is common in landscape art—e.g. Salvator Rosa, *Landscape with Erminia* (M. Kitson, *Salvator Rosa* (1973) fig. 5).
77. Ed. E. A. Horsman (1956) p. 67.
78. Cleveland, *Wat Tyler* (1654) p. 24.
79. Alexander Brome, *Songs and other Poems* (1661) p. 79.
80. Wither, *Furor-Poeticus* (1660) p. 16.
81. *The Rhetorical World of Augustan Humanism* (1965) p. 187.
82. *The Country and the City* (1973) p. 25.
83. *Poems and Fancies* (1653) pp. "153–4", i.e., ff.X1-v.
84. *Psyche* (1648) p. 382.
85. Thomas Vaughan in his brother's *Works* ed. Martin (2nd ed., 1957) p. 38.
86. *Poems* (1655) p. 18.
87. Hammond, ibid. p. 4; Cowley, *Poems* ed. A. R. Waller (1905) p. 112; Henry Bold, *Wit a Sporting* (1657) p. 91; Nicholas Hookes, *Amanda* (1653) p. 14; Robert Fletcher, *Poems and Translations* ed. D. H. Woodward (Gainesville, 1970) p. 213.
88. E.g. Hugh Crompton, *Poems* (1657) pp. 70–1.

89. *Dimagoras* (1658) p. 64.
90. *Poems* ed. G. Thorn-Drury (1929) p. 130; cp. Shakespeare, Sonnet 16.
91. *Complete Works* ed. Grosart (1881) III.234.
92. *The Queen of Aragon* in Dodsley, *Old English Plays* ed. W. C. Hazlitt (1875) XIII.349.
93. In H. E. Rollins ed., *Cavalier and Puritan* (New York, 1923) p. 364.
94. Qu. in N. Cohn, *The Pursuit of the Millenium* (1957) p. 365.
95. *Minor Poems* ed. E. Robinson (1914) p. 413.
96. (1647) p. 7.
97. *Pelecanicidium* (1653) p. 252+.
98. Wither, hymn 'For a husbandman' in *Haleluiah* (1641) p. 433.
99. Quarles, *Complete Works* ed. Grosart (1881) III.220 and 219. Joseph Beaumont's detailed picture of God as a benign farmer ('The Farm', in *Minor Poems* ed. E. Robinson (1914) pp. 405–6) would have no point if benignity was not so unusual as to be almost a paradox; Beaumont uses exclamation marks throughout.
100. Rowland Watkyns, *Flamma Sine Fumo* ed. P. C. Davies (1968) p. 88; John Taylor, *Elegy on Richard Wyan* (1638) single sheet; George Daniel, *Poems* ed. Grosart (1878) IV.233; Edward Sparke, *Appendix Sacra* (1652) f.B4; John Marsh, *Mickle Monument* (1645) p. 12; William Hammond, *Poems* (1655) p. 50; Daniel Cudmore, Ευχοδια (1965), p. 109; Benlowes, *Theophila* (1652) p. 249; Thomas Bancroft, *Epigrammes* (1639) f.C3; Quarles, *Complete Works* ed. Grosart (1881) III.204 and 208; Mildmay Fane, *Otia Sacra* (1648) p. 40; Joseph Beaumont, *Psyche* (1648) pp. 119 and 120.
101. William Chamberlayne, *Pharonnida* (1659) I p. 145; these figures appear in the long landscape description discussed in Chapter 1 above.
102. E.g. Puttenham, *Arte of English Poesie* ed. G. D. Willcock and A. Walker (1936) p. 38; Sidney, *Arcadia* (*Works* ed. Feuillerat I) pp. 27–8; Fletcher, *Faithful Shepherdess*, 'To the Reader'. Randolph (*Poems* ed. G. Thorn-Drury (1929) p. 106) distinguishes "Reapers, Loppers and Plowmen"; who are paid for their work, from shepherds, who sing; they alone are defined, like the gentry, by their leisure and not their work.
103. *Poems* (1658) pp. 13–14 and 59; cp. also pp. 60–1.
104. In H. E. Rollins ed., *Cavalier and Puritan* (New York, 1923) pp. 417–18.
105. *Grand Pluto's Progresse* (1647) p. 16.

106. *Poems and Fancies* (1653) p. "142", i.e. f.Aa3v.

107. E.g. ibid. pp. 79, 95.

108. *Miscellania* (1653) p. 28.

109. Ibid. pp. 23–4.

110. (1647) p. "7", i.e. 3 (f.A4).

111. cp. Edward Phillips's model 'letter from the country', in *The Mysteries of Love and Eloquence* (1658) p. 133.

112. *Poems* ed. K. Allott (1948) p. 77.

113. *Songs and other Poems* (1661) p. 199 and 191. Note that disgust with rustics extends to the more prosperous farmers too.

114. *Poems* (1655) p. 35.

115. *Honoria and Mammon* (1659) p. 7. This description has an obvious affinity to the pictures of Arcimboldi; cp. also J. Emerson's "picture" of an Orkney housewife made of filthy dishcloths and pieces of fish and meat (*Poetical Descriptions of Orkney* ed. J. Maidment (1835) pp. vi–vii).

116. Humphrey Mill, *A Nights Search* (1640) p. 260.

117. *Theophila* (1652) p. 236.

118. Marvell may have been fascinated by the amphibious economic status of mowers, half adjuncts of the estate, half free agents "known through all the meadows they have mown". As a tutor he was himself part servant and part gentleman, and he mentions this status several times; the Dutch are *"Half-anders*, half wet, and half dry, Nor bear *strict service*, nor *pure Liberty"* (*Poems* ed. Margoliouth (3rd ed., 1971) p. 101), and Charles II "ne're knew not he How to serve or be free" (Ibid. p. 191).

119. Joseph Beaumont, *Psyche* (1648) p. 252.

120. Benlowes, *Theophila* (1652) pp. 246–7.

121. Harvard f. MS. Eng. 645, p. 159.

122. Ed. T. Corser (1845) pp. 4–5. Note that James feels no tremor of rebuke or Wordsworthian solitude, but exclaims "Happie ould blade".

123. *Claraphil and Clarinda* (1650) ff.D5-v. This song contains a striking exception to the embargo on mentioning tools of work (ibid. f.D5v). Thomas Bushell's career is astonishing; he was the proprietor of the famous Rock at Enstone and famous also as a hermit, living on an island off the Isle of Man.

124. This sentiment derives from *Georgics* II.458–9 which says how happy the farmer would be if he were to realize his own happiness. These lines were widely imitated; Dorothy Osborne provides an especially fascinating example, since it purports to come from real life:

about sixe or seven a Clock [on a typical day in the country] I walke out into a Common that lyes hard by the house where a great many young wenches keep sheep and Cow's and sitt in the shades singing of Ballads; I goe to them and compare theire voyces and Beauty's to some Ancient Shepherdesses that I have read of and finde a vast difference there, but trust mee I think these are as innocent as those could bee. I talke to them, and finde they want nothing to make them the happiest People in the world, but the knoledge that they are soe.

(*Letters* ed. G. C. M. Smith (1928) pp. 51–2)

125. Wotton, *Reliquiae* (1651) p. 524; Suckling, 'Ballad of a Wedding'; Randolph, *Poems* ed. G. Thorn-Drury (1929) p. 80; Hugh Crompton, *Poems* (1657) p. 102.
126. *A Pastorall* in MS. Bodl. Rawl. Poet. 16, p. 61.
127. Thomas Jordan, *Fancy's Festivals* (1657) f.D3v.
128. *Psyche* (1648) p. 299.
129. E.g. John Taylor, *Ale Ale-vated* (1651) ff.B3–4 and J. Frank, *Hobbled Pegasus* (Albuquerque, 1968) p. 110.
130. Rowland Watkyns, 'The Poets Soliloquy', in *Flamma Sine Fumo* ed. P. C. Davies (1968) p. 103.

Conclusion

1. Francis Barker shows how Trotsky, grappling with the same problem, resorts to the idea that great works of genius transcend history; this is, of course, theoretically impossible. See F. Barker et al. eds., *Literature, Society and the Sociology of Literature: proceedings of the conference held at the University of Essex, June 1976* (1977) pp. 174–9 (hereafter "*Essex*"). Terry Eagleton also claims that "some works of art certainly survive their contemporary moment and others do not . . . [some also] 'transcend' their contemporary history" (*Criticism and Ideology* (1976) p. 178.
2. Commendatory poems by Joseph Howe and Edward Sherburne in William Cartwright, *Comedies, Tragi-Comedies, with other Poems* (1651); Howe's is in an unsigned sigla differently placed in the three copies I have consulted (f.1 following f.*4, f.6 following f.*8 and f.8 following f.*8), and Sherburne's is on f.*b*8. The references are to the battle of Edge Hill and the Digger community on St. George's Hill in Surrey. The contributors to

this volume are mostly royalist and Oxford–educated, and a reference to *Coopers Hill* (f.*1; hitherto unnoticed) shows that Denham was of their literary circle.

3. 'Ouverture' to *Mythologiques I: Le Cru et le Cuit* (1964) tr. as *The Raw and the Cooked* by J. and D. Weightman (1970) esp. p. 13, where he justifies filling up a gap in one myth by bringing in another from an entirely different culture to complete the structure. The phrase "goods to think with" derives from Edmund Leach's mistranslation of *bonnes à penser* (*Lévi-Strauss* (1970) p. 34). *Tristes Tropiques* (1955) tr. J. and D. Weightman (1976 ed.) pp. 253–6 also throws light on the literary process; the patterns of Caduveo body-painting express the contra-dictions of their society in a hidden "poetic" way. See also F. Jameson, *Marxism and Form* (Princeton, 1971) pp. 383–4 and M. Glucksmann, *Structural Analysis in Contemporary Social Thought: a Comparison of the Theories of Claude Lévi-Strauss and Louis Althusser* (1974) *passim*.

4. *Mythologies* (1957) sel. and tr. A. Lavers (New York, 1972) pp. 11 and 141–2; cp. his early use of myth "in its traditional sense" (p. 11) and the "necessary conjunction" of semiology and ideological analysis (p. 9).

5. Ibid. p. 109; cp. the cherry tree from *The German Ideology* (*ibid* pp. 143–4). Drouet was a child of supposed poetic gifts, then in the news. Barthes's work is very much a product of 1950s France—the renewal of affluence, the colonial war and the cult of the intellectual as outsider (p. 157). The need for "semio-clasm" (p. 9; the unmasking and destroying of hidden per-suaders) is just as strong today, however.

6. Ibid. p. 118.

7. Marxist aesthetics has, quite rightly, been concerned not with abstracting "a 'philosophy of art' from the corpus of Marx's writings" but with "tracing some crucial aesthetic themes in Marx's work in terms of their integral relations to the devel-oping totality of his thought" (T. Eagleton, intro. to M. Lif-shitz, *The Philosophy of Art of Karl Marx* tr. R. B. Winn (1973) p. 7). Nevertheless it is interesting to see that Marx approached the problem of art through the concept of mythology. In the General Introduction to the *Grundrisse* (*Selected Works* ed. D. McLellan (1977) pp. 359–60) he sees mythology as a materi-ally based "view of nature and of social relations" which "masters and dominates and shapes the forces of nature in and through the imagination"; in mythology "nature and even the form of society are *wrought up* in a popular fancy *in an unconsciously*

artistic fashion" (my emphasis; the idea is repeated two sentences later). Art is thus conscious mythology. For recent developments in Marxist aesthetics cp. *Working Papers in Cultural Studies* IV (1973) pp. 21–50.

8. Marx, op. cit. pp. 164 and 176. David Musselwhite criticizes the camera image for being too static and abstract; his case is weakened by confusing lenses with mirrors, and thus attacking reflectionism where it does not exist, and by taking the colloquial polemic phrase *auf dem Kopf* as a serious scientific proposal (*Essex* pp. 8–17).

9. "The assimilation of 'literature' to 'ideology' . . . was in practice little more than banging one inadequate category against another . . . a disastrous failure [which] fundamentally compromised, in this whole area, the status of Marxism itself" (*Marxism and Literature* (1977) pp. 52–3). His chapter on Ideology is a useful account of the various meanings the term has had. I would summarize them as follows: (i) a kind of idealism propounded in late-18th-century France; Derrida, in what seems like an attack on the Left, resurrects this meaning and criticizes (iv) below—in 'Signature Event Context' (*Glyph: John Hopkins Textual Studies* I (1977) pp. 178–9). (ii) any set of social doctrines. (iii) any (ii) which the speaker dislikes intensely. (iv) in Marxism, any form of knowledge or experience which is not fully "scientific" i.e. Marxist; this can be subdivided into the narrow and broad definitions discussed above. A non-Marxist would say that (iii) and (iv) were the same.

10. Cp. L. Althusser, *Pour Marx* (1965) tr. as *For Marx* by B. Brewster (1969) esp. glossary; *Essex* pp. 6, 10–11, 43; T. Eagleton, *Marxism and Literary Criticism* (1976) esp. pp. 16–19 and *Criticism and Ideology* (1976) esp. pp. 54. 103, 106. It is not always easy to see what Eagleton means by ideology: sometimes it is the opposite of "conceptual analysis", sometimes of "the 'world view' of a 'class-subject'", and sometimes of impoverished philosophy (empiricism, for example, "could not rise to the level of an ideology proper"). I have found an earlier Marxist text clear and useful—Franz Jakubowski, *Ideology and Superstructure in Historical Materialism* (1936) tr. A. Booth (1976) esp. pp. 98–111; the fragmentariness of my theory corresponds to my having only a "partial" theory of ideology, in his terms. I recognise that my book does not deal with the further problem of *subjectivity* and its relation to ideology, neither in its "bourgeois" form (Stanley Fish's affective

stylistics) nor within Marxism (cp. R. Coward and J. Ellis, *Language and Materialism* (1977) esp. pp. 61–92 and S. Burniston and C. Weedon, 'Ideology, Subjectivity and the Artistic Text' in *Working Papers in Cultural Studies* X (1977) pp. 203–233).

11. *Marxism and Literary Criticism* (1976) pp. 6–7 and 16 (hereafter *MLC*).

12. *Criticism and Ideology* (1976) p. 65 (hereafter *CI*); the only model he will accept is *production*. I am not clear whether this is intended as a metaphor or not, nor whether the text is to be considered raw material, processing plant or finished product. Whenever an explanation seems imminent the term changes to a theatrical metaphor (pp. 65, 177–8, 185), while Literary Mode of Production refers mostly to book manufacture, which is not the same as making texts.

13. *Pour une Théorie de la Production Litteraire* (Paris, 1966) p. 138, my translation.

14. *MLC* p. 24, developed from a statement made by Lukács long before he became a Marxist. Like Macherey, Eagleton equates form with *that which makes the literary work different from other texts*.

15. Cp. *CI* p. 184 for a sophisticated account of the dialectics of form, content, product and process.

16. In the same way, it is futile to think that criticism is any the less bourgeois if Marxist *content* has been introduced but the *institution* of criticism remains unchanged.

17. E.g. *MLC* p. 25, discussing the novel, asks us to believe that routine experience, the material fortunes of the hero, and unpredictable events are formal features, when they are obviously matters of content. The inconsistencies of George Eliot and Dickens (*CI* pp. 117–29) derive just as much from content (what topics they deal with and what events are allowed to happen) as from tone and style. *The Waste Land* is surely a poem of fragmentary form and homogenous content (repeating by allusion a few key themes), rather than vice versa (*CI* p. 148). Cp. *MLC* p. 68 for the assertion, for which there is no evidence whatsoever, that works "sold on the market to anonymous thousands will characteristically differ in form from the work produced under a patronage system". The problem is touched on by Francis Mulhern in *New Left Review* XCI (May–June 1975) p. 86.

18. And thus socially-determined; cp. the concept of genre as a *sociolect* in R. Coward and J. Ellis, *Language and Materialism* (1977) p. 38+.

19. *CI* p. 161.
20. Op. cit (n.13 above) *passim*. This aspect of Macherey's theory, which derives from Althusser, is elaborated by Terry Eagleton in *MLC* pp. 18–19 and 34–5, 'Marxist Literary Criticism' in H. Schiff ed. *Contemporary Approaches to English Studies* (1977) pp. 100–3, and *CI* ("the aesthetic is that which speaks of its historical conditions by remaining silent, inheres in them by distance and denial" p. 177).
21. Facetious commendatory verses in an edition of James Strong, *Joaneriados* (1645) f.B3v. Poor-john is dried fish.
22. "B.C." in Cartwright, op. cit. (n.2 above) f.***8. Some copies read "Bare".
23. John Norris, 'My Estate' in L. Birkett Marshall ed., *Rare Poems of the Seventeenth Century* (1936) pp. 162–3.

Index